Molly Weir's
RECIPES

BY THE SAME AUTHOR

Shoes Were for Sunday	Hutchinson & Co. (Publishers) Ltd.	(1970)
Best Foot Forward	,, ,,	(1972)
A Toe on the Ladder	,, ,,	(1973)
Stepping into the Spotlight	,, ,,	(1975)
Walking into the Lyons' Den	,, ,,	(1977)
One Small Footprint	,, ,,	(1980)
Spinning Like a Peerie	Gordon Wright Publishing	(1983)

Molly Weir's
RECIPES

•

New Ideas and Old Favourites

With 110 humorous drawings by Eric Clarke

GORDON WRIGHT PUBLISHING
55 MARCHMONT ROAD, EDINBURGH, EH9 1HT
SCOTLAND

ISBN 903065 18 5

Cover illustration by
Photo Express, Edinburgh

To

My Husband's Stomach

Without Whose Co-operation

This Book Could Never

Have Been Written

Printed and bound by Spectrum Printing Co., Edinburgh

FOREWORD

When this book was first published, I never imagined it would achieve such staggering popularity. To date, it has sold over one hundred thousand copies and become a good friend to a host of people who have felt compelled to write to me to say how well it has served them.

A few years ago, the book sold out, but the public continued to write, only now, they were imploring me to tell them "Where oh where can we obtain a copy of your recipe book?".

Daughters complained that their mothers wouldn't part with their copies. Grannies said their books were so well used they were falling to bits and they wanted to replace them. Fellow-actors declared they owed their well-fed condition entirely to my book. Wedding guests informed me that my recipe book, popped inside their "real" present, guaranteed a happy kitchen for the newly-weds!

The first edition of *Molly Weir's Recipes* was written in response to public demand. This edition, amazingly, has sprung to life for the same reason. What more could a writer ask for?

I hope you will find many things to please your palate in this volume, and that all those who have written to me will pounce upon this new edition with glad cries of recognition. I trust too, that like me, you'll have lots of fun in your kitchen trying out a collection of recipes gathered through a lifetime's interest in good cooking.

Molly Weir.

CONTENTS

CONTENTS

General Information

PREPARATIONS

(1). Have all your ingredients and utensils ready beside you before you start to cook or bake.

(2). Measure the ingredients carefully to keep the balance of recipes right.

(3). Have your baking tins greased and ready. If you leave them on top of the stove while you are preparing the mixture, you will find cakes, tarts, pies, etc. will come off the warmed tin more readily.

(4). Always remember to pre-heat your oven, before you start your preparations.

(5). Have all your ingredients at room temperature, unless the recipe says otherwise.

COMPARATIVE STOVE TEMPERATURES

Description	Gas Cookers	Electric Cookers
Very slow oven	0–½	93–121°C or 200–250°F
Slow	1–2	121–149°C or 250–300°F
Very moderate	2–3	149–177°C or 300–350°F
Moderate	3–4	177–190°C or 350–375°F
Moderately hot	4–5	190–218°C or 375–425°F
Hot	6–7	218–232°C or 425–450°F
Very hot	8–9	232–245°C or 450–475°F

Simple Metric Conversion (Approx.)

1 oz. = 25 g.

1 pint (20 fl. oz.) = ½ litre = 500 millilitres.

1 ml. of water weighs 1 g. This applies to milk, stock, beaten egg, etc.

HANDY MEASURES

All measures are LEVEL. To find correct level, for dry ingredients, fill the cup or spoon quite full, then level off the top with your knife, but DO NOT PRESS DOWN. Liquids, of course, find their own level. Fats should be packed down.

Ingredients	Table-spoons per oz	British Measuring Cup	American Measuring Cup
Breadcrumbs (fresh)	5	3 oz	2¼ oz
Butter	2	8 oz	6 oz
Cheese (grated)	4	4 oz	3 oz
Cornflour	3	5 oz	4 oz
Currants	3	4 oz	3 oz
Flour	3	5 oz	4 oz
Jam	1	12 oz	10 oz
Lard, cooking fat and margarine	2	8 oz	6 oz
Oatmeal (medium)	2	8 oz	6 oz
Sugar : Brown	2½	7 oz	5½ oz
Granulated	2	8 oz	6 oz
Icing, sifted	3½	4 oz	3 oz
Sultanas	—	6 oz	4½ oz
Syrup	1	14 oz	11 oz
Water	—	10 oz	8 oz

In addition to this table, you might like to remember that 1 walnut size piece of fat is approximately ½ oz.

When you are asked to measure 1 wineglassful of liquid, this equals approximately 2½ oz or ½ gill.

> 1 gill is equal to 5 fluid oz
> ½ pint is equal to 10 fluid oz
> 1 pint is equal to 20 fluid oz

When you are measuring out honey or syrup, or treacle, if you dip your spoon first of all in very hot water, you will find the syrup, etc., will slide off without any trouble.

RECIPES

Soups

We in Scotland are firm believers in starting the meal with soup, and the basis of practically every nourishing soup is:

(a) bone stock made by covering bones with cold water and simmering for hours, or as long as you can spare, to extract all the good from them.

(b) meat stock obtained by covering a piece of boiling beef, flank mutton or sheep tails, with warm water and simmering for as long as possible to extract all the good from the meat.

I keep a stock pot into which I put all bones, fowl carcasses, etc., and this is brought to boiling point and boiled for 20 minutes every day to keep it fresh, so I always have the wherewithal for a good soup on hand. I also save vegetable water, which I use as a basis for sauces and soups, but the water from turnip and cauliflower is not suitable as this is much too strong in flavour. If you do use vegetable water stock, be very careful, for this turns sour very quickly and should not be kept longer than two days at the most.

A SIMPLE SOUP

2 oz butter
1 chopped onion
2 or 3 small carrots, sliced
1 stick of celery, chopped
1 chopped tomato
Any vegetables in season
Water or stock
Vermicelli
Pepper/Salt
Parsley

Method. Melt the butter, and "sweat" the cut-up vegetables in this, i.e. cook gently, but do not let get brown. Add 3 breakfastcups of water or stock. If you save the water from your sprouts, potatoes and greens for two days, this provides excellent vegetable stock, but not more than two days, or it may go sour. Bring to the boil, and add a twist of vermicelli crushed into the pot from your hand. Add pepper and salt, and simmer until everything is tender. Add some chopped parsley after serving the soup, and, if liked, a spoonful of grated cheese.

MUTTON BROTH

¾ lb mutton neck or
    knuckle
1½ pints cold water
1 dessertspoon rice or
    barley
1 large leek or 1 onion
1 small piece each:
    carrot
    turnip
    celery
1 dessertspoon chopped
    parsley
Pepper/Salt

Method. Prepare the vegetables and cut them in small neat pieces, allowing about ½ teacup of each. Put the meat and water into a saucepan with a little salt, put on the lid and bring slowly to the boil. Skim well, add the rice, well washed, and the prepared vegetables. If you are using barley, it should have been soaked overnight before adding to the soup. Simmer for about 2 hours or until the vegetables are well cooked. Skim off any fat from the top of the broth, add the parsley, pepper, and more salt if necessary, before serving.

The meat can be served as a separate course with parsley sauce and boiled potatoes, or, if preferred, it can be cut small at the beginning and served with the soup, with all the bones taken out.

SCOTCH BROTH

1 lb bones
1 tablespoon barley
1 tablespoon peas
2 pints water
Carrot
Turnip
Leek
Parsley
Salt/Pepper

Method. Soak the barley and the peas overnight. Wash the bones and cover with the cold water and a teaspoon salt and bring slowly to the boil. Dice the vegetables, cut the leek into rings, and add to the bone stock, with the steeped barley and the peas, but keep back the parsley which should be chopped and laid in the tureen so that the soup may be poured over it just before serving.

Do not put too much turnip in broth, as it makes it very strong in flavour. If you wish, you may add a diced potato, and a grated onion, and indeed any other vegetable which is to your taste.

Remove the soup from the fire after it has simmered for about 1 hour, and season to taste with salt and pepper. Lift out the bone, which can be used again for second stock, and pour into the tureen.

NOTE. You can make this bone stock at any time and keep it until you wish to use it, provided you boil for 20 minutes each day to prevent it turning sour. If too much fat is released, you may skim the surplus to prevent having too greasy a soup.

IF YOU like mustard mixed with water only, but find it gets rather dry, try adding a little salt and a drop of oil to the mixture and you will be pleased how moist it keeps.

MIX mustard with vinegar for a nice change. You will find, too, that it keeps the mustard fresh longer.

CABBAGE SOUP

1 cabbage
1 onion or 2 leeks
2 pints meat stock
1 tablespoon rice
1 small ham bone
1 teaspoon chopped
    parsley
White pepper/Salt
1 slice of toasted bread

This is a great favourite on the Continent, and many a time I have been grateful for its sustaining warmth after a long walk or cycle ride.
Method. Wash the cabbage in cold water, remove the coarse outside leaves and any hard pieces of stalk, separate all the leaves and let them soak in cold water for ½ hour. Drain off the water and shred the leaves finely. Put them in a pan of fast-boiling water, slightly salted, boil quickly for five minutes, and throw this water away too. Now slice the onion or leek finely, and put it into a saucepan with the shredded, blanched cabbage, ham bone, and meat stock and boil steadily for ½ hour. Sprinkle in the rice, add the seasoning, and cook until the rice is thoroughly cooked. Add the parsley just before serving. Cut the toast into small square pieces, put them in a soup tureen, and pour the boiling hot soup over them.

CELERY AND RICE SOUP

1 pint light stock
2 or 3 sticks white celery
¼ oz butter
2 tablespoons top of milk
1 teaspoon rice
Seasoning

Method. Well wash and brush the celery and cut in small pieces, then put it into a saucepan with the stock, piece of butter about the size of a walnut and the rice, well washed. Cook slowly, stirring now and again, till the ingredients are quite soft. Rub as much as possible through a fine sieve and return to the saucepan to reheat. Add the top of milk and season to taste. Serve with small strips of toast.

ITALIAN MINESTRONE

1 onion
1 carrot
1 cup chopped cabbage
2 leeks
½ small turnip, chopped
1 cup tomato pulp
1 stalk of celery
1 sprig of parsley
½ teaspoon white pepper
Salt to taste
3 pints water or stock
1 level tablespoon rice
1 level tablespoon
    macaroni
2 oz fat

Method. Heat the fat (butter, margarine or some fine olive oil) in a big saucepan, and stir in the onion, parsley, carrot and turnip. Cook till the vegetables are golden brown, stirring occasionally. Add the salt to taste, pepper, tomato pulp, cabbage, leeks, celery and water. Bring to the boil. Chop the macaroni (spaghetti or vermicelli) into inch pieces and add. Stir in the rice, and cover the pan. Simmer for about ¾ hour till the macaroni, rice and vegetables are tender.

When the soup is served, grated Parmesan cheese should be handed round and sprinkled on top of the soup at the table. It is more economical to buy a piece and grate it yourself, than to buy it already grated. *For 8 persons.*

LENTIL SOUP

Stock
1 teacup lentils
Carrot, turnip, onion,
    parsley and seasoning

Method 1. Wash lentils and braise in hot fat till they swell up. Add stock and other vegetables and cook gently till ready.

Method 2. Put lentils into cold stock, add other vegetables and seasoning, and cook for about 1 hour, or until all vegetables are tender.

ONION SOUP (Brown)

1 or 2 Spanish onions
1 oz butter
1 slice toast, buttered
1 quart brown stock
Grated Parmesan

Method. Skin the onions and cut them in thin slices so that they fall in rings. Cook them a few minutes in the butter, letting them get nicely brown, but *not* black as this will spoil the flavour of the soup. Heat the stock and pour it into the saucepan over the onions. Season to taste. Butter a slice of toast and dice, toss in grated Parmesan, brown in the oven for a minute or two, and float pieces on the top of the soup. This is a very quickly-made soup, and only takes about 15 minutes altogether.

ONION SOUP (White)

4 or 5 medium-sized
    onions
1 oz butter
2 pints meat boilings or
    white stock
1 bay leaf
A few parsley stalks
6 white peppercorns
1 blade of mace (if liked)
1 oz flour
½ pint milk
Salt to taste

Method. Skin the onions and scald them in boiling water for a minute or two to take away some of the pungent flavour. Then slice them down very thinly so that they fall into rings. Melt the butter in a saucepan and into it put the sliced onion, bay leaf, parsley stalks, peppercorns and mace. Put the lid on the pan and cook gently for 10 minutes without browning. Pour on the stock or meat boilings and simmer until the onions are very soft, then rub through a fine sieve. Rinse out the saucepan and return the soup to it. Blend the flour gradually with the milk, add this to the soup and stir over a gentle heat until boiling. Boil for at least 5 minutes and season to taste. Serve with little snippets of fried bread, and hand round grated cheese separately. This soup takes about 1–1½ hours to cook.

FOR EASY basting, fill a muslin bag with shredded suet, herbs and seasoning, and tie to the bars above the baking pan on which the roast is placed. When the oven gets hot, fat and seasoning drips on to the joint and keeps it continually basted.

COOKING salt which is solid will crush more easily if the block is allowed to stand on the cold tiles, or on a stone sill for ½ hour beforehand.

PIG'S FEET SOUP WITH LENTILS

½ pint lentils
2 quarts of cold water
2 pig's feet (salted)
1 onion
1 carrot
2 sticks of celery
Seasoning

Method. Wash the lentils and soak them overnight in
1 quart of the cold water. Put the feet in a saucepan
with cold water, bring to the boil, pour the water away
and rinse the feet. Now return the feet to the saucepan
with a quart of fresh cold water, and add the lentils
along with the water in which they were soaked.
Bring to the boil, add the vegetables, all prepared and
cut in small pieces, and allow the soup to simmer
slowly till the feet and lentils are very tender (about
2 hours). Lift out the feet and cut them into neat
pieces, then put them back to reheat, add seasoning
to taste, and serve.
NOTE. You can, if you like, sieve the lentils and
vegetables before returning the feet to the soup to be
reheated.

TOMATO AND GREEN PEA SOUP

½ pint shelled green peas
3 or 4 tomatoes
½ pint water
1 quart stock
1 dessertspoon cornflour
2 oz butter
Seasoning
1 cup cooked green peas

Method. Wipe the tomatoes, cut them in slices and
put them into a saucepan with the ½ pint of green peas.
Add the water, which should well cover them, and
cook slowly until the vegetables are tender. Then
rub as much as possible through a sieve, keeping
back the seeds and skins. Return this purée to a
clean saucepan, add to it the cornflour mixed to a
smooth paste with a little of the stock, and then the
remainder of the stock. Bring to the boil, boil for
a few minutes to cook the cornflour, and season to
taste. Then add the cooked peas and the butter
broken in tiny pieces. Do not boil again. If possible,
serve with fried, crisp pieces of bread.

TOMATO SOUP (1)

Piece of mutton, ham
   bone, or sheep's tail
1 lb peeled tomatoes
1 or 2 potatoes
1 onion
Seasoning

Method. Cover meat with water and bring to the boil,
and simmer as long as possible to extract all the good
into the stock. Add tomatoes, cut-up potatoes, cut-up
onion and seasoning. Boil till potato is quite soft,
then strain through colander, rubbing the vegetables
well through to make a fine pulp. Return to pot, and
serve very hot.
NOTE. Meat should go into warm water, bones into
cold water.

TOMATO SOUP (2)

1 lb tomatoes (or 1 tin)
1 gill water
1 quart stock
1 oz butter
1 piece of onion
A little chopped celery
1 oz cornflour
Salt/Pepper

Method. Melt butter in white-lined pan. Cut the onion finely and fry gently in the butter, add celery and fry gently also. Add the gill of water and the tomatoes, and cook over a low gas for 20 minutes. Strain through sieve. Add stock. Blend cornflour with a little milk or water, add to the soup, and stir until it boils. Serve at once, with fried, diced bread if possible.

QUICK TOMATO SOUP (3)

1 lb tomatoes
1 oz butter or olive oil
1½ pints white stock
Seasoning
Parsley

Method. Peel and slice the tomatoes and cook very gently in the melted butter or warmed oil for 4 or 5 minutes. Then add the stock (chicken stock if possible) and seasoning, bring to the boil, and simmer for 5 minutes. Add freshly-chopped parsley after serving the soup and, if you like, little squares of crisply-fried bread.

VELVET SOUP

½ lb red carrots
2 oz butter
1½ pints white stock
1 onion or leek
1 dessertspoon fine tapioca
Pepper/Salt

Method. Choose the reddest carrots you can find, and cut in thin slices. Put these slices in a saucepan with the onion or leek, also sliced thinly, and half the butter. Cook slowly for a few minutes and season with pepper and salt. Moisten with ½ pint of the stock and simmer until the carrot is completely soft, then rub through a sieve. Put the rest of the stock into a clean saucepan and bring to the boil, sprinkle in the tapioca and let it cook until it turns clear. Then add to it the carrot purée and cook the two together for a few minutes. Add the rest of the butter in tiny pieces, but do not boil after this is added.

NOTE. Pastry croûtons are delicious with this soup. To make these, roll out any scraps of puff or other good pastry you may have left over, and cut in shreds from 1 to 1½ inches in length and either bake or fry these until lightly browned. Drain carefully and serve very hot and crisp. The pastry can be flavoured with grated cheese if you like. It is not worth making pastry specially for this purpose though, and little pieces of bread fried to a crisp golden brown are an excellent substitute, but remember to drain well before using.

ANGUS POTATO SOUP

6 potatoes, peeled
1½ pints of water
1 large scraped carrot
¾-1 lb roast beef bones
1 large peeled tomato
1 large peeled onion
Seasoning
Parsley

Method. Put the bones in a saucepan, add water, cover with a lid and simmer for 1 hour. Then add the chopped onion, potatoes and tomato. Grate and add the carrot. Cover and simmer slowly for at least 1 hour. Remove the bones. Season to taste. Serve very hot, and at the last minute sprinkle with freshly chopped parsley.

PADDY'S POTATO SOUP

6 large potatoes, grated
1 tablespoon lentils
1 leek, chopped
1 small piece of dripping
    or bacon fat
1 quart water or vegetable
    stock

Method. Wash and cook the lentils in the water for 15 minutes. Add the rest of the vegetables and the fat, and simmer gently for 1¼ hours. Season well and serve very hot.

A sprinkling of chopped parsley on top is an improvement.

WATERCRESS CREAM SOUP

2 bunches watercress
2 oz butter
½ lb sieved potato
1 quart white stock
Seasoning
¼ pint cream (if desired)

Method. Pick and wash the cress carefully, then drain and chop it roughly, reserving a few good leaves to serve as a garnish for the soup. Put the chopped cress into a saucepan with the butter and let it cook for a few minutes without browning. Then add the cooked and sieved potato and thin it gradually with the stock. Simmer all together for about 20 minutes, and then rub through a sieve. Return the soup to the saucepan and reheat, season to taste, and if you are using it, add the cream. Garnish with a few leaves of watercress, which have been boiled in salted water for 5 minutes. If possible, serve with croûtons of cheese pastry.

Meat Dishes

I have tried to cover a wide range in this section, both as to prices and types of meat. You will find a few Scottish dishes which may be strange to you, and these I think you will discover are very economical and well worth attempting. Do not be put off by queer-sounding names like "potted hough," because this simply means brawn made from shin of beef and shin bone.

BEEF

AUSTRALIAN STEW

1 lb chuck steak
1 tablespoon flour
½ teaspoon salt
1 tablespoon fat
1 small onion
½ green pepper
Pinch marjoram or thyme
1 dessertspoon chutney
¼ cup stock or water
1 teaspoon Worcester sauce
¼ cup chopped tomatoes

Method. Trim the steak and cut into neat pieces, and coat well with salted flour. Brown on both sides in hot fat, and sprinkle the rest of the flour over the meat while it is browning, stirring it well round in the fat. Add the sliced onion, chopped green pepper, herbs (if available), chutney (sweet, if possible), stock or water and the sauce. Blend all smoothly. Lay the chopped tomatoes on top of the stew and add a little more seasoning if necessary. Cover with a lid or plate and simmer very gently for about 1½ hours until all the ingredients are cooked.

AMERICAN MEAT LOAF

2 lbs chopped, raw steak
2 eggs
1 large onion
¼ lb green peppers
¼ lb red peppers
1 cup breadcrumbs
Seasoning to taste

Method. Put chopped steak, onion and peppers through the mincer, mix with the breadcrumbs, season to taste, and mould into a softish mixture with the beaten eggs. Put in a loaf tin, and bake for 1–1½ hours, or until everything is thoroughly cooked.

This gives a very meaty loaf, as Americans use a much higher proportion of meat than we do, but you can halve all quantities, of course, if you want to try out a smaller one first.

BACHELOR STEAK

¾ lb thick stewing steak
Walnut of margarine
1 good teaspoon flour
Small piece of dripping
1 teaspoon ketchup
Salt/Pepper

Carefully cooked in this way, stewing steak tastes like a good juicy fillet.
Method. Wipe the steak and beat it hard on both sides with a rolling pin, then rub in the margarine and flour till well engrained. Score the steak with a knife, and brown it on both sides in the hot dripping in a thick stewpan. Sprinkle with the ketchup, and seasonings, reduce the heat, and cook gently from ¾–1 hour. Remove to hot serving dish. Make a little gravy by adding hot water to the pan and serve this in a sauceboat, or pour over the steak. The steak can be garnished with fried tomatoes, mushrooms or a mixture of cooked vegetables.

BEEF CASSEROLE

¾ lb thick runner of beef
2 onions, diced
1 teacup diced carrot
1 teacup diced turnip
¼ teacup diced celery
3 teacups stock or water
Salt/Pepper to taste
1 bunch of herbs

Method. Wipe the meat and cut it into small cubes. Heat and grease the frying pan with a piece of fat cut from the meat. Brown the meat all over, turning it over and over, then brown the onion. Put a layer of the prepared vegetables in a casserole, lay the browned meat and onion on top, then cover with the remainder of the vegetables. Pour over the seasoned liquid, and lay the herbs on top. Put on lid, and cook in a steady, moderate oven from 2½–3 hours, till the meat is quite tender. Remove the herbs before serving.
NOTE. This is an excellent way of cooking inexpensive cuts, and is economical because quantities of meat can be combined with generous helpings of vegetables to make a substantial meal.

BEFORE frying sausages, try part-boiling them. This makes them more digestible, especially for people with weak tummies, and the scalding prevents the skins from breaking.

BELGIAN STEW (1)

1 lb stewing steak
2 onions, sliced thinly
2 carrots, sliced thinly
2 oz dripping
1 bay leaf
1 thick slice of bread
Seasoning to taste
Made mustard
1¼ pints water

Method. Cut the meat in neat pieces, season fairly highly, and fry in the hot fat with the sliced onions until golden brown. Add the carrots and the water, put in the bay leaf and simmer in a saucepan with the lid on until the meat is really tender (about 2–2¼ hours). Take the crusts off the bread, spread the bread on both sides with the mustard, and lay this on top of the stew. Let it simmer with the stew for 5 or 6 minutes, then beat the bread into the stew.

BELGIAN STEW (2)

1½ lb stewing steak
1½ oz lean bacon or gammon
1¼ oz butter or dripping
2 onions, chopped or minced
1 tablespoon flour
½ garlic clove, peeled
Small sprig of parsley
Small bay leaf
Small sprig of thyme
1 lump of sugar
Salt/Pepper to taste
½ tablespoon vinegar
½ pint dark beer

Method. Wipe and cut the meat into small pieces. Cut the bacon or gammon into small cubes. Melt the fat in a shallow pan, and fry the beef slowly until brown all over, turning over and over till it is thoroughly browned. Remove it from the pan. Now fry the bacon or gammon in the same way, and remove and place with the meat. Fry the onion too, till brown. Strain off 2 tablespoons of fat into another pan, and blend in the flour, stirring till it is a nice light brown colour, then gradually stir in the beer. Pour the beer sauce into a casserole, and place a layer of onion in the bottom, then a layer of meat and gammon. Crush and add the garlic, with the parsley, thyme (if available), bay leaf, sugar and salt and pepper to taste. Cover, and bring to the boil. Cook slowly in a slow oven for 2½–3 hours, adding more boiling beer if it boils away too much, for the meat must stay covered all the time. When ready, add the vinegar, and serve from the casserole accompanied by plain boiled potatoes.

MEAT ROLL

1 lb lean beef, minced
¼ lb bacon trimmings
½ lb fine breadcrumbs
½–1 level teaspoon grated nutmeg
Pepper/Salt to taste
1 large egg

Method. Mix together the minced beef and chopped bacon, add breadcrumbs, and seasonings, and the large egg whipped till frothy. Form into a roll. Wring a cloth in hot water, flour the inside, wrap it tightly round the roll, tie at each end, and boil or steam for 2½–3 hours. Remove. Tighten the cloth then, when cold, remove the cloth and roll the meat in browned fine breadcrumbs.

TO KEEP milk from turning sour, stand the bottles on a layer of coarse salt on a plate (not a tin) and place in coolest, shadiest spot in larder.

BEEF STEAK AND KIDNEY PUDDING

1 lb beef, cut thin
2 sheep's kidneys
1 tablespoon flour
Seasoning
3 tablespoons stock or
   water
1 dessertspoon ketchup
Suet pastry

Method. Cut the steak into pieces and dip in seasoned flour. Remove skin and core from the kidneys, slice them thinly, and dip in seasoned flour. Take a 1½ pint basin and grease it well, then line it with suet crust about ¼″ thick, keeping it smooth and of an even thickness all over. Trim off round the edges and roll out these pieces to form a cover. Fill up with the prepared meat, and pour in the ketchup and stock or water. Pile up fairly high in the middle as they sink in the cooking. Double down the edge of the pastry lining the basin over the meat, and wet with cold water. Lay the round piece of pastry on top and press the edges well together. Cover with a scalded and floured pudding cloth, or a greased paper, and put the pudding into a saucepan of boiling water and boil till thoroughly cooked. The water must not be allowed to go off the boil, and more boiling water may be added as required. When ready (3 hours at least must be allowed), lift out and let it stand for a minute or two. Then remove the covering, and wipe the basin. Fold a table napkin neatly round, and serve in the basin in which it was cooked. A small jug of nice gravy or stock must *always* be sent to the table with this pudding, as it will need filling up when the crust is cut.

NOTE. You can add chopped onions and/or mushrooms to this mixture if you want to add extra flavour.

MEAT AND VEGETABLE LOAF

4–6 oz minced meat (veal,
   beef, ham or tongue)
2 tablespoons flour
2 tablespoons bread-
   crumbs
Pieces of onion, celery,
   turnip (finely-chopped)
1 grated carrot
½ teaspoon salt
Shake of pepper
1 egg
A little stock or water

Method. Mix all ingredients together and then mix into a stiff paste with beaten egg, and a little stock or water if necessary. Turn into a greased jar or basin, cover with a greased paper, tie down securely, and steam for about 1½ hours. Turn out on to a dish and serve hot with gravy.

This loaf can also be eaten cold with salad, and is equally delicious.

NOTE. If you wish to use cooked meat, you can, but only 1 hour is then necessary for cooking.

LEFT-OVER TONGUE. If you have cooked a tongue and are getting a bit tired of it towards the end, take the last piece, which may be a bit dry by this time, put it through the mincer with 3 skinned tomatoes, and beat up with a fork and 1 tablespoon home-made chutney. Pile on slices of buttered toast.

BEEF OLIVES

1 lb thin stewing steak
1 oz butter or dripping
1 oz flour
½ pint stock
1 dessertspoon mushroom ketchup
Seasoning
Sausage meat or forcemeat stuffing (see p. 32)
Border of potatoes
Parsley

Method. Cut the meat into small oblong-shaped pieces, suitable for rolling up, and as much one size and shape as possible. Beat them lightly with the rolling-pin and spread out all the strips on a board or your baking top. Put a little sausage meat or forcemeat stuffing on the centre of each and roll them up. Tie round like little parcels with fine string or coarse thread and coat them with the flour. Melt the dripping or butter in a stewpan, and when smoking hot put in the rolls of meat and turn them over and over until they are browned on all sides. Lift them on to a plate as they are ready, and when they are all browned, pour away the fat from the pan and add the stock. Add the seasonings, bring to the boil, and skim well. Return the rolls of meat, put on the lid, and simmer very slowly until the meat feels really tender (1½–2 hours). When ready, lift the olives on to a hot plate and take off the strings. Arrange a border of potatoes round about, with the beef olives in the centre, strain the gravy over and round them, and sprinkle with a little finely-chopped parsley. If any of the stuffing is left over, it can be made into little balls, baked in the oven and used as a garnish to the beef olives.

NOTE. Green peas and mixed vegetables are also delicious with this dish.

OXTAIL CASSEROLE

1 oxtail, jointed
4 onions
4 potatoes
4 carrots
Flour
Pepper/Salt
2 cloves
2 peppercorns
1 bay leaf

Method. Put the oxtail in a stewpan with enough water to cover, and a dessertspoon of salt. Add a muslin bag containing the spices, and stew slowly for about 2 hours. Take it off the heat and let it cool. Skim off the fat.

Chop the onions, and the carrots, slice the potatoes in three, and put into the casserole with the oxtail and some of the stock in which it had its first stewing. Make a thick gravy with the rest of the stock and the flour, and get it to a rich brown colour. Add this to the casserole when it is simmering, and cook for another 1½–2 hours in a slow oven until the oxtail is so tender that it falls from the bones when tested.

THE OLD-FASHIONED blue bag placed in the rinsing water when washing out the cloth gives a grand sparkle to mirrors and windows.

BAKED MINCE

1 lb cooked meat
Thick slice of bread
Pepper/Salt to taste
1 egg
Hard-boiled egg

GRAVY

Meat bones
Onion, carrot and turnip
Flour
A walnut of butter
Seasoning

This is a nice way of using up left-over meat and of course you can reduce the quantities to suit what you have in hand.

Method. Mince or chop the meat finely. Soak a thick slice of bread in milk and when it is well soaked, press the milk well out and beat it up with a fork, then add to the meat and mix thoroughly together. Add seasoning to taste, and blend well with a well-beaten egg. Butter a deep pudding dish and ornament the bottom and sides with a hard-boiled egg cut up. Press the mixture in and bake in a moderate oven for 1 hour. Turn out when well cooked and ready.

For the gravy, break up any bones of the meat and simmer for 2 hours with carrot and turnip. Melt a walnut of butter, and fry a cut-up onion in this till it is brown, then sprinkle in about 1 dessertspoon flour and blend smoothly. Draw off the heat and stir in about ½ pint of the bone-vegetable stock, season with pepper and salt and a little ketchup if you like. Return to the heat, stir till boiling, but do not let it get thick. Strain round the meat and serve very hot.

MINCE PUDDING

½ lb mince
1 well-beaten egg
1 tablespoon flour
Salt/Pepper to taste
½–¾ cup milk

Method. Pass mince twice through the mincer, put it into a basin and mix into it the well-beaten egg, the flour, and the seasoning. Gradually add the milk to give a consistency rather like a thick porridge, and turn into a greased basin. Cover with a greaseproof paper, tie securely, and steam for about 1 hour until firm. Serve with a brown or tomato sauce, and, if liked, some cooked macaroni.

NOTE. This pudding can also be cooked in a border mould, the macaroni served in the centre, and sauce poured over.

Another alternative is to line the basin with suet pastry and put the pudding mixture inside as a filling, but this requires at least 2 hours steaming. A few onions can be cooked in the surrounding water, and these, coated with a good white sauce, make an excellent garnish for the pudding.

BATTER puddings can be made lighter by adding 2 teaspoons of ground rice to the flour before mixing.

BRAISED BEEF

3 lbs round of beef
¼ cup each:
    carrot
    turnip
    onion
    celery
2 oz good dripping
1 pint stock
A little flour
Trimmings of ham or
    bacon
12 peppercorns
2 or 3 cloves

Method. Prepare the vegetables and cut them in small neat pieces. Then put the dripping and some ham or bacon trimmings into a stewpan and when melted put in half the vegetables. Coat the meat lightly with flour, lay it on top, with any bones round the side, and cover with the rest of the vegetables. Cook gently until the contents are just coloured, then add the stock and the spices tied in muslin. Cook very very slowly until the meat is thoroughly tender. When ready, lift the meat on to a hot dish, strain the gravy into a sauce boat, serve the vegetables round about, with some freshly-cooked potatoes.

PICKLED OX TONGUE

Soak for several hours or overnight. Wash. Run a skewer under the tip and into the root. Put on in cold water to cover, and skim when it boils. Add a few vegetables (onion, carrot, bay leaf), and simmer for 3–4 hours according to size. Dip in cold water and skin. It is ready when the skin peels back easily from tip. Remove skewer, trim root and remove any small bones. Fit tongue tightly into a round glass dish, keeping the arch tightly formed. Place a plate on top, and a heavy weight, such as an iron, to press it down. Leave till cold. *To serve hot.* Trim, and reheat in the liquor. Serve whole or sliced, with a good brown or tomato sauce.

POT ROAST

3 lbs beef, round or topside
Salt/Pepper
1 breakfastcup stock or
    water

Method. Wipe and trim the meat, and if necessary, tie it into a neat shape with a piece of tape. Grease a large stewpan with a piece of suet or fat from the meat, and when it is hot put in the meat and brown quickly on all sides. Pour in the stock or water, season with pepper and salt, put the lid on the pan, and cook it slowly until the meat is tender, basting it frequently with the stock. If necessary, you can add a little more stock or water, but be very careful with this, as too much liquid will spoil the roast effect. Success depends on slow and steady cooking. If you like, you can add a few small onions to the meat and cook them at the same time.

NOTE. This meat is nice served with horse-radish sauce, and a few baked potatoes and tomatoes. It is also delicious served cold.

Beef

PILAU OF COLD BEEF

½ lb cold roast beef
2 tablespoons chopped
  onion
1 oz butter or dripping
Salt/Pepper
2 tablespoons rice
3 tomatoes
Stock or meat boilings

Method. This is an interesting method of using up your cold left-overs. Trim the meat, removing all the skin, gristle and superfluous fat, then cut it in fine shreds. Melt the butter or dripping in a stewpan, and fry the chopped onion without browning. Add the prepared meat, pepper and salt, and cook again for a few minutes, stirring it about with your wooden spoon. Meantime, wash the rice and put it into another small saucepan with cold water to cover and bring to the boil. Let it boil for 5 minutes, then strain and rinse with fresh cold water, and add to the meat, etc., in the other saucepan, along with two of the tomatoes, wiped and cut in small pieces. Pour in enough hot stock or meat boilings to cover, and simmer slowly with the lid on, for about 1 hour, stirring occasionally. Arrange the pilau neatly on a hot dish and garnish with the third tomato, cut in 6 or 8 pieces and cooked for a few minutes in the oven or under the grill to get hot.

PICKLED BRISKET

2 lbs pickled brisket
1 onion
1 bay leaf
1 carrot
Water

Method. Cover the brisket with cold water, add the vegetables and bay leaf, and bring it to the boil. Simmer until ready, giving 25 minutes to the pound and 25 minutes over. This can be served hot, with boiled potatoes and carrots, but if wanted cold, let it cool in the water, then lift it out and press between two plates, under a heavy weight. It will cut down beautifully when cold.
NOTE. Add a pinch of sugar to the water when boiling carrots, to bring out all the sweetness.

POTATO BRIDIES

1 lb short crust or potato
  pastry

FILLING
½ lb raw beef or mince
2 or 3 raw potatoes, diced
1 or 2 whites of leek or
  onion, finely-chopped
Salt/Pepper
3 tablespoons water/stock

Method. Roll pastry thinly and cut into rounds about the size of a saucer. If using beef, cut it very small. Mix beef or mince with the other ingredients and put a good spoonful on each round of pastry. Damp the edges, fold over, press well together, and flute with the fingers. Place on a greased baking tin, brush over with egg or milk, and bake in a warm oven for ¾–1 hour. Regulo 6 for 10–15 minutes, then Regulo 4 for the rest of the time.

POTTED HOUGH

1 large piece of shin bone
1 lb shin of beef
1 onion
1 carrot
1 bay leaf
Pepper/Salt to taste

Method. Choose a piece of bone from the shiny, knobbly end, wash it, and put in a pan with enough cold water to cover. When the water is warm, add the shin of beef, the vegetables, and seasonings, and bring slowly to boiling point. Simmer for 3 or 4 hours, until the meat is so tender that it will separate when you put a fork into it. If you are out all day, you can safely leave this dish on a tiny peep of gas, or by the side of the fire, and it will not spoil, for it requires long slow cooking.

When tender, remove the meat into a basin and break it up roughly with a fork into small pieces. Mincing makes it too fine, and it is better to handle it with a fork. Return the meat to a small saucepan, and just cover with the boiling stock. Add salt and pepper to taste, and boil all together fiercely for 10 minutes. Rinse out ovenware glass dishes in cold water, and divide the mixture into your bowls or jars. I find the best method is to pour off all the liquor equally into the jars, and then spoon out the meat evenly. Leave until cold and set. This is a delicious jellied meat, ideal for serving with salads or with hot vegetables.

SOUTHERN STEW

1 lb stewing steak
3 oz butter
4 shallots
Clove of garlic
4 oz mushrooms
4 oz bacon
Salt/Pepper
1 dessertspoon flour
1 dessertspoon tomato
　　purée
½ pint stock
5 oz rice
3 tomatoes

Method. Trim and cut the meat into neat cubes. Put 2 oz of the butter in a pan and brown the meat in this. Remove it, then add sliced shallots, the crushed garlic, half of the mushrooms, sliced, and the bacon cut up small. Cook together for a minute or two, season, then sprinkle in the flour and let it brown gently. Add the tomato purée and the stock and stir till boiling. Return the meat to the pan, cover with a lid, and simmer slowly for about 2 hours. When the stew is nearly ready, boil the rice in salted water, drain it well and keep it hot. Melt the rest of the butter in a pan and fry the rest of the sliced mushrooms with peeled, sliced tomatoes, then add the warm, drained rice and mix lightly together. Arrange this savoury rice mixture into a border, and pour the stew in the centre.

STALE bread can be improved if placed in a steamer over boiling water and allowed to steam slowly for 15 to 20 minutes. This gives a very light loaf and is more effective than reheating in the oven.

Beef

SCOTCH COLLOPS WITH SUET DUMPLINGS

1 lb best steak
2 oz butter
Flour
Salt/Pepper

DUMPLINGS
4 oz self-raising flour
2 oz shredded suet
Good pinch of salt
Parsley

Method. Skin the steak, remove any gristle, and mince it. Melt the butter in a stewpan and add the mince, stirring well to dissolve lumps. Let it simmer. Dredge flour over the mixture, then add enough boiling water or stock to keep moist. Season with salt and pepper, cover and cook for about ½ hour.

A few minutes before serving, add suet dumplings.

DUMPLINGS

Method. Mix into a firm dough with water, and roll into small balls. Drop into the hot mince and leave for a few minutes until cooked.

SCOTS SLICED SAUSAGE

½ lb minced beef
¼ teaspoon black pepper
¼ teaspoon salt
2 slices bread

Method. Moisten the bread slightly and beat it into the finely-ground minced beef and seasonings. Form into sausage-shape, wrap closely with greaseproof paper and leave in a cool place till firm. Slice with sharp knife and fry with egg or tomato for breakfast or high tea.

POTATO BEEF PIE

Boiled potatoes
Pepper/Salt
Butter
2 egg yolks
2 onions, chopped
2 oz butter
2 oz flour
Stock
Parsley
1 bay leaf
Sieved tomatoes
Worcester sauce
Minced beef as desired

Method. Boil some potatoes, and mash together with pepper, salt, a little butter, and the egg yolks. Butter a pudding basin and line it with the potatoes. Fry the chopped onions in the butter, and when lightly browned, blend in about 2 oz flour to make a thick sauce with some stock. Stir in about a tablespoon chopped parsley, a chopped bay leaf, some sieved tomatoes, and a dash of Worcester sauce. Add some minced beef to these ingredients and fill up the basin. Cover with more potatoes and bake or steam for 1½ hours till well browned. Serve with gravy.

WHEN the potatoes are very new, you may enjoy a complete meal from them this way. After pouring off the water, shake a lump of butter round them in the saucepan, add a good tablespoon of medium oatmeal, a chopped spring onion, or a few chives cut up, and serve with a piece of cheese. This makes a very nourishing meal, especially if accompanied by a glass of milk.

TO KEEP milk from turning sour, place milk jug in bowl of cold salted water, and cover with a muslin cloth. Leave the ends of muslin trailing in the water so that the cloth is always moist, and place in cool spot.

SCOTTISH MEAT ROLL

1 lb raw minced beef
¼ lb bacon pieces
1 breakfastcup bread-
    crumbs
1 teaspoon black pepper
1 teaspoon salt
1 egg

Method. Chop the bacon or put it through the mincer and add to the minced beef. Add your flavourings and crumbs (these should be soft) and beat the egg till light and frothy, then add to the mixture to bind it all together. If too dry, you may add a little milk, but do not get it sloppy. It should just be nicely sticky.

Press the mixture tightly into a greased straight-sided stone jar, cover with greaseproof paper, then a clean cloth securely fastened, and steam for 1–1¼ hours. Be sure to keep the boiling water well up the jar, and add more boiling water if it evaporates too much.

When cooking time is up, have ready a paper sprinkled with dried breadcrumbs. Turn your meat roll on to this and roll round and round so that the crumbs will stick to the sides and make a nice finish.

STEWED OXTAIL

1 oxtail, jointed
Seasoned flour
1 onion
1 bay leaf
1 sliced carrot
1 oz dripping

Method. Dip the jointed oxtail pieces into seasoned flour and brown all over in the melted dripping. Pack into a casserole, and place sliced carrot and onion round about. Add the bay leaf, cover with water, put on the lid, and cook very gently in a moderate oven until the meat is tender. Cook for 2 hours or more. Serve with plain boiled potatoes.

STEAK AND KIDNEY PIE

¾ lb stewing steak
¼ lb kidney
Seasoned flour
1 onion
¼ lb flaky pastry
1 oz dripping

Method. Cut the steak and kidney into neat pieces, dip in seasoned flour, and lightly brown all over in the heated dripping. Slice the onion, and toss about in the dripping with the steak and kidney. Cover with water and bring to the boil, then simmer *very slowly* and *gently* until the meat is tender (about 1½ hours). Thicken the gravy with a little blended cornflour, and colour with a little gravy salt, then leave to get cold. Pour into a pie-dish and cover with good flaky pastry, paint the top with milk, and put in a moderately hot oven until pastry is golden and meat heated through. Serve with mashed potatoes and vegetables in season.

DO NOT leave food in the papers you have bought it in. Turn everything into bowls or plates at once, and place in coolest part of the larder.

STUFFED BEEF ROLL (1)

1½ lbs lean stewing steak
6 tablespoons white
   breadcrumbs
2 oz grated suet
1 teaspoon chopped
   parsley
1 teaspoon dried herbs
Salt/Pepper
A little milk or beaten egg
1 oz dripping
¾ pint stock or water

Method. If possible have the steak cut in one ½″ thick slice. Beat the meat lightly with a rolling pin into a neat flat shape. Mix breadcrumbs, suet, herbs and seasonings and bind with milk or egg. Spread over the meat and roll up like a roly-poly. Tie securely, then brown in a pan with the dripping, pour in the stock and simmer for about 2½ hours. When ready, lift out the meat, thicken and brown the stock to form a good gravy and pour over and round roll. Can also be eaten cold with salad.

STUFFED BEEF ROLL (2)

1 lb stewing steak
Seasoning
Forcemeat stuffing
A little flour
1 tablespoon dripping or
   bacon fat
2 teacups stock

FORCEMEAT STUFFING

¼ lb breadcrumbs
2 tablespoons chopped
   suet
1 dessertspoon chopped
   parsley
Grated rind of ¼ lemon
Salt/Pepper
Egg or milk

Method. Have the meat cut in one slice, less than ½″ thick. Remove the skin and any fat. Lay the meat on a board and beat it out a little with the rolling-pin, then season well with pepper and salt and lay any trimmings in the middle. Prepare the stuffing as follows : Put the breadcrumbs into a basin, add the finely-chopped suet, the chopped parsley, lemon rind and seasonings, and bind with a little beaten egg or milk. If you like, you can add 1 oz chopped ham, and you can use melted butter instead of suet. Lay it in the centre of the meat, roll up and bind round with tape or string. Coat this roll with flour. Melt the dripping or bacon fat in a stewpan, and when smoking hot put in the meat and turn it over and over until you have browned it on all sides. Pour in the stock, or enough to about half-cover the meat. Put the lid on the pan and stew very slowly until the meat is tender, turning it over once or twice during the cooking. When it is ready, lift on to a hot plate, remove the tape or string and keep it warm. Blend a teaspoonful of flour with a little water, add it to the gravy in the saucepan and stir till boiling. If this is too thick, depending on how much gravy has evaporated, you may have to add a little more stock or water. Season again if necessary, and strain this gravy over the meat. This is delicious served with green peas and small baked potatoes and tomatoes. (Stewing time—about 2 hours.)

WHEN you have finished with the oven and there is still plenty of heat there, pop your kettle in, and you will find it only requires very little heat to bring to boiling point when you want it for a cup of tea.

STEWED OX KIDNEY

1 ox kidney
2 oz dripping or butter
2 tablespoons flour
½ teaspoon mixed spice
Salt/Pepper
3 teacups stock
1 tablespoon chopped
    onion
1 dessertspoon ketchup
Boiled rice

Method. Wash the kidney and scald it for **2 or 3** minutes in boiling water. Dry it and cut in thin slices, removing any fat. Mix the flour with the spice, pepper and salt, and dip the kidney slices in this, coating them well. Melt the butter or dripping in a stewpan, and when smoking hot put in the pieces of kidney and the chopped onion and turn them over and over with a spoon till they are well browned on all sides. Add the stock and ketchup and stir till almost boiling, then cover the saucepan and stew very slowly until the kidney is really tender (1½–2 hours). When ready, remove any grease from the top of the gravy, add more seasoning if necessary, and serve on a hot dish with a border of rice, potatoes or macaroni. NOTE. Chopped mushrooms, bacon or tomatoes can be added if wished, or a little wine can be added to the gravy.

STEWED OX CHEEK

½ ox cheek
Vegetables, for flavouring
1 bunch of herbs (if liked)
Seasoning
Cold water or stock
1 oz butter
1 oz flour

Method. Get the butcher to bone the ox cheek, wash it well, and let it soak for an hour or two in cold water. Wash it now in warm water, and cut it into convenient pieces. Put the pieces of cheek and the bones into a saucepan, cover them with cold water or stock, and bring to the boil. Skim well, and add the vegetables for flavouring, the herbs, pepper and salt, and stew very slowly until the cheek pieces are quite tender (3–4 hours), keeping them just covered with the liquid all the time. When ready, strain, keeping the liquid aside. Melt the butter in the saucepan and let it brown, add the flour and blend it in, letting it brown too, then pour in 1 pint of the liquid and stir till boiling. Add more seasoning, if necessary, and put in the pieces of cheek to reheat. Serve with potatoes and nicely-cooked spinach, and, if you like, some of the vegetables cut into neat shapes. NOTE. You can add a little wine to this gravy if you like, or the juice of half a lemon. The bones and remains of the vegetables can be used for making stock or soup. If you like the "goo-iness" of it, you can add a cow-heel to the cheek.

THE WHITE of egg beaten to a froth, mixed with a teaspoon of vinegar and a teaspoon of sugar makes a nice soothing drink for an obstinate cough.

STEAK AND RICE KEDGEREE

¼ lb stewing steak
1 onion
1 carrot
Good tablespoon dripping
   or margarine
1 teacup rice
2 teacups stock or water
Salt/Pepper

This is an economical Scottish dish.
Method. Wipe and dice the steak. Clean and dice the vegetables. Melt the fat in a stewpan, and fry the meat and vegetables till lightly-browned. Add the washed rice and toss over heat for a few minutes. Add the liquid and seasonings and simmer for 30 minutes or longer, until the meat and vegetables are tender and the rice swollen and soft. If the mixture gets too dry, add a little more stock during the cooking. Serve nicely moist, not too wet, with potatoes, piled up in a hot serving dish.

STUFFED BRAISED OX CHEEK

1 ox cheek
Stuffing (see p. 32)
Vegetables for braising
Stock
Tomatoes to garnish
2 oz butter or dripping,
   or fat bacon
Seasoning

Method. Melt the butter, dripping or bacon fat in the bottom of a deep stewpan, then put in a layer of diced vegetables—carrot, turnip, onion and celery in equal proportions and, if you like, a little tomato and leek. Make a good bed of the vegetables, about 1½–2 inches say, according to the size of your stewpan. Season with pepper and salt, and a small bunch of herbs, if available. On top of this lay the ox cheek, prepared like this : Have the butcher bone it. Wash it well and let it soak for an hour or so in cold water. Keeping it in one piece, dry it thoroughly and spread it out on a board. Season well with pepper and salt, and spread it with the stuffing mentioned. Roll up and tie securely with tape or string. Put the lid on the pan, and cook gently for about ¼ hour, shaking the pan occasionally to prevent sticking. Now pour in enough stock or water to cover the vegetables and just touch the cheek, and cover everything with a piece of well-greased paper. Do not let it get too dry, and baste the cheek frequently with the liquid. Cook very, very slowly (4–5 hours) until the cheek is tender. When it is ready, lift the meat out of the braising pan and brown it in the oven for a few minutes. Strain the stock and boil it down till it is almost a glaze. Remove the tape or string from the meat, pour the glaze over, and garnish with small baked tomatoes or any other vegetable you prefer, in addition to the vegetables cooked in the braising pot.

BACON for boiling will have a better flavour if a dessertspoon of vinegar is added to the water.

SWEDISH MEAT BALLS

¼ lb minced beef
1 large onion
1 teacup fine breadcrumbs
A pinch of sage
A pinch of mace
Pepper/Salt to taste
1 egg to bind
1 oz butter
A little flour
Stock or water
1 meat cube

Method. Chop the onion finely and mix with the beef, breadcrumbs, sage, mace, seasonings in a basin and blend thoroughly together. Bind with the egg and form into small balls just a little larger than egg size. Melt the butter in a stewpan and lightly brown the balls on all sides, using your floured hands before putting them into the butter so that they will keep their shape. Remove from the pan when they are all browned, and blend in a little flour with the butter, add a breakfastcup of stock or water with a little meat cube melted in it, stirring all the time, to make a nice brown gravy. Return the meat balls to this, and simmer gently for about ½ hour till the meat is well cooked right through. Serve very hot, surrounded with the gravy and creamy mashed potatoes.

MUTTON AND LAMB

KIDNEYS WITH RICE

4 lamb's kidneys
6 oz butter
¼ lb mushrooms (or stalks)
1 small onion, shredded
6 oz rice
Seasoning to taste
Stock

Method. Skin, chop and flour the kidneys and toss in 2 oz of the butter made very hot, turning and cooking till tender. Wash and chop the mushrooms, or the stalks, shred the onion, and sweat them together in 2 oz of the butter till both are tender, then mix in with the kidneys. Stir in ½ teacup of weak stock (you can use part of a meat cube), and blend all thoroughly. Meantime boil the rice till tender, drain well, and then toss in the remaining butter till thoroughly mixed. Dish up the kidney mixture and surround with the buttered rice. During the cooking, season everything to your own taste.

ISLAND PIE

1 lb scrag of mutton
    cutlets
2 onions, chopped
1 lb potatoes, sliced
1 lb suet crust
Stock
Seasoning to taste

Method. Put a layer of cutlets at the bottom of the casserole, season to taste, then a layer of sliced potatoes, then one of chopped or sliced onions, then a thin layer of suet crust. Repeat the layers until the final layer of onions, pour in mutton stock, add more seasoning to taste, then the top lid of suet crust. Bake in a moderate oven for about 2 hours.

35

Mutton and Lamb

IRISH STEW

1 lb neck of mutton or
    scraps of any meat
8 large potatoes
1 teacup water
2 large onions
Pepper/Salt

Method. Cut the meat up neatly, make the pan hot and brown the meat in it. If meat is very lean, a little dripping may be used for browning. Wash, peel and slice the potatoes. Skin the onions and cut into rings. Put alternate layers of meat, potatoes, onions and seasonings in pan, add the water, cover closely, and stew gently for 2 hours. Dish piled up on a hot plate and serve very hot.

HOT POT

1 lb mutton
1 lb potatoes
1 sheep's kidney
1 oz butter or dripping
½ pint stock
1 dessertspoon chopped
    parsley
Seasoning
2 onions

Method. Trim the meat and cut in small pieces, removing most of the fat. Split the kidney, skin, trim away the gristly part from the centre, and cut in small pieces. Slice the onions thinly and scald in boiling water for a few minutes. Peel the potatoes, cut a few in halves or quarters and slice the rest fairly thickly. Arrange the ingredients in layers in a casserole, seasoning each with a little pepper and salt. The last layer should be the biggish pieces of potato. Pour in the stock and dot with butter or dripping. Cook with the lid on for 1½ hours, and then for the next ½ hour without the lid so that the top gets nicely browned. Sprinkle with finely-chopped parsley and serve from the casserole.

NOTE. Beef, veal or a mixture can be used instead of mutton. A few mushrooms or oysters may be added for extra tastiness.

DEVILLED KIDNEYS

3 or 4 sheep's kidneys
1 oz butter
1 tablespoon chopped
    onion
Cayenne/Salt
1 teaspoon chutney
A squeeze of lemon juice
¼ teaspoon made mustard
1 teacup stock
2 yolks of eggs
A few breadcrumbs.

Method. Split the kidneys, remove the white centre and the skin, and cut them in small pieces. Melt the butter in a small stewpan and cook the onions in it for a few minutes without browning. Add the kidney with the seasonings and mix well, then pour in the stock. Stew with the lid on, over a gentle heat, until kidney is tender (about 15 minutes). When ready, draw the pan to the side and stir in egg yolks. Fill small scallop shells or individual dishes with the mixture, sprinkle with fine breadcrumbs and pour over a little melted butter. Brown under the grill and serve.

36

BRAISED BREAST OF MUTTON

2 lbs breast of mutton
Forcemeat stuffing
   (see p. 32)
Stock
Flavouring vegetables
A little browning
Seasoning

Method. Have the butcher bone the mutton. Remove the skin and some of the fat, then spread the meat out on a board and flatten it with the rolling-pin. Trim again if necessary, wipe with a damp cloth on both sides and season with pepper and salt. Spread the forcemeat stuffing in the centre of the mutton, roll up and sew together with a needle and fine string. Place a bed of mixed vegetables (carrot, turnip, onion and celery, cut in dice), at the bottom of a large stewpan, barely cover with stock and bring to the boil. Lay the meat on top of this, cover with a greased paper, put a tight-fitting lid on the pan, and cook slowly until the meat is tender, turning the roll once during the cooking time (about 2 hours).

To serve hot. Lift the meat on to a hot dish and draw out the string. Strain the liquid from the vegetables and serve them round the dish. Return liquid to the saucepan, and add to it some browning to make a nice gravy and pour this over the meat. Red currant jelly makes a nice accompaniment, served separately.

To serve cold. Lift the meat out of the saucepan and press it between two boards with a weight on top, until cold. Then draw out the string, trim the ends, and serve with salad.

SAVOURY CHOPS

3 mutton chops
2 tablespoons chopped
   onion
1 carrot
1 small turnip
½ pint stock
1 tablespoon rice
Seasoning

Method. Wipe the chops with a damp cloth and trim off most of the fat. Melt some of this fat in a frying pan and fry the chops for two or three minutes, browning them on both sides. Cut the carrot and turnip into small pieces (there should be about a teacupful of each) and put them at the bottom of a stewpan with the chopped onion, and well-washed rice. Pour in the stock, season with pepper and salt and bring to the boil. Then put in the chops, cover, and cook slowly until meat and vegetables are tender (about ¾ hour). Serve the vegetables on a hot dish with the chops on top, and garnish with snippets of toast.

TO KEEP butter from melting, place it inside a polythene bag, fasten securely, and drop into a bowl of cold, salted water. Keep in coolest spot in larder.

TO REMOVE onion taste from breath, brush teeth immediately afterwards and sip a glass of cold milk.

Mutton and Lamb

LAMB'S SWEETBREADS

½ lb lamb's sweetbreads
A little flour
Seasoning
Egg and breadcrumbs
Rolls of bacon, if liked
Lemon
Gravy. if liked

Method. Wash the sweetbreads thoroughly, then let them soak in cold water for an hour or so and wash again. Put them in a lined stewpan with enough cold water to cover, bring to the boil, skim if necessary and then simmer slowly for 10–15 minutes. Then lift them out, and press them between two dishes until cold. Toss them, when cold, in flour seasoned with pepper and salt, then egg and breadcrumb them neatly, and fry in hot fat till a golden brown. Serve garnished with cut lemon and, if you like, little rolls of bacon fried to a crisp brown. If you like, you can serve a little good gravy separately.

MUTTON STEW WITH TOMATOES, AND RICE

1 lb lean mutton
1 oz butter
1 tablespoon chopped
    onion
Salt/Pepper
2 tomatoes
1 pint water or stock
¼ cup parboiled rice

Method. Choose meat which is not too fat, wipe it with a damp cloth, cut in pieces about 2 inches square, and season with pepper and salt. Melt the butter in a stewpan, put in the chopped onion and cook for a few minutes without colouring. Now add the meat and stir and cook for about 15 minutes. Pour in the water or stock and add the tomatoes, wiped and cut in small pieces. Put the lid on, and stew slowly for about 1 hour. Then add the parboiled rice and cook for another ½ hour. Arrange the stew neatly on a hot dish and sprinkle with a little finely-chopped parsley. NOTE. If you get any bones with the mutton, cook them with the stew and lift them out before serving—they add goodness to the dish.

STEW IN CASSEROLE

½ lb mutton (best end
    neck)
1 carrot
1 onion
1 small turnip
1 or 2 potatoes
Boiling water
Salt/Pepper

Method. Chop meat in fairly small pieces, remove any excess fat, and put in casserole. Cover with sliced potato, turnip and carrot. Add about 1 inch of boiling water and 1 teaspoon salt. Add sliced onion. Cook slowly in the oven for 1¼ hours. Add pepper and serve.

IF YOU have made too much Yorkshire pudding for one meal, it can be reheated perfectly if you get the grill red-hot, pop the pudding underneath, and toast till crisp and brown, turning from side to side every quarter-minute or so, so that the fat runs right through.

DO NOT cook lamb's liver more than a minute on each side, or you will overcook and ruin it.

SPRING STEW

1 lb neck of lamb
½ dozen young carrots
3 young turnips
3 spring onions
½ dozen new potatoes
1 cos lettuce
½ cup green peas
Warm water
Salt

Method. Have the lamb cut into chops. Wipe and trim them neatly. Put them into a stewpan or casserole with warm water to cover and a little salt. Bring to the boil and skim well. Prepare the vegetables. Cut lettuce and onions in shreds and cut the potatoes, turnips and carrots in equal-sized pieces. When all the scum has been removed from the meat, put in the lettuce, onion, carrot and turnip and add a little more salt. Put the lid on and stew slowly for ½ hour. Then add the new potatoes and green peas and stew for another ½ hour. Serve the meat in the centre of a hot dish with the vegetables and gravy round about.

SHEEP'S HEAD BRAWN

1 sheep's head
½ lb bacon
Pepper/Salt

Method. Boil the head for 3 hours with the bacon. When cooked, remove flesh, skin the tongue, and mince both finely, together with the bacon. Season with salt and pepper and press firmly into basin. Put plate on top, and a weight on top of that till next day. Turn out when cold and firm.

SHEEP'S HEART, POT ROASTED

1 sheep's heart
Forcemeat stuffing
    (see p. 32)
2 oz dripping
1 teaspoon flour
1 teacup stock
1 teaspoon lemon juice
Seasoning

Method. Thoroughly wash the heart in several cold waters, cutting away the pipes and flaps. Let it lie in cold salted water for ½ hour, then dry well, and fill the cavities with the forcemeat stuffing. Tie a strong piece of greased paper over the stuffing to keep it in place, or sew the opening, just as you prefer. Melt the dripping in a strong stewpan, put in the heart and baste it well. Then let it roast slowly over a gentle heat, with the lid on the pan, until tender, basting it occasionally. If it gets too dry, you can add a tiny quantity of hot water, but do not get it wet. When ready (about ¾ hour), lift the heart on to a hot dish, and remove the paper or stitching. Pour away most of the fat from the pan, sprinkle in the flour and stir until brown. Then add the stock, stir till boiling and skim well. Season to taste, adding the lemon juice last of all. Strain this sauce round the heart and serve with red currant jelly.

Mutton and Lamb

LARGE MUTTON PIE

1¼ lbs mutton
2 sheep's kidneys
1 shallot (or onion)
1 tablespoon flour
1 teaspoon chopped
    parsley
4/5 parboiled potatoes
1/2 tablespoons chopped
    mushrooms (optional)
Pepper/Salt
A little stock or water
Rough puff pastry

Method. Choose mutton without much bone or fat, wipe it and cut it in small pieces. Remove skin and core from the kidneys and cut them in thin slices. Toss meat and kidney in the flour, sprinkle them with chopped parsley, mushrooms and shallot. Season with pepper and salt, and mix with the potatoes cut in slices. Put the mixture in a pie-dish, piling it fairly high in the centre, and pour in a little stock or water. Cover the pie with the pastry and bake in a good oven until cooked through (1½–2 hours).

NOTE. A few tomatoes will give a nice flavour. As mutton by itself can be a bit greasy, the potatoes are put in to absorb some of this grease.

SMALL MUTTON PIES

¼ lb lean mutton
Seasoning
Gravy
Raised pie crust

Method. Any scraps or trimmings of mutton can be used for making small pies, but they must not be too fat. Cut them in small pieces, removing all skin, bone and gristle. Season with pepper, salt, and, if liked, a pinch of nutmeg, and just moisten with water or gravy. For six pies use double the quantity of raised pie crust given in my pastry recipe, and mix it up as hot as possible. Put aside about a third of the paste to keep warm and divide the rest into six equal-sized pieces. Form each piece into a small ball, and then into little cases, either round a tumbler or with thumbs and fingers. Fill with the meat, and then raise up the sides again with the hands. Roll out the paste which has been keeping warm, and cut out rounds to make covers for the pies. Wet round the edges, lay them over the pies, wetted side down, and press the two edges firmly together. Trim round with scissors, make a small hole in the top, brush over with a little milk or egg and bake in a good oven for about ½ hour. When ready, fill up with a little hot gravy.

ALWAYS let boiled meat get cold in its own broth if you want it to be tender when cold. Even a joint which you can carve hot may be put back in the broth to get cold.

ORANGE peel can be dried in the oven and small pieces used for flavouring puddings, cakes and custards. When very dry, the rinds make grand fire-lighters.

WHEN boiling milk, rinse the pan out with cold water first and it will prevent burning.

MUTTON ROLL

¼ lb lean mutton
3 oz lean bacon
½ teacup breadcrumbs
1 dessertspoon chopped
    onion
1 teaspoon chopped
    parsley
Salt/Pepper
Little lemon rind (if liked)
1 dessertspoon chopped
    pickles
1 egg to bind
A pinch of mixed spice

Method. Scrag or any of the cheap cuts of mutton will do for this, but trim off all the fat, and put the meat, trimmed and cut in pieces, through the mincer twice with the bacon. Mix with the breadcrumbs, chopped parsley, chopped onion, pickles, seasonings, until thoroughly blended, and bind with the egg, well-beaten. Form the mixture into a roll, wrap it in a double sheet of greased paper, lay it in a baking tin or fireproof dish with a little melted fat and about two tablespoons hot water in the bottom to prevent sticking, and bake in a moderate oven for about 1 hour, turning it over once or twice to cook evenly all through, and basting to keep the paper moist. When nearly ready, remove the paper, sprinkle the roll with breadcrumbs and return to the oven to brown and finish cooking.

This is delicious hot with green vegetables and a nice tomato sauce, or cold with salad.

PORK AND HAM

BAKED HAM IN PASTE COVERING

Soak the ham in lukewarm water for an hour or so, to remove the saltiness. If it is very highly smoked or salted, you may have to let it soak overnight, and if possible the water ought to be changed once or twice. Scrape the ham, removing all rust and any discoloured parts, and put it into a saucepan with sufficient lukewarm water to cover it. Bring to the boil, and skim well. Simmer it for 1 hour. Meantime prepare a plain paste made with flour and water and roll out on a pastry board. Drain the ham well, dry it and wrap it up in the paste, covering it thoroughly. Lay in a roasting tin with 3 or 4 tablespoons of dripping and bake in a moderate oven, basting frequently. The time taken will depend on the size and thickness of the ham—20 minutes to the pound and 20 minutes over should be allowed. When ready, remove the crust, and the skin, coat all over with breadcrumbs, and return to the oven for a few minutes to make the crumbs brown and crisp. Spinach, Brussels sprouts, greens or green peas are all delicious served with hot, boiled ham.

FROSTED GRAPES. If you want to make these exotic-looking grapes for decorative purposes, just beat up an egg white till slightly frothy, spread it on a bunch of grapes, sprinkle with caster sugar and leave aside till the sugar and egg white is dry.

IF THE paper sticks to your table jellies, hold them under a running tap for a minute or so, and the paper will come away easily.

BACON KNUCKLE

1 bacon knuckle
Bay leaf
Few peppercorns
1 onion
Breadcrumbs

Method. Cover knuckle with cold water, bring to the boil, then throw this water away and with it any excess salt which has been boiled out. If knuckle is very salt, repeat this process twice. Then simmer it with the bay leaf, peppercorns and the onions for about 2 hours until skin can easily be lifted up when tested with a fork. Skin the knuckle, rub it with breadcrumbs, and serve with cauliflower and sliced carrots, and a few mushrooms if available, all masked in a creamy white sauce, with boiled potatoes.

NOTE. If any bacon scraps are left, mince them, add to mashed potato, season, form into cakes with floured hands, and fry in shallow fat.

PORK AND APPLE PIE

1 lb fresh lean pork
1 lb potatoes
1 onion
1 large apple
½ teaspoon powdered sage
Salt/Pepper
1 teacup stock
1 oz dripping

Method. Wipe the pork and cut in small pieces, cutting away all skin and bone and any superfluous fat. Season with pepper, salt and powdered sage, and mix well together. Slice onions thinly, and slice also the apples and potatoes. Grease a casserole and put in the different ingredients in layers, making the top a thick layer of sliced potatoes. Pour the stock over and dot the dripping on top. Cover with a lid and bake in a good oven for about 2 hours, but about ½ hour before it is ready, take off the lid and let the pie brown.

NOTE. You can use any cheap cut of pork for this dish, for the long slow cooking makes the cheapest cuts tender, but be sure to trim away all the fat, or the dish might be too rich in grease. If you do not like sage, mixed spice may be used instead.

BELLY OF PORK

About 2 lbs belly of pork
1 lb sliced carrots
1 onion
Seasoning

Method. If using fresh pork, cover with boiling water. If salt or pickled pork is used, cover with cold water. Place in a casserole with the sliced carrots and the onion, season to taste, and cook in a slow oven for 2–2½ hours. Serve with pease pudding mixed with a knob of butter, or with potatoes as required.

WARM the tea leaves before putting them into your warmed teapot and you will find you get a stronger cup than if the tea leaves are put cold into the warmed teapot.

PORK CHOPS IN THE OVEN

2 pork chops
2 apples
2 onions
2 potatoes
½ pint stock or water
Salt/Pepper

Method. Wipe chops and cut into four pieces. Place in greased pie-dish and sprinkle with sage, if liked. Peel and slice onions. Peel, slice and core apples. Place onion and apple mixture on top of chops. Sprinkle seasonings over, and pour on water or stock. Cover the dish with greased paper, then place a flat enamel or fireproof plate on top and bake in a moderate oven for 1½ hours.

VEAL

MINCED VEAL STEAKS

½ lb veal
2 oz ham or bacon
1 oz chopped suet
1 tablespoon breadcrumbs
A little grated lemon rind
1 teaspoon chopped
    parsley
Pepper/Salt
A pinch of nutmeg
Egg and breadcrumbs

Method. Cut veal and ham in small pieces and put them through the mincer. Mix with the chopped parsley, suet, breadcrumbs and seasonings, and bind all together with a little beaten egg. Form into flat cakes, using a little flour on your hands if necessary. Egg and breadcrumb them and fry to a golden-brown in a little hot butter in a frying pan. They must be well cooked, so turn frequently to make sure they are cooked right through to the middle, and this prevents them getting too hard on the outside. Drain, and serve either plain or with a good tomato or brown sauce. Garnish with small pieces of cut lemon. Spinach is very nice with this dish.

BOSTON VEAL WITH PINEAPPLE

6 veal chops
2 tablespoons flour
Salt/Pepper to taste
¾ cup pineapple juice
2 tablespoons lemon juice
1 tablespoon Worcester
    sauce
6 pineapple slices
Little extra flour
Fat

Method. Trim the chops, wipe with a damp cloth, and coat with seasoned flour. Brown lightly in hot fat, then remove from the pan and place in fireproof dish. Mix the pineapple juice with the lemon juice and the Worcester sauce and pour this mixture over the chops. Cover and bake in a moderate oven for 1¼–1½ hours, or until the meat is really tender. Drain the pineapple slices well, and coat lightly with the extra flour. Fry lightly on both sides in a little hot fat, then arrange chops and pineapple alternately on a flat serving dish and pour the sauce over. Serve very hot. NOTE. Peas and creamed potatoes make a nice vegetable accompaniment for this dish.

VEAL AND HAM PIE

PASTRY
1 lb flour
1 teaspoon salt
4 oz lard
¼ pint of hot water, or
   hot milk and water

FILLING
¾-1 lb veal
Some veal bones
4 oz chopped bacon or
   gammon
Salt/Pepper
2 hard-boiled eggs
Beaten egg to glaze

Method. Sieve the flour with the salt, and then put the fat and the liquid into a saucepan and bring to boiling point. Pour this hot liquid into the flour and salt, and mix to a dough with a wooden spoon and the hands, making it very flexible so that it can be moulded with the fingers into any shape. Knead until the paste is smooth, then cut off a quarter of the paste and keep it warm by putting it into a bowl sitting in a pan of hot water and covering with a cloth or it will not be pliable when you want it for the lid. Mould the main piece of the pastry into a round pie-case, but you can fit it inside a cake tin with a loose base if you find this easier. A 6″ diameter tin, about 3″ deep is a suitable size for this quantity. Roll to about ½″ thick.

Now make the filling : Cut the meat into very small pieces, having removed any skin and bone from the veal. Add the ham and a sprinkling of chopped parsley, if liked, season well, and moisten with a little stock or cold water. The bottom ring of pastry should be put in first, if you are using a tin, and all edges painted with beaten egg to keep the juices in. Then line the sides, pressing pastry well to the shape of the tin, and let it stand above the top edge about ½″, to form part of decoration later. Pinch all joins well together to make an efficient casing. Fill the pie halfway with meat, then put in the hard-boiled eggs. Cover with the rest of the meat. Roll out the remaining piece of pastry for the lid. Damp the inner edge of the pastry and press the edges together to form a rim. Cut at ½″ intervals and bend in alternate tabs to form a decoration, leaving the ones in between standing upright. Use scissors for this cutting to get a firm pattern. Make a hole in the centre to let the steam out, and brush all over with beaten egg to form a good glaze. Bake in a hot oven for about 15 minutes to brown the pastry, then lower to moderate heat and cook for another 1½-2 hours, or until the meat feels tender when you test it with a skewer.

Stock. Meantime, you have been simmering the veal bones, and any trimmings, to form a rich stock which will provide the jelly, and when you take the pie out of the oven, fill this stock through the centre hole, and this will set in a jelly inside the pie.

Serve cold with salad.

BEEF AND VEAL MOULD

¼ lb lean beef
¼ lb fleshy veal
¼ lb fat bacon
2 oz stale bread
1 small onion
1 egg
Salt/Pepper
Pinch grated nutmeg
¼ pint stock
¼ teaspoon made mustard
1 teaspoon chopped
   parsley
1 tablespoon breadcrumbs

Method. Soak the stale bread in cold water until soft, then squeeze it as dry as possible, and beat it with a fork until smooth and free from lumps. Add the minced beef, veal and bacon, which you have put through the mincing machine twice, the finely-chopped or grated onion, the chopped parsley and seasoning. Mix all together and add the stock. Beat the egg and add to the other ingredients and mix again. Carefully grease a plain mould and coat the inside with the breadcrumbs which you have browned. Pack the mixture into it, cover with greased paper and steam until the meat is thoroughly cooked. When ready, turn out on to a hot dish and pour brown, tomato, mushroom, caper or any other preferred sauce around. Spinach and potatoes are a grand accompaniment to this dish, and of course this mould is excellent served cold with salad. (Steaming time about 2½–3 hours.)

VEAL AND HAM PASTY

½ lb cooked veal
3/4 oz cooked ham or
   bacon
½ pint white sauce
2/3 hard-boiled eggs
Rind of 1 lemon
1 dessertspoon chopped
   parsley
Grated nutmeg
Seasoning
Rough puff or flaky
   pastry

Method. Cut the veal and ham in small pieces, or, if they are a bit scrappy, put them through the mincer. Make about ½ pint of good white sauce of a fairly thick consistency, and mix in the meat, seasoning with the grated lemon rind, a little nutmeg, pepper and salt and chopped parsley. Cut the hard-boiled eggs in slices, and fold in. Let everything get cold before using.

Line a greased tin with rough puff or flaky pastry, put in the meat mixture, and wet the edge of the pastry with cold water. Cover with another round of pastry, pressing the edges well together. Mark round nicely with the back of the knife and flute the edges. Make a hole in the centre, and brush over with beaten egg or a little milk. Bake in a good oven till the pastry is well browned and thoroughly cooked (¾–1 hour). Cut across in triangular-shaped pieces and serve hot.

DO NOT throw away any crusts of bread. Crisp them in the oven, then put through the mincer. This sharpens the blades and the crumbs are excellent for fish dressing.

SOAK almonds overnight in cold water, and you will find the skins come off easily.

Veal

BROWNED KNUCKLE OF VEAL

2 lbs knuckle of veal
2 onions
3 celery stalks
Hot water
Salt/Pepper
1 yolk of egg
Breadcrumbs
Seasoning
1 oz butter
1 oz flour
Juice of ½ lemon
Rolls of bacon

Method. Wipe the meat and put it into a saucepan with hot water to cover it. Bring to the boil and skim well. Add the onions and celery prepared and cut in small pieces, season with pepper and salt and stew slowly for about 2 hours, until tender. When tender, lift it out and remove as much of the bone as possible. Fold into a neat shape and fix in position with a skewer. Then brush over with egg yolk, season with pepper and salt and coat with fine breadcrumbs. Now place the joint of veal in a good oven until it is nicely browned. Meantime, make a sauce with the butter, flour and a pint of the liquid in which the veal was cooked. Season to taste. Add the lemon juice and strain into a sauce boat. Serve the veal on a hot dish and garnish with rolls of bacon fried to a crisp brown, and cut lemon.

GALANTINE OF VEAL

3/4 lbs breast of veal
1 lb pork sausage meat
Seasoning
2 hard-boiled eggs
6 oz ham or tongue
1 dessertspoon chopped
    parsley
Cold water
Vegetables for flavouring

Method. Have the meat boned by the butcher, but be sure to get the bones back. Spread the meat on a board, skin side underneath, and spread the seasoned sausage meat on top. Cut the hard-boiled eggs in long sections, and the ham or tongue in strips and place these in rows on top of the sausage meat. Sprinkle the parsley over. Roll and sew up the meat, then tie in a cloth very firmly, in the shape of a roll.

Put the veal bones in a saucepan with cold water to cover, a little salt and a few pieces of flavouring vegetable (carrot and onion, etc.). Bring to the boil, then lay in the roll of veal and simmer it slowly until tender (2½–3 hours). When done, lift it out, and if there has been any shrinkage of the meat and the cloth looks loose, take it off and re-roll it. Press the galantine between two dishes with a weight on top, and leave it until it is quite cold. Then take off the cloth and trim the ends, and if you want a nice glazed finish, melt a little aspic or gelatine and paint over the roll, giving two coats if necessary. Serve garnished with parsley, and with a nice salad.

WHEN you are making cakes, and in danger of being interrupted, a good memory-jogger is to put all the needed ingredients at the right-hand side of your mixing bowl, and then as you use them transfer them to the left-hand. So if you are interrupted, you know which ingredients have been used and which not.

VEAL AND HAM MOULD

1 lb fleshy veal
1 good veal bone
Vegetables for flavouring
6 oz fat bacon
2 hard-boiled eggs
1 teaspoon chopped
    parsley
Grated rind of ¼ lemon
Salt/Pepper
Lemon juice

Method. Make a good cupful of jellied stock by boiling the veal bone, plus any bones from the 1 lb of veal, for ½ hour or so with a little water and small pieces of flavouring vegetables. Strain and keep aside till wanted.

Take a plain mould and decorate the bottom with a few slices of hard-boiled egg and a little chopped parsley. Wipe the veal with a damp cloth, remove all skin and bone, and cut into small pieces. Remove all rind and gristle from the bacon and cut it in narrow strips. Mix veal and bacon together on a plate with the rest of the eggs cut in small pieces and the seasonings. Pack the mixture loosely into the mould, filling it to within an inch from the top. If the stock has jellied, melt it and strain it over, or if it has not jellied, strain it straight over. Fill up the mould with this jellied stock, cover with a greased paper, and bake in slow oven until cooked. (Baking time 2 hours.)

When it is ready, the veal should feel quite tender when tested with a skewer. If necessary, fill up with a little more stock, then leave aside to cool. When wanted, turn it out on a dish, surround with a nice salad, and decorate with parsley.

NOTE. Rabbit can be prepared in the same way.

VEAL HOT POT WITH DUMPLINGS

1 lb fleshy veal
2 oz fat bacon
Hot water
Salt/Pepper

DUMPLINGS

6 oz flour
1 or 2 oz butter
1½ teaspoons baking
    powder
Milk or water
Salt

Method. Wipe the veal and cut it into small pieces free from skin and bone. Cut the bacon in small pieces and put them both in a saucepan with hot water to cover. Season with pepper, and salt if necessary (if the bacon is very salt you may not want to add any more salt). If you like, you can also add a little sliced onion at this stage. Stew slowly with the lid on for about 1 hour, or until the veal is tender. When nearly ready, prepare the dumplings. Sieve the flour, salt and baking powder into a basin and rub in the butter till the mixture is like fine breadcrumbs. Then mix very lightly with water or milk, or a milk and water mixture, to a softish dough.

Turn the veal into a casserole, and put the dough, shaped in spoonfuls, on the top. Bake in a moderate oven till the dumplings have risen and are well cooked (about ½ hour).

Veal

VEAL ESCALOPES WITH MUSHROOMS

¼ lb fillet of veal
Egg and breadcrumbs
Chopped ham
Lemon rind
Seasoning
Mushrooms

Method. Have the butcher slice the veal fairly thinly, and then beat it yourself on a wooden board with the rolling-pin until it is really thin. Cut it into small cutlets or escalopes about 3″ in diameter, and season these with pepper and salt, brush them over with beaten egg and toss in fine breadcrumbs with which a little finely-chopped ham and grated lemon rind have been mixed. Pat the escalopes, making them as smooth and neat as possible, and fry them in butter until a golden brown on both sides and thoroughly cooked. Rather keep turning them than let them cook too long on one side or you will make them hard. Drain on kitchen paper until free from grease. Trim and wash the mushrooms. Peel them and cut in small thin slices, using the best of the stalks too. Put them in a small saucepan with a little butter, season with pepper and salt and fry gently for a minute or two, then add a little water, or stock, or wine if you like it and can spare it, and cook for a few minutes longer when they will be ready to serve. Arrange the escalopes in a circle on a hot dish, put the mushrooms in the centre, and pour the sauce in which they have been cooked around. Spaghetti and cheese makes a delicious accompaniment to this dish, or a border of creamy mashed potatoes.

STEWED VEAL WITH POTATOES

1 lb fleshy veal
Hot water
6 small white onions
Salt/Pepper
2 oz ham
3 or 4 potatoes
1 oz butter
1 oz flour
1 tablespoon chopped
    parsley

Method. Wipe the meat with a damp cloth and put it into a stewpan with hot water to cover. Bring to the boil and skim well. Prepare the onions and add them with the ham cut in small pieces, pepper and salt. Cover and simmer slowly for 1¼ hours. Then add the potatoes, peeled and cut in quarters, and the butter and flour which have been blended smoothly together on a plate. Continue cooking slowly until the potatoes are ready, and add the chopped parsley at the very last. Arrange neatly on a hot dish and serve very hot.

BEFORE baking potatoes, let them stand in boiling water for 15 minutes. This will partly cook them and they will take only half the time to bake.

TO SKIN tomatoes quickly and easily, pop them in boiling water for a few seconds. This will loosen the skin and they can be peeled easily.

SCRAMBLED VEAL AND TOMATOES

¼ lb cooked veal
2 eggs
1 cup tomato purée
1 oz butter or bacon fat
1 teaspoon chopped
    parsley
Salt/Pepper
Slices of toast

Method. Remove all skin and gristle from the veal, then chop it finely or put it through the mincer. You can use either fresh or tinned tomatoes, and they should be rubbed through a wire or hair sieve to make the purée. Melt the butter or bacon fat in a saucepan, add the purée, meat, eggs slightly beaten, pepper and salt, and stir over a moderate heat until thoroughly hot and thick. Serve on neat pieces of toast or fried bread, and decorate with small sprigs of parsley. This is a nice way to use your left-over meat, and when the eggs are dear, it stretches them a bit too.

OTHER MEAT DISHES

INDIAN PISH PASH

¼ lb rice
1 lb chicken or mutton
Few slices green ginger
2 onions
2 bay leaves
Peppercorns
Salt
1 or 2 oz butter
Water to cover

Method. Wash the rice in several waters, then put into a saucepan with the chicken or mutton cut up in neat pieces, the ginger (if available), sliced onions, bay leaves, pepper-corns and salt. Dot with the butter and add enough water to just cover. Simmer with the lid on over a gentle heat until the meat is tender and the rice pappy, and serve very hot.

TRIPE WITH TOMATOES (from Italy)

1½ lbs prepared tripe
1 cup tomato sauce or
    purée
1½ oz butter
¼ lb fresh mushrooms
Stock
2 tablespoons bread-
    crumbs
2 tablespoons grated
    cheese
Seasoning

Method. Cut the tripe into narrow strips of smallish size and put into the stewpan with the mushrooms, carefully washed, peeled and cut in slices. Add half the butter and a seasoning of pepper and salt, and cook for about 10 minutes, very gently, but do not let it get brown. Pour in enough light stock to cover the tripe and mushrooms, put the lid on the pan and stew slowly until tender. Add the tomato sauce, or a purée made from tinned tomatoes rubbed through a sieve, and cook a few minutes longer. Pour the stew into a fireproof dish, sprinkle the breadcrumbs and cheese on top, dot the rest of the butter over this, and brown in the oven or under the grill.
NOTE. If you like you can cook a little finely-chopped onion along with the tripe and mushrooms.

FARMHOUSE CURRY

¼ lb of any cold meat
1 tablespoon chutney
1 dessertspoon curry
    powder
1 dessertspoon flour
1 onion, chopped
1 apple
2 oz butter or margarine
¼ pint stock or water
1 tablespoon sultanas
Salt to taste
Rice

Method. Melt the fat, and when it is really hot, fry the chopped onion, flour and curry powder all together for a minute or two, stirring all the time. Do not worry if it looks a bit dry, just make sure you do not burn it. Add your stock, chopped apple, and salt to taste, and keep stirring all the time until the sauce is smoothly boiling. Turn down the gas, or put the pan by the side of the fire, and simmer for a good ½ hour, or longer if you like, for it is impossible to overcook this, so long as you give it a stir from time to time to prevent sticking. Then add the chopped meat, stir in either apple or tomato chutney, add the sultanas, and, if available, a squeeze of lemon juice, and heat all through very thoroughly. Simmer all together to blend smoothly, and to swell up the sultanas, and serve piping hot in a hot dish in a border of boiled rice, and, if you like, a few plain boiled potatoes.

Boil the rice in the usual way in boiling salted water, and when cooked, turn into a colander and pour boiling water through to remove sticky starchiness. Put in a cool oven for a short time to dry off, when grains should be white and separate and perfect for the curry accompaniment.

GALANTINE

1 lb sausage meat
¼ lb lean bacon, cut thick
1 hard-boiled egg
Grated rind of 1 lemon

Method. Divide sausage meat in two, and lay one half on a floured board in oblong shape. Cut bacon in long strips and lay on top of sausage meat. Lay egg, cut in slices on top of bacon, then sprinkle the grated lemon rind on top, and lastly cover with the other half of the sausage meat. Roll all in greased paper, then in floured cloth and tie well at each end. Place into pan of boiling water and simmer for 1½ hours. When cooked, take out and lay on plate without taking out of cloth or paper, and lay something very heavy on top to press it. Leave until next day, then take off cloth and paper, and use as required for breakfast or supper. If you wish, you can glaze with a little gelatine (with a little gravy browning added as colouring) as a finishing touch.

WHEN frying onions for curry, a tablespoon of boiling water poured over them a minute before removing from the pan, will make them a golden brown colour, and more digestible.

SAUSAGE AND LEEKS

3 or 4 large leeks
¼ lb liver sausage
1 oz butter
1 oz flour
1½ teacups stock
Seasoning

Method. Prepare and wash the leeks thoroughly, and cut them into short lengths. Throw them into a saucepan of boiling, salted water and boil for 5 minutes, then drain. Return the leeks to the saucepan with the butter and seasoning and shake over the heat for a few minutes. Mix in the flour smoothly, then stir in the stock, and stir till boiling. Now add the liver sausage in one piece, put the lid on the pan and stew slowly over a gentle heat. To serve, arrange the leeks neatly in the centre of a hot dish, and lay the sausage, cut in slices, round about.

MEAT SURPRISES

½ lb cooked meat
3 oz breadcrumbs
1 teacup stock
Seasoning
1 egg yolk
Chopped parsley
4 or 5 eggs

This is a tasty way of using your left-over meat when the eggs are cheap.
Method. Simmer the bread-crumbs in the stock for a few minutes until they swell and absorb the liquid, then add the meat, seasoning and the egg yolk. Mix well together, and turn the mixture on to a plate to cool. Well-grease four or five individual moulds or teacups, and sprinkle in a little chopped parsley at the bottom of each. Now line them with the meat mixture, leaving a little hollow in the centre. Into each hollow drop an egg. Place the moulds in a deepish tin, cover them with greased paper, and pour some boiling water round to come well up the moulds. Cook in the oven until the eggs are set (about 10–15 minutes), then turn out carefully, and pour a little brown sauce or gravy around if liked.

SPANISH STEW

1 lb of any stewing meat
Seasoned flour
½ lb cut-up tomatoes
½ lb sliced onions
1 oz dripping
Crushed clove of garlic

Method. Cut up the meat into small pieces, dip in the seasoned flour, and pack into a greased casserole in layers, with the cut-up tomatoes and sliced onions, making your top and bottom layers tomatoes. Dot the top with the dripping broken into tiny pieces, then sprinkle in the crushed garlic. Add more salt and pepper if desired, and pour in ½ teacup hot water. Cover and cook *very* gently for 2½–3 hours. If it goes a little dry, add a little more water, but if cooked really gently this should not be necessary. Serve with boiled rice or spaghetti.

TRIPE AND ONIONS

1 lb prepared tripe
2 large onions
Salt/Pepper to taste
White sauce

Method. Cut the onions into quarters and put on in a saucepan of cold salted water and bring to boil. Simmer until half-tender, then add the cut-up tripe, and simmer all together until everything is tender. Make a rich white sauce, with melted butter into which a tablespoon of flour is stirred, then add half tripe liquor and half warm milk. Bring to the boil, add the tripe and onions spooned from their saucepan, and blend all together until creamily mixed. Add pepper and more salt if necessary. Serve very hot with buttery mashed potatoes.

MEAT ACCOMPANIMENTS

BORDER OF RICE

¼ lb rice
1 pint white stock
1 egg
½ oz butter
Pepper/Salt

Method. Wash the rice well in several waters then put it into a saucepan with the white stock, or milk and water. Add the butter and seasonings and simmer slowly till the rice is soft and has absorbed all the liquid. Stir occasionally to prevent sticking. When ready, remove the pan from the heat and add the well-beaten egg.

Pour the mixture into a well-greased border mould, cover with greased paper, tied down and steam slowly in a pan until firm to the touch. Lift from the pan, let it stand for a few minutes and turn out carefully on to a dish. The centre can be filled with green peas, mixed vegetables, mince, or any meat mixture you fancy.

SAVOURY BALLS

2 oz flour
1 oz chopped suet (or 2
   teaspoons chopped
   margarine)
Pinch baking powder
A little chopped onion
A little chopped parsley
Water to mix
Seasoning
Herbs, if liked

Method. Mix all dry ingredients together, then add sufficient water to form a dough with an elastic consistency. Turn on to a floured board and work gently into a roll. Cut into four. Form these pieces into balls and put on top of simmering stew until cooked.

This dough can also be used as a lid to cover the stew and the stew then becomes sea-pie.

YORKSHIRE PUDDING

4 oz flour
1 egg
½ pint milk and water
   mixed
Pinch of salt

Method. Break egg into flour and salt mixture, and mix well. Gradually add milk and water, beating continuously, and allow to stand for a time. Beat it up again before putting into a well-greased tin which has been heated in the oven so that fat and tin are piping hot, and bake in moderate oven for ½ hour. *For 3 persons*.

RICE PILAFF

6 oz rice
1½ oz butter
1 tablespoon chopped
   onion
1 pint light stock
Seasoning
2 dozen stoned raisins
1 dozen shredded almonds

Method. Melt half the butter in a saucepan, and cook the finely-chopped onion in this for a minute or two. Add the well-washed rice (having dried it thoroughly), and stir until well coated with butter but do not brown it. Add the stock, almonds, raisins and seasoning, and cover with a lid. Cook until the rice is tender without being broken (about ½ hour), then add the rest of the butter, and mix lightly with a fork.

This can be served by itself, or as an accompaniment to some meat dishes. Hard-boiled eggs or cooked mushrooms can be used as a garnish if the rice is being eaten on its own.

NEAPOLITAN RICE

¼ lb Patna rice
2 tomatoes (fresh or
   tinned)
2 oz grated cheese
1 oz butter
Salt/Pepper to taste

Method. Boil the rice in salted water in the usual way and make it very dry. Slice the tomatoes, rub them through a sieve and grate the cheese. Melt the butter in a saucepan, put in the rice, mix well, season with pepper and salt to taste, add the tomato purée, then the cheese, and stir all together over the heat until thoroughly hot. Serve at once.

Poultry and Game

As this book is intended principally to be of use to those with light purses, I have not put a great deal in this section. However, as chickens are more reasonably priced nowadays and as the budget may sometimes run to game, I think you will find safe guidance here for dealing with them.

POULTRY

CHICKEN WITH RICE

1 tender fowl or chicken
2 oz butter
6 oz rice
3 teacups light stock
2 onions
2/3 tablespoons tomato
    purée
Salt/Pepper

Method. Cut the chicken into small neat joints and melt the butter in a saucepan. Fry the chicken joints gently, turning them over and over until brown on all sides, then lift them out and keep them aside for the moment. Into the same saucepan put the rice, well washed and dried. Stir until it begins to colour, then add the stock, seasoning, finely-cut onions, and the tomato purée made by rubbing 2 or 3 tomatoes through a fine sieve. When the rice begins to cook, return the pieces of chicken to the saucepan, put the lid on, and cook gently until the flesh of the chicken is quite tender. Do not let the rice stick to the pan, and add a little stock from time to time if necessary to prevent this. When ready, the stock should be completely absorbed by the rice. Serve very hot in a deep dish. This method takes about 1½–2 hours cooking time.

BOILING FOWL

1 boiling fowl
Salt
1 onion
1 carrot
1 bay leaf

SAUCE
Skimmed fat from stock
1 dessertspoon vinegar
1 teaspoon dry mustard
1 teaspoon ground ginger
Soft breadcrumbs

This is cooked to eat as a roaster.

Method. Put the fowl, stuffed or unstuffed, into a big pan of *warm* water, just enough to cover. Add the salt, onion, carrot and bay leaf, and bring to the boil. Simmer gently for about 3 hours, or until the bird is tender, and leave in the liquid all night. In the morning, lift it out, and put it in a roasting tin, a self-baster if possible.

Now make the sauce: Skim off the yellow fat from the top of the stock into a cup. Add to this the vinegar, mustard and ground ginger and blend together into a smooth sauce. Spread this over the bird, then sprinkle on top a good handful of breadcrumbs which will stick to the sauce. Pop the bird into a warm oven and heat thoroughly, (about 1 hour). NOTE. Use the stock to make chicken broth. Bring to the boil and add ½ teacup rice or noodles, a chopped onion, and before serving, some chopped parsley.

ROAST CHICKEN IN CASSEROLE

1 roast chicken, jointed
1 oz butter or margarine
1 tablespoon flour
2 chopped tomatoes
1 tablespoon tomato purée
¼ cup stock or water and milk
1 or 2 mushrooms
2 onions

Method. Fry the jointed chicken in the melted fat, then pack it into a casserole. Stir a tablespoon of flour and the chopped tomatoes in the fat left in the pan, then add the tomato purée, and the stock or water and milk. Cook for a few minutes, then pour this sauce over the chicken. Place the chopped mushrooms and the quartered onions on top, put on the lid, and cook in a moderate oven for about 1 hour. Use carcase and giblets to make an excellent soup.

POT ROAST CHICKEN

Put chicken into pot in which you have melted a little good fat. Heat the chicken through, which takes about ½ hour, turning continually. Add 2 or 3 tablespoons of water, and cook very slowly for about 1½–2 hours, depending on size of bird. When chicken is removed, skim off fat, and use the remaining liquid for sauce.

TURKEY

Slow roasted, as for chicken (see above), if you have a large enough pot. Otherwise wrap in aluminium foil, place on roasting tin and slow roast in oven. Foil keeps in all juices. Cooking time according to size.

JELLIED CHICKEN AND HAM

A boiling fowl
About 1 lb raw ham (in one piece)
About 4 pints water
Small blade of mace
1 onion
Salt/Pepper
¼ oz powdered gelatine
1 teaspoon chopped parsley
2 hard-boiled eggs

Method. Clean the fowl and wipe it out thoroughly, then put into a pan and cover with boiling water. When it comes to the boil again, skim, and add the mace, onion and seasonings. Simmer for about 2 hours. Now add the ham and cook for another ½ hour. When both are tender, lift from the pan and skin them. Divide the fowl into joints and remove all the meat.

Return the bones and skin to the pan and boil briskly without a lid until the liquid is reduced to a third of its original measure. Strain it on to the gelatine in a basin and stir till gelatine is well dissolved. Add the chicken and ham diced, and the parsley, and reheat all in the rinsed pan.

Decorate some moulds with the sliced hard-boiled eggs and set in position with a little of the stock. When firm, fill up with the cooled chicken and ham mixture. Put aside to firm and get cold, then turn out by dipping each mould into a basin of warm water and slipping the jelly on to a serving dish. Garnish with green salad and tomatoes.

CHICKEN EN CASSEROLE

Cut-up chicken
Oil or margarine
1 cut-up garlic section
1 tablespoon flour
2 tomatoes
1 tablespoon tomato purée
6 tablespoons water
6 tablespoons white wine (or cider or water)
12 mushrooms
12 tiny onions

Method. Fry the cut-up chicken in the oil or margarine, till pale golden, and then arrange in casserole.

Make the sauce thus : Into the oil remaining in the frying pan, stir the flour, the tomatoes, the purée, and add the water and wine (or all water if preferred). Pour this sauce over the chicken, add the mushrooms and the onions, season to taste, and cook in casserole with the lid on for about 1 hour.

Serve with plain boiled potatoes, and any other vegetable you fancy.

THE BIRD. If you have to pluck your own fowl, then it must be singed afterwards, and a quick easy way to do this is to pour a little methylated spirits on to an old tin plate and set it alight. Hold the bird over the blue flame, and you will find it will become perfectly white and clean in half the time.

IF YOU spill hot fat on the kitchen floor, pour cold water on it immediately. This hardens the grease before it can soak in and makes it easy to scrape off with a dull-bladed knife.

DUCK CASSEROLE WITH ORANGE SAUCE

1 medium-sized duck
1 oz butter
2 small oranges
¼ pint white wine
¼ pint stock
2 dessertspoons flour

Method. Joint the duck and fry the pieces in the butter for a few minutes, then transfer to a large casserole and cook in the oven till the pieces are brown all over. Peel one of the oranges very finely and cut this peel into very thin strips. Divide the orange into sections, and put peel and sections into the casserole. Add the stock and season to taste, then cover with the lid and cook in a moderate oven for about 1 hour, or till tender. Remove the duck to a hot dish and keep it warm. Lift out the pieces of orange and as much fat as you can from the stock, and thicken stock with the flour blended with a little of the wine (or stock if you are not using wine). Add the rest of the wine, or stock, bring to the boil and add more seasoning if required. Pour this sauce over the duck and decorate with the second orange, cut in thin slices with the peel left on. As duck is rather fatty, a green salad is an excellent accompaniment to this dish.

NOTE. If you like, you can leave the duck whole, and cook in a large, covered dish.

INDIAN PILAU

Small boiling fowl
2 oz butter
½ lb rice
1 onion, sliced
Few cloves
1 piece cinnamon stick
Peppercorns
A pinch of mace
Salt to taste
1 oz raisins (if liked)
1 onion, shredded
Almonds, shredded

Method. Put the fowl in a saucepan, cover with water, and boil for 1 hour, or until tender. Take it out, and put it into a saucepan with the melted butter and let it brown nicely all over, turning it over and over to colour evenly. Then remove the fowl and keep it hot. Now put the well-washed rice into the butter, stir it well for 5 or 10 minutes with the sliced onion, and the seasonings (cloves, cinnamon, peppercorns, mace and salt to taste). Add the liquor from the fowl and boil till the rice is really tender, adding the raisins if you are using them. Fry the shredded onion and a few shredded almonds till crisp and brown. Serve the fowl in the centre of a large dish with the savoury rice in a border, and over the fowl sprinkle the crisply-fried shredded onions and almonds.

NOTE. Another decorative touch, if you like, is to hard-boil an egg, quarter it, and place round the fowl with the onions and almonds.

CHICKEN SAVOURY

2 tablespoons rice
1 large onion
1 oz margarine or lard
2 or 3 chopped mushrooms
2 or 3 tomatoes
Left-over chicken
Lettuce

Method. Boil the rice in boiling salted water until almost tender, and then drain. Slice the onion thinly, melt the fat, and fry the onion until tender. Add the mushrooms and the tomatoes and fry gently. Stir the rice into this mixture and cook until lightly browned. Finally stir in the left-over chicken and heat all through. Serve piled inside a ring of lettuce, and eat with bread and butter.

NOTE. Any left-over meat can be used instead of chicken, or any sort of shellfish like shrimps, prawns or crayfish.

GAME

STUFFED ROAST RABBIT

1 rabbit
Forcemeat stuffing
   (see p. 32)
A little flour
Fat bacon
Butter or dripping
Gravy

Method. Wash and clean the rabbit. Prepare the forcemeat stuffing and add to it the liver, heart and kidney of the rabbit, parboiled and chopped. Now dry the rabbit, season it, and stuff with the forcemeat. Sew it up. Rub it all over with flour and truss into shape with skewers, fixing the legs to lie close to the body. Tie a few slices of fat bacon over the back of the rabbit, and it is ready for roasting. Put it into a hot oven to begin with, to brown it and seal the juices, then lower the heat and cook till tender (about 1 hour). A short time before it is cooked, remove the bacon slices to let the back of the rabbit brown. It is also a good idea to cover the roasting rabbit with a greaseproof paper or cook in a self-basting roaster as the flesh is inclined to be dry.

For the gravy, pour away most of the fat from the roasting pan, leaving only about a dessertspoonful. Add to this 1 dessertspoon flour and mix it in until smooth and brown. Now draw the tin to the side, and mix in ½ pint of water or stock and stir again over the heat till boiling. Simmer for a few minutes, season to taste, and pour a little round the rabbit and the rest in a sauce boat. You can serve bread sauce if you like too, and red currant or any other sort of acid jelly if you like this.

59

Game

RABBIT MOULD

1 tender rabbit
1 pint water
¼ lb sausage meat
2 or 3 hard-boiled eggs
1 tablespoon chopped
    parsley
Grated rind of ½ lemon
Seasoning
½ oz gelatine
Pieces of tomato

Method. Wash the rabbit carefully and dry it, then cut the flesh into small neat pieces, taking it all off the bones. Break up the bones and put them into a saucepan with the water and a little salt and let these simmer slowly for 1 hour at least, till the liquid is reduced to about half the quantity. Then strain it over the gelatine, to be used as stock for the mould. Cook the rabbit liver in the stock for a few minutes, then chop it finely and mix with the parsley and grated lemon rind. Hard boil the eggs and slice them. Take a plain mould large enough to hold everything, and arrange a few slices of hard-boiled egg in the bottom. Then put in some rabbit, season with pepper and salt, sprinkle over this some of the liver mixture, then a layer of sausage meat, more egg and so on until everything is used up. Do not pack too tightly, and then fill up with the stock from the bones. Tie a piece of strong greaseproof paper over the top, and bake in a moderate oven for at least 1 hour, or until the rabbit feels tender when tested with a skewer. Leave till cold, then turn out when wanted and decorate with parsley and pieces of tomato and serve with a green salad.

NOTE. If you do not want to use the liver in the mould, just omit it, in which case you can also leave out the parsley and lemon rind, and have a straightforward mixture of rabbit, sausage meat and hard-boiled eggs.

STEWED PIGEONS WITH MACARONI

2 pigeons
1 oz dripping or butter
1 tablespoon flour
Seasoning
2 tablespoons chopped
    onion
¼ pint brown stock
1 dessertspoon chopped
    parsley
3 or 4 oz macaroni

Method. Clean the pigeons and cut each in four pieces. Season with pepper and salt, and coat them with flour. Melt the butter or dripping in a stewpan, put in the pigeon joints with chopped onion and cook gently until well browned, turning them over and over. Add the stock, and (if you like it and can spare it) a little wine. Simmer slowly until the pigeons are ready. About 20 minutes before they are completely tender, add the macaroni (or spaghetti), parboiled and cut in small pieces, and cook this with pigeons for the rest of the time. Add more seasoning if necessary and serve very hot, sprinkling the chopped parsley over. This method takes 1–1½ hours.

STEWED RABBIT

1 rabbit
2 or 3 oz bacon
1 oz flour
2 onions, chopped
1 pint stock
Pinch of nutmeg
Salt/Pepper

Method. Clean and wash the rabbit, then drain and dry it and cut into neat joints. Remove the rind from the bacon, cut it into small pieces, put in a stewpan, and cook over a gentle heat until the fat is transparent. Lift it out on to a plate and prepare the rabbit joints for browning by coating them in the flour. Fry them in the bacon fat until brown on all sides, adding a little more fat if necessary. Add the chopped onions and brown them also, then return the bacon to the pan, pour in the stock, and season to taste. Stew very slowly with the lid on until the rabbit is quite tender. (1½–2 hours.)

NOTE. If you like them, a few mushrooms or a little tomato purée could be added to the gravy to give extra flavour, and a little finely-chopped parsley could be sprinkled over at the last minute.

PIGEON CASSEROLE (1)

1 pigeon per person
Salt/Pepper
Bacon "pieces" or streaky
    rashers
1 shallot or onion
Seasonings
Stock or water

Method. Quarter the birds by splitting them down the centre and then across, season the quarters with salt and pepper and tie the four pieces together. Fry lightly in butter until golden brown, then put in a casserole, covered with bacon "pieces" or rashers, a chopped shallot or onion, a bay leaf, if liked, some peppercorns, and as an extra, a few button mushrooms. Add a small cupful of stock or water. Stew until quite tender, and serve with diced, mixed vegetables, potato crisps, and, if liked, cranberry sauce.

PIGEON CASSEROLE (2)

1 wood-pigeon per person
Two pieces of streaky
    bacon per pigeon
1 onion
Peppercorns
Bay leaf
Pepper/Salt
1 oz butter

Method. Quarter the pigeons, salt and pepper them and brown with the bacon in hot butter until golden brown. Place them in a casserole with the onion, peppercorns and the bay leaf, and a little stock made by rinsing out the pan in which the bird has been browned. Cook in a moderate oven for 1 hour. Serve with potato crisps and, if available, buttered mushrooms.

WHEN a joint is too much underdone, re-cook it the next day for 30 to 40 minutes in a saucepan in which you have heated a little fat. Turn once and keep it covered.

VENISON CASSEROLE

1 lb venison
¼ lb bacon
1 oz flour
2 teacups water
1 dessertspoon chopped
    onion
1 teaspoon red currant
    jelly
½ teaspoon lemon juice
Seasoning

Method. Choose a fleshy piece of venison, wipe and trim it and cut in pieces about 1 inch square. Take rind off the bacon, cut in pieces, and fry gently in hot fat for a minute or two, without browning, and remove to the bottom of a fireproof casserole. Coat the venison pieces in flour and fry in the bacon fat, turning over and over until they are nicely browned on all sides, then put them in the casserole beside the bacon. Pour the water into the frying pan and stir all the residue up to make a nice rich gravy. Pour this over the venison, add the chopped onion, red currant jelly, lemon juice, and seasoning to taste. Put the lid on and cook slowly in a moderate oven until the meat is tender (2–2½ hours).
NOTE. You can add some forcemeat balls 15 minutes before serving (see p. 32). If you prefer, you can use a little wine, and less water. Mashed potatoes and spinach are excellent accompaniments.

ROAST GROUSE

Have the butcher pluck the bird very carefully and draw it, as I do not expect you want to tackle this job yourself. It requires expert treatment and few of us are experienced in this field these days. Wipe the bird inside and out with a damp cloth, but do not wash it. Take a piece of butter the size of a nutmeg, work it up with a little pepper and salt and a squeeze of lemon juice, and put it inside the body along with the liver. Truss in the same way as roast fowl, but use a fine needle and string, as large holes let the juices escape. Tie a slice of fat bacon over the breast and roast in a good oven, basting frequently with butter or bacon fat as the flesh of grouse is inclined to be dry. Remove the slice of bacon a few minutes before serving, dredge the breast with flour and roast again until nicely browned. Time depends on the age and size of the bird, but a young and tender one will cook in 25–30 minutes, while an older one might require ¾ hour. When ready, remove to a hot dish and take out the trussing thread or string. Serve separately a good brown gravy made from the residue in the roasting tin, and garnish with watercress. Game chips and fried breadcrumbs are the perfect accompaniments with the watercress and the gravy.
NOTE.—*Roast Partridge* is prepared and served in exactly the same way. *Roast Pheasant* also is treated in this way, but it should be hung for some days before cooking to improve the flavour.

TO MAKE old potatoes nice and floury, pour off the water when cooked, then cover with a clean cloth or white tissue paper, replace the lid, and let them steam for 5 minutes.

PIGEONS WITH GREEN PEAS

2 young pigeons
1½ oz butter
3 small onions
¼ lb bacon
1 dessertspoon flour
½ pint light stock
½ pint fresh green peas
Seasoning

Method. Truss the pigeons. Melt the butter in a saucepan and when smoking-hot put in the pigeons and turn them over and over until well browned on all sides. Lift them out, and put into the butter the peeled, chopped onions and the bacon cut in small pieces. Cook them for a few minutes, sprinkle with the flour, blending this well in, and pour in the stock. Stir till boiling. Return the pigeons to this sauce along with the green peas, season to taste, cover with a lid and simmer everything slowly until the pigeons are tender (¾–1 hour). When ready, serve the pigeons in the centre of a hot dish with the green peas and onions round about.

Fish

This is a very extensive section, because I consider that fish provides a most welcome change for every meal of the day. It is light; it is nourishing, and with the sauces I have given, you will be able to vary your fish menus without repetition for many, many meals.

WHEN BUYING FISH

Fish to be good must be very fresh and in season. The flesh should be firm and stiff, the gills red, and the eyes bright, and there should be no unpleasant odour

In choosing cut fish, such as cod, halibut, salmon, etc., the flesh should have a close grain. If it looks watery and fibrous it is not good. Fish that is bruised or has the skin broken will not keep well.

COD

BAKED COD FILLET

2 cod fillets
1 onion
Salt

SAUCE
1 dessertspoon cornflour
½ teaspoon dry mustard
Salt/Pepper
½ pint milk
1 oz butter

Method. Put the cod in a greased pie-dish and cover with an onion, thinly-sliced, and sprinkled with salt.

Now make a thin paste with the cornflour, dry mustard, salt and pepper, and a little milk taken from the ½ pint, then blend this with the rest of the milk and pour over the fish. Dot the top with butter, and bake in a moderate oven for ¾ hour, depending on the thickness of the fish.

For greater quantity of fillets, double all quantities for the sauce.

Fish

SALT COD BALLS

½ lb cooked, salt cod
A lit le warm water and
    milk
½ lb cooked potatoes
1 tablespoon melted butter
1 egg
Pepper
A little flour
Egg and breadcrumbs

Method. Soak the cod for 12 hours in lukewarm water, changing the water once or twice. When sufficiently fresh, cover it with warm water and milk in a saucepan, bring slowly to the boil and simmer very slowly for about 1 hour. Do not cook it too quickly or it will become tough and leathery. Drain well, and let it cool. Pick to pieces with two forks and shred it finely, removing all skin and bone. This is a better way than chopping with a knife, which is inclined to make it heavy. Mix the prepared fish in a basin with the sieved potatoes, season with pepper and, if liked, a little anchovy essence and bind together with the melted butter and beaten egg. Form into balls, using your floured hands, then egg and breadcrumb and fry in boiling fat to a nice golden brown. Drain well and decorate with parsley. Caper or tomato sauce can be served separately.

NOTE. As an alternative, you can form the mixture into flat cakes instead of balls, and a poached and well-drained egg can be placed on top of each after it is fried.

POACHED COD (from Norway)

Piece of tail cod
Melted butter
Chopped parsley
Buttered carrots
New potatoes

Method. Poach the fish gently in salted boiling water, until the bone can be moved when you touch it. Skin and bone it, and cover with plenty of melted butter and chopped parsley. Serve with the buttered carrots and new potatoes.

PORTUGUESE COD STEAKS

2 cod steaks
Salt/Pepper

SAUCE
1 oz butter or margarine
1 chopped onion
Section of garlic, if liked
2 good-sized tomatoes
Juice of 1 lemon
Chopped parsley
Cornflour

Method. Place the cod steaks in a well-buttered pan, season with salt and pepper. Cover and cook over a gentle heat for about 15 minutes. When they are ready, place them in a heat-proof dish in a slow oven to keep warm.

Now make the sauce: Melt the butter or margarine in a pan, and lightly fry the onion, garlic (if used) and chopped, peeled tomatoes for a few minutes. Add ½ teacup water and the lemon juice, the parsley and a little seasoning, and stir till thick and cooked. Thicken with a little cornflour and pour over the fish. *For 2 or 3 persons.*

MUSTARD-COATED COD

2 cod steaks
Salt/Pepper
French mustard
Butter

Method. Spread the top of the steaks, after washing, with French mustard and place the fish, mustard side down, in a well-buttered oven dish. Spread the uncovered parts of the fish with another generous layer of the mustard. Sprinkle with salt and pepper, and dot with butter. Bake for 30–40 minutes in a moderate oven, basting frequently. A greased paper on top will keep it from drying, but if it does dry out, add a very little hot water. *For 2 persons.*

The surprising thing about this dish is that the mustard taste vanishes as a definite "mustard," and there is just the knowledge that this is a most excellent flavour.

FILLETS OF COD WITH PARMESAN

1 lb cod steaks
1 oz butter
1 oz flour
½ pint fish stock
2 oz grated Parmesan
Pepper/Salt
2 tablespoons top of
  milk
Squeeze of lemon juice
Milk and water
Bay leaf
Parsley stalks
1 small onion

Method. Remove all the skin and bone from the fish, and wash these trimmings in cold water. Put these trimmings and bones into a saucepan with equal parts of milk and water to cover them, a bay leaf if liked, a few parsley stalks, and a small onion. Simmer this for up to ½ hour, then strain this stock, and use ½ pint to make the sauce.

Meanwhile cut the fish into neat pieces, lay them on a greased fireproof dish and sprinkle with pepper, salt and a squeeze of lemon juice. Cover with a greased paper and cook in a moderate oven until quite tender (about 30 minutes). Make a sauce with the butter, flour and fish stock, and cook it well. Add the top of the milk, and most of the cheese and season to taste.

Before coating the fish with this sauce, add to it any liquid in the fireproof dish from the fish, for this gives all the flavour and goodness from the fish to the sauce, and increases its tastiness. When you have coated the fish with the sauce, sprinkle with the rest of the cheese and brown in the oven or under the grill. If you wish, a few slices of fried tomato may be added as a colourful garnish.

FISH BATTER. When making batter for fish, add ¼ teaspoon dry mustard, and leave for about 1 hour before using. This makes a tasty change from the usual batter.

MOCK LOBSTER

2 good-sized cod steaks
1 tin lobster soup
1 small tin lobster meat

Method. Simmer the cod steaks very gently in a little salted water, drain, and place in a fireproof dish. Pour the lobster soup over, then empty the small tin of lobster meat on top. Bake all together in a moderate oven for about ½ hour. Serve with boiled, fluffy, dry rice.

SPANISH COD

1 lb cod fillet
¼ lb tomatoes
1 chopped shallot
2 oz butter or margarine
Salt/Pepper
Chopped parsley

Method. Cut the cod fillet into neat portions, and well season with salt and pepper. Place them in a well-greased fireproof dish. Arrange a layer of finely-sliced raw tomatoes over the top. Sprinkle these with the shallot (or onion), fried to a golden brown, some more salt and pepper, and dot with butter or margarine. Cover with a greased paper and bake for 25 minutes in a moderate oven. Serve very hot and at the last minute sprinkle with 2 tablespoons chopped parsley.

NOTE. To make this dish more "gooey" for serving on toast, make a flour and butter "roux", thin with milk and liquid from fish mixture, cook to a smooth sauce, and pour over the fish before adding the parsley.

HADDOCK

BAKED HADDOCK

2 small haddocks
3 tablespoons bread-
    crumbs
A little butter
Salt/Pepper
1 teaspoon chopped
    parsley
A few slices of bacon

Method. Clean the fish, cut off the heads and remove the skin. Lay them in a greased fireproof dish and sprinkle with the breadcrumbs, which have been mixed with the parsley and seasonings. Lay some small slices of bacon round the dish and cover all with a piece of greased paper. Bake in a good oven for 15–20 minutes and serve hot in the same dish.

MEXICAN SAVOURY HADDOCK

1 cooked, smoked haddock
4 tomatoes
1 minced onion
2 oz butter
Cayenne pepper
Chopped parsley
Boiled rice

Method. Fry minced onion and tomatoes in the butter. Add skinned and sliced haddock, and stew all together very gently for 15–20 minutes, seasoning to taste. Serve on a bed of boiled rice, sprinkled with chopped parsley.

FRESH HADDOCK IN SAVOURY SAUCE

2 pieces of fresh haddock
Seasoned crumbs
Butter

SAUCE
1 oz butter
3 mushrooms
2 or 3 tomatoes
1 dessertspoon flour
Milk and water
Seasoning

Method. Dip the fish in seasoned crumbs, and plain fry in butter. Put in a casserole and into the oven to keep warm.

Now make the sauce: Melt the butter in a pan, then gently fry the mushrooms, chopped, and the sliced tomatoes. Stir in the flour, seasoning and milk and water and cook for a few minutes. Pour over the fish and, if available, decorate with a few thin slices of cucumber.

SMOKED HADDOCK WITH EGG SAUCE

1 smoked haddock
½ pint egg sauce
¼ teaspoon anchovy
  essence
¼ teaspoon chopped
  parsley

Method. Trim the fish and cut off the fins. Put it into a frying pan with warm water to cover, bring to the boil, and simmer slowly for 10–12 minutes according to the thickness of the fish. Lift out, drain, remove the flesh quickly from the bones, break it into flakes and put it neatly in a hot deep dish. Have ready some good egg sauce (made by making a rich white sauce and chopping two hard boiled eggs in it, all piping hot), add to it the anchovy essence, and, when boiling hot, pour it over the fish. Sprinkle the parsley lightly over and serve very hot.

NOTE. This can be piled up on toast for tea, or served for lunch or dinner with creamy mashed potatoes in a ring of green peas. If you do not wish potatoes, another way to make it more substantial for hungry mouths is to poach an egg for each person and serve in the middle of the fish mixture. This is particularly tasty and very nourishing.

FILLETS OF HADDOCK IN CUSTARD

Baby haddocks
Lemon juice
Salt/Pepper
Nutmeg
1 egg
1 teacup milk
Chopped parsley

Method. Sprinkle the fillets with lemon juice, salt and pepper. Roll up and place in a buttered fireproof dish. Beat up an egg till frothy, then add white pepper, salt and nutmeg, and a small teacup of milk. Pour this mixture over the fish, sprinkle chopped parsley on top, and bake for 20 minutes in a moderate oven.

VINEGAR added to the water in which you boil the fish, not only whitens the flesh but keeps it firm.

GEESE, wild ducks, etc., are improved if hot water is poured over and through them before cooking.

SMOKED HADDOCK SAVOURY

2 eggs
3 tablespoons smoked
    haddock, cooked
3 tablespoons milk
Cayenne pepper
1 teaspoon anchovy
    essence
Walnut of butter
Browned breadcrumbs

Method. Take the skin and bones from the cooked, smoked haddock and break it into small flakes. Melt a small piece of butter in a saucepan, pour in the milk, and then the well-beaten eggs, and stir over a gentle heat till the mixture is just beginning to thicken. Draw the pan off the heat, and add the fish, anchovy essence (if available), a good pinch of cayenne, and salt if necessary. Make the mixture thoroughly hot, but do not let it boil. Put it into scallop shells or small fireproof dishes that have been greased and sprinkled with breadcrumbs, then sprinkle a few browned breadcrumbs over. Dot with tiny pieces of butter, and brown quickly in the oven or under the grill. Serve very hot, decorated with parsley.

NOTE. Cooked kipper can be used this way too, and the mixture can be served on hot buttered toast instead of in the scallop shells.

SMOKED HADDOCK OMELETTE (Northern dish)

Some mildly-smoked
    haddock
Milk
Plain omelette
Creamy sauce
Grated cheese

Method. Cook the smoked haddock in a little milk and flake it. Make a plain omelette, but *before* it is ready for rolling up, spread the surface with big flakes of the fish. Roll up quickly. Turn on to a fireproof plate, and gently pour over it a creamy white sauce to which has been added a generous helping of grated cheese. Slip under the grill to brown and glaze.

Be sure not to overcook the omelette before adding the fish and rolling up, or it will be overdone with the extra grilling.

SAVOURY HADDOCK CUSTARDS

2 tablespoons cooked,
    smoked haddock
2 yolks and 1 white of egg
1 teaspoon anchovy
    essence
Seasoning
1 teaspoon chopped
    pickles
Chopped parsley
Rounds of hot toast

Method. Beat up the egg yolks with the white until light and fluffy, then add the cooked smoked haddock, chopped finely. Stir in the anchovy essence and a little chopped green pickle and season to taste. Pour the mixture into very small greased moulds and poach them carefully until firm to the touch. Turn out, when ready, on to rounds of hot buttered toast sprinkled with finely-chopped parsley, and serve very hot.

SMOKED HADDOCK PASTIES

¼ lb smoked haddock
1/2 tablespoons white
    sauce
Seasoning
Some scraps of pastry
Egg and breadcrumbs

Method. Cook the smoked haddock and chop it roughly, removing all skin and bone. Moisten with a little thick white sauce and season to taste. Roll out some scraps of left-over unsweetened pastry very thinly, and cut out in rounds about 3 inches in diameter. Put a little of the fish mixture in the centre of half the number of rounds. Wet round the edges of the other half with a little beaten egg or water and place them on top, pressing the edges firmly together. Egg the pasties evenly, then toss in fine breadcrumbs, and fry in deep boiling fat to a golden brown colour. Drain on kitchen paper and serve garnished with parsley.

FINNAN HADDY AND HAM

1 Finnan haddock
Rashers of streaky bacon

Method. Steam the haddock for about 5 minutes in a little water, to soften and partly cook. Meantime fry bacon slices as usual, then when nearly ready, put the haddock into the bacon fat, cover with the almost cooked bacon, and finish all off together under a top covering plate, so that the fish absorbs the bacon flavour and the bacon completes cooking. Serve with hot buttered toast.

HERRING

GRILLED HERRINGS

3 herrings
Oatmeal
Seasoning

Method. Wash the fish, scrape the scales off, cut off heads and pull out guts, but leave any roe where it is. Then with a sharp knife, score deeply across the thickest part of the fish to the backbone about five times, turn it over and do the same to the other side. Dip in seasoned oatmeal, put under a fiery hot grill and grill for a minute on each side. Then turn the grill down to half, and give it another five minutes each side, making twelve minutes altogether, just as for a steak.

If you wish, serve with a mustard sauce, made by making an ordinary white sauce, and adding a spoonful of made mustard. Do not add the mustard dry or it might lump and burn the tongue.

BAKED STUFFED HERRINGS

4 herrings, boned

FORCEMEAT

2 oz breadcrumbs
2 tablespoons chopped
    parsley
A little grated lemon rind
Salt/Pepper to taste
¼ oz melted dripping or
    other fat
1 egg

Method. Mix all forcemeat ingredients together, and spread inside the fish. Roll up each fish, and pack closely into a greased pie-dish or casserole. Sprinkle top with a little salt and a few peppercorns, cover with a piece of greaseproof paper and bake in a moderate oven for about 15 minutes. Before taking it out of the oven remove the paper and allow the fish to brown for a further 5 minutes.

HERRINGS AND STUFFED TOMATOES

6 fresh herrings
6 tomatoes
4 tablespoons bread-
    crumbs
1 tablespoon margarine
½ teaspoon lemon rind
1 tablespoon chopped
    parsley
A little grated onion
Some small skewers
Seasoning

Method. Scale, clean and behead the herrings. Twist them, head to tail and secure with a small skewer or cocktail stick.

Slice the top off each tomato with a sharp knife, but keep the slice. Scoop the inside out, and mix the pulp with the breadcrumbs, lemon, parsley, onion and seasoning. Fill each tomato with this mixture and dot with margarine, then replace the slice you cut off, to form a lid.

Put the curled herrings into a well-greased fireproof dish, and set a stuffed tomato in the centre of each fish. Bake for about 20 minutes in a fairly hot oven. Serve in the dish straight from the oven.

POTTED HERRINGS

4 herrings, boned
1 onion
1 cup water
1 cup vinegar
Peppercorns
Salt

Method. Roll up the fish with a slice of onion inside each fish and pack closely together in a baking dish. Scatter peppercorns between the rolls, and add the remainder of the sliced onion around. Sprinkle in 1 teaspoon of salt, pour on vinegar and water mixed together, and bake in a slow oven for 1½ hours. Serve hot or cold.

POTATOES will cook much more quickly if you cut them lengthwise, instead of crosswise.

TO GET all the juice out of a lemon, heat it by leaving it on top of stove for a few minutes, then roll it over and over, pressing with your hand to break down the cells and release the juice.

BUTTER PATS. To make butter pats quickly, just scoop out a large roll of butter with your apple-corer, then cut into little wheels with a knife.

MACKEREL

POTTED MACKEREL (from Cornwall)

4 mackerel, filleted
½ cup vinegar
½ cup water
½ dozen cloves
A bay leaf

Method. Roll the filleted mackerel from tail upwards and pack into a fireproof dish. Cover with vinegar and water, add the cloves round about, and the bay leaf, and cover with a greased paper. Cook in a slow oven for 1 hour. Serve hot or cold.

BAKED MACKEREL (from Cornwall)

4 mackerel, cleaned
Spring onions
Pepper/Salt
Milk

Method. Put a spring onion inside each cleaned mackerel, and season with salt and pepper. Roll up and put in a baking dish, cover with milk, and bake in a slow oven until ready (about 40–50 minutes).

SOUSED MACKEREL

3 mackerel
1 onion
2 or 3 cloves
1 bay leaf
12 white peppercorns
A few parsley stalks
A sprig of thyme
A blade of mace
Brown vinegar
Salt

Method. Clean and wash the fish, cut off the heads and fins, and lay them in a baking dish with the onion, finely-chopped, the spices, herbs (if available) and salt to taste. Cover with the vinegar and bake in a warm oven till thoroughly cooked (30–40 minutes).

Lift the fish carefully on to a long deep dish, strain the vinegar over them, and serve when cold with salad.

SALMON

POTTED SALMON

6 oz cooked salmon
2 oz butter
1 teaspoon anchovy or
   shrimp essence
½ teaspoon vinegar
Pepper/Salt
A pinch of powdered
   mace
A pinch of cayenne

With tinned salmon the price it is, you might like to try potting some yourself, for summer sandwiches.
Method. Free the salmon from all skin and bone, and put it in a basin with most of the butter, melted, and beat till smooth, seasoning to taste rather highly. If you want it really smooth, rub it through a sieve. Pack into a small pot or jar, and run the rest of the butter over the top, which will preserve the paste and prevent it getting dry. When making the sandwiches, thinly-sliced cucumber and some small cress make excellent extras.

73

FRESH SALMON (1)

Put piece of salmon or cutlets in water which has been brought almost to boiling point. Put a little salt and vinegar in the water, and bring to boiling point again. Allow salmon to simmer exactly 5 minutes—no longer. Add 1 teacup of cold water. Bring to the boil once more. Simmer *very slowly* for 20 minutes. Allow to cool in the water. Do not put lid on pan.

FRESH SALMON (2)

Piece of salmon or
  2 or 3 cutlets
Small slice carrot
Parsley stalks
Piece of onion
Bay leaf
Pepper

Method. Prepare a panful of salted hot water with pepper, the carrot, parsley stalks, onion, bay leaf, and if liked, thyme. Put in the salmon, bring the water to the boil. Now draw the pan to the side of the stove and let it poach gently for 10–15 minutes, according to the thickness of your salmon cutlets. If it is a large piece, allow 10 minutes per pound.

Drain it well, lay it on a hot serving dish surrounded by sprigs of parsley, buttery-minty new potatoes, and, if liked, some watercress.

If you are having it cold, surround it with crisp fresh lettuce and watercress, cucumber, tomatoes and radishes and any other salad vegetable you prefer.

NOTE. After a long walk in the Highlands, we once arrived at a manse and the minister took us in for "supper, bed and breakfast". Supper was hot salmon with buttery-minty potatoes. Never was food so good.

SALMON GATEAU

12 oz tin salmon
2 tablespoons fine
  breadcrumbs
1 oz margarine
3 tablespoons milk
2 eggs
Salt/Pepper

Method. Remove skin and bones from the fish. Mix it well with the breadcrumbs, salt and pepper. Warm milk and margarine gently and add this to the well-beaten *yolks* of the eggs. Mix this liquid with the fish, breadcrumbs and seasoning. Fold in the stiffly-beaten whites of the eggs. Turn the mixture into a well-greased bowl and cover with a double layer of greaseproof paper, securely tied on. Place in boiling water in a pan with a firmly-fitting lid and steam for 1 hour. Serve with parsley sauce poured over the gâteau if you are sure everyone likes it, otherwise serve it separately in a sauce-boat. Garnish with slices of lemon, green peas, and, if liked, cucumber. Potatoes also may be served with this dish.

IF THE hinged tail of the lobster is folded back, this is a sure sign that the lobster was put into the boiling pot alive—proof of its freshness.

SALMON or TUNA FISH MOULD (from Australia)

¼ lb tin salmon or tuna
¼ lb margarine
2 eggs
1 cup fresh breadcrumbs
Salt/Pepper to taste

Method. Melt the margarine. Beat the eggs till frothy, then blend margarine and eggs with the flaked, tinned fish and salt and pepper to taste. Beat in the breadcrumbs. Press into a mould or a bowl and cover with greaseproof paper. Steam for about ¾ hour, until risen and cooked. Turn out and serve either hot with a good white sauce and vegetables, or cold with salad.

OTHER FISH

HALIBUT WITH TOMATOES

1 lb halibut
3 or 4 fresh tomatoes
1 tablespoon flour
Pepper/Salt
Juice of ½ lemon
2 tablespoons bread-
    crumbs
1 oz butter

Method. Wipe the halibut, cut it into small neat pieces free from skin and bone, and coat each piece lightly in the flour. Soak the tomatoes in boiling water for a few minutes to loosen the skins, then lift out, dry and skin them, and cut them into slices. Lay a few pieces of the floured fish in a well-buttered fireproof dish, season with pepper, salt and lemon juice, and cover with some of the sliced tomato. Put in another layer of fish and seasoning, then sliced tomato, and so on until all is used up, finishing with a layer of tomato. Sprinkle the breadcrumbs on top and dot with the butter in tiny pieces. Bake in a moderate oven until the fish is thoroughly cooked and browned nicely on the top (about ¾ hour). Garnish with parsley and serve very hot. A little finely-chopped onion or shallot can be added to this mixture, if liked.

FRIED SCALLOPS

6 to 8 scallops
2 tablespoons salad oil
1 tablespoon lemon juice
Pepper/Salt
A little flour
Egg and breadcrumbs

Method. Wash the scallops thoroughly, cut away the beard and black part and leave them on a cloth to drain. Mix the salad oil with the lemon juice, pepper and salt, and leave the scallops to soak in this mixture for about ½ hour. Drain them, roll lightly in flour, egg and breadcrumb them, and fry in deep fat to a delicate brown colour. Drain very well and serve piping hot, garnished with parsley.
NOTE. Do not prepare too many scallops with their dressing at a time, for they must not be allowed to get moist again before going into the deep fat.

Fish

SOLE WITH SHRIMP STUFFING

1 medium-sized lemon
   sole

STUFFING

2 or 3 oz picked shrimps
3 tablespoons bread-
   crumbs
1 teaspoon chopped
   parsley
Seasoning
2 tablespoons white sauce,
   or some beaten egg
1 gill fish stock or white
   wine
1 tablespoon browned
   breadcrumbs
A little butter

Method. Clean the fish carefully and remove the dark skin. On the skinned side, make an incision right down the centre of the fish to the back bone. Slip the knife along close to the bone and raise the fillets a little bit, so as to make pockets for the stuffing.

To make the stuffing, put the shrimps and the soft breadcrumbs into a basin, add the chopped parsley and, if liked and available, a small teaspoon anchovy essence, but this can be omitted without harm to the recipe. Bind all together with the white sauce or some beaten egg. Season to taste, and put this stuffing into the fish, piling it fairly high and smoothing it over the top. Lay the fish in a well-buttered fireproof dish, pour the stock or wine around, sprinkle the browned crumbs on top, and dot with butter. Bake in a moderate oven (20–30 minutes), serve from the dish, and garnish with parsley and lemon.

BAKED HAKE CUTLETS

1 lb hake
A little flour
¼ lb breadcrumbs
½ pint fish stock, or milk
   and water
1 teaspoon lemon juice
1 tablespoon chopped
   parsley
1 teaspoon chopped shallot
   or onion
1 oz butter
Seasoning

Method. Mix together the breadcrumbs, shallot and parsley with a little pepper and salt, and sprinkle a little of this mixture into a well-greased fireproof dish. Have the hake cut in small slices about 1″ thick, remove all skin and bone and boil these trimmings to make a fish stock. Lay in a few pieces of fish on top of the layer of breadcrumb mixture, cover with another layer of the mixture, then a layer of fish and so on, making the top layer breadcrumbs. Add the lemon juice to the fish stock and pour this over. Dot the top with the butter in tiny pieces, and cover with a greaseproof paper. Bake in a moderate oven until ready (about ½ hour).

COLD TURBOT

Piece of turbot
Bay leaf
Peppercorns
Piece of carrot
Some parsley stalks
1 onion

Method. Prepare a panful of salted hot water, add the bay leaf, the peppercorns, the piece of carrot, parsley stalks and onion, and slip in the fish. Poach *very* gently for about 10–15 minutes according to size. Leave in the water until cold, to absorb all the flavour. Lift it out, drain carefully, skin it, and serve on a bed of watercress or lettuce, with slices of cucumber and tomato along the top.

SCALLOPS IN CHEESE SAUCE

Scallops
Butter or margarine
Grated cheese
Flour
Milk
Seasoning

Method. Allow one or two scallops for each person, and, after cleaning them well, poach them gently in a little butter and milk until they go opaque. Lift them out and put them in a fireproof dish, covered with a rich white sauce. Make this sauce in the usual way, using half the fish liquor and half warm milk, and adding a generous helping of grated cheese. Pour this sauce over the scallops, then sprinkle a tablespoon of grated cheese over the top, pop the dish under the red-hot grill until the cheese bubbles and browns. Serve with brown bread and butter for tea, or with peas and mashed potatoes for lunch or dinner.

BAKED SOLE WITH MUSHROOMS

1 medium-sized plump
    sole
1 dessertspoon chopped
    parsley
6 button mushrooms
1 shallot or onion
½ oz butter
Grated lemon rind
Lemon juice
Salt/Pepper
1 tablespoon browned
    breadcrumbs
1 glass white wine or
    stock

Method. Chop the shallot or onion and mushrooms, mix them with the chopped parsley and a little grated rind, and sprinkle half this mixture over the bottom of a well-greased fireproof dish. Clean the fish, remove the black skin, and cut off the head and fins (these trimmings can be used to make a stock, if you are not using wine). Score the sole across on both sides, and lay it on top of the mushroom mixture, white skin downwards. Sprinkle the remainder of the chopped ingredients on top, season with pepper, salt and a little lemon juice. Cover with the breadcrumbs and dot with butter. Pour the wine or stock round and bake in a moderate oven for about 20 minutes. Serve from the dish in which it is cooked. A few button mushrooms or some parsley and cut lemon may be used as a garnish.

If you are not using wine, a little butter should be melted into the stock to give it a richer flavour.

BAKED RIVER TROUT

2 river trout
1 oz butter
1 teaspoon capers
Seasoning
A few breadcrumbs
A little lemon juice

Method. Thoroughly clean the fish and lay them head to tail on a well-buttered fireproof dish. Sprinkle them with pepper, salt, lemon juice and the capers, roughly chopped. Put a light coating of breadcrumbs on top and dot with butter. Cover with a buttered paper and bake in a moderate oven for 15–20 minutes. Serve hot, garnished with thin slices of lemon.

FRIED WHITEBAIT

1 pint whitebait
Flour
Salt

Method. Make sure the fish are perfectly fresh and look them over for weeds or any other undesirable matter. Wash and rinse them in icy cold water, handling them as little as possible and leave them in a colander or a basin with a lump of ice, if possible, until wanted. Meantime have a saucepan of boiling fat ready for the fish. Spread the fish on a clean cloth to drain, and in another cloth put 2 or 3 tablespoons of flour. Place a few of the whitebait on the top and toss them in the flour until lightly and evenly coated, and separate the fish from each other. Empty the fish without delay into the frying basket, and shake it well to let the loose flour fall out. Plunge it into the hot fat and fry about 2 minutes, shaking the basket gently all the time. The whitebait must not be coloured this first frying. Lift out the basket, allow the fat to drip from it, and turn the fish on to soft paper to drain. Cook the rest of the fish in the same way until all are finished. Let the fat get smoking hot again, put the fish back into the basket (putting in as many as the fat will cover this time) and fry them a second time until brown and crisp, about 2 minutes. Drain on soft paper, and season with salt. Serve immediately on a paper doily on a hot plate, garnish with quarters of fresh lemon, and eat with thin brown bread and butter.

STUFFED TROUT IN PAPER

4 or 5 small ½-lb trout
2 oz butter
1 teaspoon chopped
  parsley
1 tablespoon chopped
  mushrooms
3 tablespoons bread-
  crumbs
Squeeze of lemon juice
1 egg yolk
Seasoning

Method. For the stuffing, beat the butter to a cream, add the other ingredients, binding all together with the egg yolk. Clean the trout carefully without cutting and fill with the stuffing. Wrap each fish in a piece of greased white paper, or tinfoil, and place on a greased baking tin. Bake in a brisk oven, turning the fish once during the cooking (15–20 minutes). Serve on a hot dish without removing the paper, and garnish with parsley. The paper should only be removed when the fish is on the point of being eaten.

ADD a sprinkling of nutmeg to your buttered shrimps—it makes a mouth-watering difference.

LEMONS that have become hard and dry can be plumped up very easily by putting them in a saucepan of hot water (not boiling), and leaving for about 2 hours. Wipe and let them get cold before using.

BAKED SPRATS

1½ dozen sprats
1 dessertspoon chopped
    onion
1 bay leaf
1 dozen black peppercorns
A few parsley stalks
A little salt
Grated nutmeg
Vinegar
1 oz butter

Method. Prepare the sprats, cutting off heads and tails, and lay them in a pie-dish or fireproof dish with the seasonings. Pour in enough good vinegar, or a mixture of vinegar and water to cover them. Lay a few small pieces of butter on the top and bake in a moderate oven until the fish are cooked (20–30 minutes).

Serve cold with salad.

JUGGED KIPPERS

Pair of kippers
Boiling water

Method. Trim off the fins and clean off any scales. Cut kippers in half, place in a heatproof jug and pour over them plenty of boiling water. Place a plate on top and leave for 10 minutes. Lift out and drain. Serve with hot buttered toast if wanted for a warm dish.

If wanted for summer, let them cool, and serve them in a ring of watercress, with slices of tomato and cucumber to garnish.

BAKED HALIBUT

Halibut
A little flour
Salt/Pepper
Pinch of mace
Butter
1 tablespoon water or
    water and milk

Method. Wash the fish, then dredge lightly with flour. Season rather highly with salt, pepper, and a little powdered mace if liked, and place in a greased baking dish. Dot the fish with pieces of butter, and add 1 tablespoon water or milk and water. Bake for ½ hour in a moderate oven, length of time depending on thickness of fish.

Serve with a good white sauce, made with half milk and half the fish stock, sprinkled with chopped parsley.

FRIED SPRATS

Clean the sprats and draw them through the gills. Wipe them very dry and dip in flour, coating them lightly. Then run a skewer through the heads of about a dozen at a time and fry them on the skewer in plenty of hot fat until they are nicely browned. Drain them well, draw out the skewer and serve very hot, garnished with parsley and lemon. Thin slices of brown bread and butter are the perfect accompaniment to sprats cooked this way.

BAKED WHITING

4 whiting
2 oz butter
1 tablespoon flour
Pepper/Salt
Juice of ½ lemon

Method. Skin the whiting, cut off the heads and clean them thoroughly. Dip each fish in seasoned flour, coating it lightly, and lay them in a well-buttered fireproof dish. Strain the lemon juice over, dot the top with butter, bake in a moderate oven for 10–15 minutes, and serve hot, garnished with parsley.

NOTE. This is particularly nice for invalids or anybody with a delicate stomach as it is very easily digested.

POTTED BLOATER

Grilled bloater
Pepper
Pinch of mace
Pinch of nutmeg
Butter

Method. Carefully skin and bone the cooked bloater, and beat it till smooth, adding gradually enough melted butter to make a soft paste. Season with pepper, salt (if necessary), and a small pinch of nutmeg and mace. If you want it very smooth, you can rub it through a sieve. Pack the paste into small pots or jars, and if you want to keep it for any length of time, run some melted butter over the top. This is delicious on hot buttered toast and for small sandwiches.

NOTE. You can pot other kinds of fish this way, regulating the seasoning and the butter according to the kind of fish used.

FISH DISHES

BAKED FISH SOUFFLE

6 oz cooked fish
4 oz cooked potato, sieved
2 oz butter
¼ teacup milk
2 eggs
Grated lemon rind
Pepper/Salt

Method. Put the butter and milk into a saucepan, and when boiling add the sieved cooked potato. Beat with a wooden spoon until very light and creamy, then add the fish, which has been freed from all skin and bone and chopped finely, then the yolks of eggs, the rind and seasonings, and beat again. Whip the egg whites to a stiff froth and stir them lightly in at the very last. Pour the mixture into a greased pie-dish or soufflé dish and bake in a moderate oven for about ½ hour, until nicely browned and well risen. Serve at once in the dish in which it was baked.

BAKED FISH WITH CHEESE

3 pieces of white fish
Seasoning
1 tablespoon grated onion
1 tablespoon breadcrumbs
    or crushed cornflakes
1 tablespoon grated
    cheese
1 oz butter or margarine

Method. Put the seasoned fish (cod, haddock or halibut) into a well-greased pie-dish or fireproof dish and cover with the grated onion, breadcrumbs and grated cheese. Dot the top with butter or margarine and bake for ½ hour in a moderate oven until the cheese is crisp and golden. Serve very hot.

FISH CAKES

½ lb cooked fish
½ lb cooked potatoes
1 oz butter
1 yolk of egg
1 teaspoon chopped
    parsley
1 teaspoon anchovy or
    shrimp essence, or
    paste
Pepper/Salt
A little flour
Egg and breadcrumbs

The remains of any cold, cooked fish can be used for fish cakes, and a mixture of fish is very good, such as smoked and fresh fish combined.
Method. Free the fish from all skin and bone, and chop it finely. Sieve the potatoes and chop the parsley very finely. Melt the butter in a saucepan, add the fish, potatoes, parsley, egg yolk and seasonings, and mix well together over the heat. When it is all nicely hot and blended, turn out on to a plate, smooth it over with a knife and let it cool. When the mixture feels firm, divide it into ten or twelve smallish pieces, flour the hands, and roll each piece into a ball, laying them on a floured board and flattening them with a floured knife into neat little round cakes. Paint each cake quickly with a brush dipped in beaten egg, and cover smoothly with fine dry crumbs, shaking any loose ones off. Deep fry in boiling fat to a nice brown colour. Drain well on soft paper and serve on a hot dish on a paper doily, garnished with parsley.
NOTE. If you happen to have a little good fish sauce available, then you can use this instead of the butter and egg yolk for mixing the ingredients. To vary the flavour, you can add a chopped, hard-boiled egg if you like, and one or two sardines will also give variety.

FISH PIE

Any cooked fish
White sauce
Hard-boiled egg or eggs
Mashed potatoes

Method. Fold the cooked fish (which can be white or smoked) into a good, rich white sauce, together with the chopped, boiled egg(s). Cover with a layer of creamy mashed potatoes, and heat all through in the oven until potatoes are lightly browned.

FISH OMELETTE

About 1 dessertspoon cold, flaked fish (cooked)
2 eggs
1 dessertspoon grated cheese
Salt/Pepper
1 oz butter

Method. Chop the cooked, flaked fish very small and put it to one side. Separate the yolks from the whites of the eggs. Beat the yolks in a basin, stir in the grated cheese, and season with salt and pepper to taste. Whisk the egg whites, to which a pinch of salt has been added, then fold them gently into the yolk mixture.

Melt the butter in the omelette pan, then pour in the egg mixture and stir very lightly. Just as it is beginning to set, add the prepared fish and stir again for a second or two. When almost cooked, fold over quickly, leave for just a few seconds, and serve at once on a hot dish.

FRICASSEE OF FISH

½ lb white fish
½ pint fish stock (made from the trimmings)
1 gill milk
1 oz butter
1 oz flour
1 hard-boiled egg
Squeeze of lemon juice
White pepper/Salt
1 or 2 tablespoons top of the milk

Method. Make a sauce with the butter, flour, fish stock and milk and season it with pepper and salt. If using cooked fish, flake it, add to this sauce and heat through. If using raw fish, cut it in small pieces and allow it to simmer for a few minutes until it is cooked. Add a squeeze of lemon juice and the top of the milk. Serve inside a border of mashed potato and garnish with the hard-boiled egg, a few thin slices of lemon and a little finely-chopped parsley. This makes an appetising and colourful finish.

SCALLOPED FISH

½ lb cooked fish
½ pint good white sauce
Breadcrumbs
A little butter

Method. Take 4 or 5 natural or fireproof scallop shells and grease them with a little butter. Coat the insides with some fine breadcrumbs and lay in some pieces or flakes of nicely cooked fish, piling them quite high in the centre. Then take some good, well-seasoned white sauce and pour it over the fish, coating it well. Smooth over with a knife and sprinkle with more breadcrumbs. Dot with butter and bake in the oven for 10–12 minutes, until nicely browned on top. Serve with a tiny slice of cut lemon and a sprig of parsley on the top of each.

NOTE. If you like, you can add a little grated cheese to the breadcrumbs, and another nice addition for extra flavour is to add a few picked shrimps to the flaked fish.

GATEAU OF FISH AND RICE

¼ lb rice
⅓ pint fish stock or milk
2 eggs
½ lb cooked fish
1 oz butter
Grated rind of ½ lemon
Pepper/Salt
1 teaspoon chopped
    parsley

Method. Wash the rice and put it into a saucepan with the milk or fish stock, and let it cook slowly until quite soft, adding more liquid if necessary. Then add to it the chopped fish, butter, pepper, salt and grated lemon rind. Beat up the eggs and add them, mixing well. Grease a bowl and in the bottom sprinkle the chopped parsley, and pour the mixture on top. Cover with a greased paper and steam slowly until firm to the touch (1–1½ hours). Turn on to a hot dish and serve with or without sauce, as you like, and decorate with more parsley.

FISH CURRY

½ lb cooked fish
2 hard-boiled eggs
1 cup boiled rice
1 dessertspoon curry
    powder
1 dessertspoon chutney
2 oz butter
1 oz flour
½ pint milk or fish stock
Salt
½ lemon

Method. Remove all skin and bone from the cooked fish and break it into pieces. Have the rice boiled in salted water, and very dry. Cut the hard-boiled eggs in slices. Melt the butter in a saucepan, stir in the flour, and mix well together. Add the chutney, salt, curry powder, and fry for a minute, stirring well, then add the milk or fish stock and stir until boiling. Put in the fish, rice and eggs and mix all very gently together until thoroughly hot, and serve on a hot dish garnished with thin slices of lemon.

FISH SOUFFLE

1 large cup cooked fish
4 eggs
Salt/Pepper

WHITE SAUCE
¼ cup butter
⅓ cup flour
1½ cups milk
Pinch grated nutmeg

Method. First make the white sauce by melting the butter, working in the flour, then blending in the milk. Add pinch of grated nutmeg, then stir and cook to thicken. Add the cooked fish, minced, and then beat in the egg yolks very thoroughly. Season with 1 teaspoon salt and a good pinch of pepper.

Fold in the stiffly-beaten egg whites. Turn into a buttered and breadcrumbed mould or soufflé dish, filling it two-thirds full. (There will be about 5 cups of the mixture and it will rise.) Bake for 45 minutes in a moderate oven. Serve from the dish with melted butter.

IF YOUR poached egg usually scatters all over the pan and you have no proper poaching utensil, put a small pastry cutter in the pan and drop the egg inside.

THREE things at least which go harder the longer they are boiled, are eggs, winkles, and corn-on-the-cob.

KEDGEREE

Any cold, cooked fish
1 teacup well-boiled rice
1 oz butter
1 teaspoon mixed mustard
2 boiled eggs
Salt/Cayenne pepper
Tomato sauce

Method. To the well-boiled rice add butter, seasonings, eggs cut up, and lastly the pieces of fish which should be free from bones. Stir over heat till piping hot, pile on dish, and pour over warmed tomato sauce. If tomato sauce is not liked, sprinkle with chopped parsley and chopped yolk of egg which has been kept back for this purpose.

Vegetables

I hope you may find some interesting ways of dealing with vegetables in this section. Many of the recipes would make complete meals without the addition of any meat or fish, so may appeal to the vegetarians among my readers.

GLAZED CARROTS

Young carrots
Stock
Butter
Sugar

Method. Use young carrots if possible, but if they are not in season, cut large carrots in small rounds with a vegetable cutter, or in some other fancy shape. Put the prepared carrots into a shallow stewpan with enough stock to cover, a small piece of butter and a good pinch of sugar. Cook in the oven or over a slow gas, or by the side of the fire, without covering the pan, so that by the time the cooking is finished the liquid has evaporated and the carrots are coated with a thick gravy or glaze.

These make a lovely garnish for meat dishes.

BRITTANY CABBAGE

1 cabbage
Grated nutmeg
Butter
Flour
Black pepper

Method. Cook the cabbage in well-salted, boiling water, then drain and press out all the water you can. Cut it up quite small. Measure the chopped cabbage and return it to the pan. For every two breakfastcups of cabbage allow 1 level saltspoon grated nutmeg, 1 oz butter, 1 heaped teaspoon flour and a pinch of pepper. Melt the butter and blend the flour and nutmeg in with it. Then stir this mixture into the cabbage, bring to the boil and boil for 2 minutes. Add pepper and serve.

SCALLOPED JERUSALEM ARTICHOKES

Artichokes as required
White sauce, with grated
  Parmesan
A little butter
Few browned crumbs
Salt/Pepper to taste
Grated cheese
Breadcrumbs
Melted butter

Method. Peel and boil in milk and water the number of artichokes required, having added salt to the water, and cook till tender. Drain and cut into pieces, and mix them with a little good white sauce to which you can add a little grated Parmesan cheese. Butter some shells or a fireproof dish, then sprinkle in a few browned crumbs. Now put in the mixture, seasoned to taste with salt and pepper, cover with a mixture of grated cheese and breadcrumbs, and pour over a little melted butter. Brown in the oven till golden and thoroughly heated through.

HOT BEETROOT WITH BUTTER

3 small beetroots
1 or 2 oz butter
Seasoning
Parsley

Method. Cut the tops off the beetroot and wash carefully in cold water, making sure the skin is not broken or the juice will run out and the colour be spoilt. Put them into a saucepan of boiling water, giving them plenty of room, and add salt (1 dessertspoon to a quart), and boil gently with the lid on until they feel tender when you press them with a finger. *Never* use a fork to test beetroot. When ready, peel quickly, quarter or slice and lay in a hot dish. Pour melted butter (with a little chopped onion, if liked) over them and sprinkle with finely-chopped parsley.

BACON AND CAULIFLOWER WITH CHEESE

1 cauliflower
2 teacups milk
1 tablespoon flour
3 tablespoons melted
  butter
1 teacup grated cheese
Slices of fried bacon

Method. Leave the tender green leaves on the cauliflower, and soak it in salted water for 10 minutes. Boil till tender, but do not let it break. Blend the flour into the melted butter, add the milk and the grated cheese and stir till boiling. Cook for a minute or two. Cut a slice from the bottom of the cauliflower and stand it on a hot dish. Arrange some pieces of crisply-fried bacon round about and pour the sauce over. Serve very hot.

NEVER buy oysters or mussels if they are open.

DO NOT use a knife for peeling cooked beetroot. Hold the beetroot under a running tap, rub the skin with your hands and it will slide off without difficulty.

RED CABBAGE WITH APPLES

1 medium-sized red
   cabbage
1 onion
2 or 3 apples
2 oz butter or dripping
Salt/Pepper
1 teacup milk

Method. Cut the cabbage in four, removing any outer leaves and the hard part of the stalk, wash it well and let it soak for about 1 hour in cold water with a few drops of vinegar added. Rinse well after this soaking, drain well, and then shred it with a sharp knife. Have ready a panful of boiling salted water and plunge the shredded cabbage into this, boil quickly from 5–10 minutes and drain it again. Peel the onion and chop it or slice it thinly. Peel and slice the apples, removing the cores. Melt the butter or dripping in a stewpan, and cook the onion for a few minutes but do not let it get brown. Add the prepared cabbage with the apples, and season with pepper and salt. Stew slowly until tender (about ¾ hour), stirring occasionally. Add the milk (top of milk if you can spare it) at the very end, and cook for a few minutes longer.

This is very good with salt meat or with sausages.

CABBAGE WITH BACON

1 lb cooked cabbage
Seasoning
10 thin rashers of bacon

Method. Fry the rashers in a frying pan until cooked as you like them, then lift them on to a plate and keep them warm. Have the cabbage well-drained and chopped, and put it into the bacon fat. Season it with pepper and salt, and stir over the heat until thoroughly hot. Grease a hot basin and press the cabbage into it. Then carefully turn it out, not to break the shape, put it in the centre of a hot dish and put the bacon round about.

NOTE. This is a very nourishing economical dish when meat is scarce or expensive. You can use any greens in this way.

HOT RED CABBAGE

1 small firm red cabbage
Salt
3 sour apples
1 large onion
Nutmeg
1 tablespoon vinegar
3 oz butter
2 oz sugar

Method. Remove the outer leaves of cabbage. Wash and drain thoroughly. Shred cabbage and put in a pot with a little boiling water, adding some salt. Add apples, onion, nutmeg and vinegar. Simmer until liquid is completely evaporated (about ¾ hour). Add butter and sugar. Mix well and simmer for another 10 minutes.

STUFFED CABBAGE

1 medium-sized firm
  cabbage
1 pint of stock

STUFFING
4 tablespoons cooked
  meat
3 tablespoons bread-
  crumbs
1 teaspoon chopped onion
1 teaspoon chopped
  parsley
1 tablespoon melted butter
  or bacon fat
1 egg

Method. Wash the cabbage well, removing any discoloured leaves, and the hard end of the stalk, then
put into a basin, cover with boiling water, put a plate
on top, and let it stand for ½–¾ hour to soften.

Meantime make the stuffing: Chop the meat, onion
and parsley finely, mix them together, add the breadcrumbs and season to taste. Pour in the melted butter
or fat and bind it all to a stiffish paste with beaten egg.

Lift the cabbage out of the water and drain well,
then pull the leaves apart and put a good spoonful of
the stuffing in the centre, and the remainder between
the leaves. Wrap the cabbage in a piece of well-
greased paper, tie it with string and place it in a
baking tin with the stock poured round, and bake in a
good oven for about 1 hour. Baste it every now and
then with the stock. When ready, remove paper and
string and serve the cabbage on a hot dish. Boil
down the stock in the tin until there is just enough
for a gravy, removing any grease from the top, and
pouring it round.

STEWED RED CABBAGE

1 red cabbage
1 pint light stock
1 oz butter
1 oz flour
2 tablespoons vinegar
Salt/Pepper
2 oz bacon
A pinch of nutmeg, if
  liked

Method. Trim the cabbage, removing any damaged
leaves and the hard part of the stalk. Cut it in half
and shred it fairly finely. Wash it carefully, drain, and
scald in boiling water for a minute or two. Drain
again, and put into a stewpan with the stock to cover
it. Add the butter and flour melted and mixed
together, the vinegar, seasonings, and bacon cut in
small pieces. Put the lid on the pan, and simmer
slowly by the side of the fire, on a low gas, or in the
oven until quite tender (about 1 hour).

Cooked this way, it makes a nice accompaniment
to game or sausages.

RED CABBAGE IN CASSEROLE

Red cabbage
Chopped onion
Salt
1 dessertspoon vinegar
1 dessertspoon brown
  sugar

Method. Plunge cabbage into boiling water for 5
minutes, then rinse through with cold water. Place
chopped onion in bottom of casserole. Slice the
cabbage and put into the dish with salt, vinegar and
sugar, and cook slowly for 1½–2 hours.

NEW CARROTS A LA MAITRE D'HOTEL

1 or 2 bunches young
    carrots
½ teaspoon sugar
Salt/Pepper
1 dessertspoon chopped
    parsley
1 oz butter
1 dessertspoon lemon
    juice

Method. Wash and scrape the carrots very lightly, cutting off the green tops. Put into a saucepan with enough boiling water to cover, add a little salt and boil with the lid on until tender (about 15 minutes). When ready, drain off every drop of water (you can keep this for your stock pot), add the butter, lemon juice and seasoning and toss over the heat until thoroughly mixed. Serve very hot, sprinkled with chopped parsley.

You can use older carrots this way too, but they must be cut in pieces.

CAULIFLOWER A LA POLONAISE

1 cauliflower
½ or 1 hard-boiled egg
2 oz butter
2 tablespoons white
    breadcrumbs
1 dessertspoon chopped
    parsley

This is a good way of serving cauliflower past its best. *Method.* Cook the cauliflower, but not too much, drain it well and press gently in a cloth to make it a nice round shape. Place it in a vegetable dish and sprinkle with a mixture of chopped parsley, chopped white of the egg, and sieved yolk, but do not use all the chopped mixture for this—keep a little back. Keep the cauliflower warm over a bowl of hot water.

Melt the butter in a saucepan and let it brown slightly, then put in the breadcrumbs and fry slowly until golden brown. The sauce must not get too thick, nd the crumbs should float in the butter when ʃrowned. Pour this over the cauliflower and sprinkle with the rest of the chopped parsley and egg mixture.

CELERY WITH CREAM SAUCE

1 head of celery
½ pint milk
1 oz butter
1 dessertspoon flour
2 tablespoons top of
    milk
Seasoning

Method. Wash and brush the celery, dividing the stalks and removing any brown or decayed bits. Cut into small pieces and put into saucepan with enough boiling water to cover. Boil for 5 to 10 minutes, then pour the water off. Add the milk and stew the celery slowly until it is really tender, then strain and keep the milk aside. Melt the butter in a saucepan, stir in the flour, then add the milk in which the celery was cooked and stir till boiling. Put the celery into the sauce, add the top of milk and seasoning. Simmer together for a minute or two, and serve nice and hot, garnished with snippets of dry toast ($\frac{1}{2}$–$\frac{3}{4}$ hour).

BAKED CAULIFLOWER (1)

1 cooked cauliflower
3 tablespoons bread-
    crumbs
1 egg
1 teacup milk
Seasoning
1 oz butter

Method. Grease a fireproof dish and sprinkle in half the crumbs. Break the cauliflower in small pieces and arrange them neatly in the dish. Beat up the egg in a bowl with the milk, add a little salt, pepper and, if liked, a pinch of nutmeg and strain over the cauliflower. Sprinkle in the rest of the crumbs, dot with butter and bake in a moderate oven until nicely browned (15–20 minutes).

BAKED CAULIFLOWER (2)

1 cauliflower
1 teacup breadcrumbs
1 tablespoon chopped
    onion
Salt/Pepper
A little nutmeg (if liked)
3 tablespoons grated
    cheese
½ pint white sauce
1 or 2 egg yolks

Method. Cook the cauliflower and break it into pieces. Grease a fireproof dish and lay in half the cauliflower. Sprinkle over this some of the grated cheese, chopped onion and breadcrumbs and season with pepper, salt and a little grated nutmeg. Then add the rest of the cauliflower and more breadcrumbs, cheese, etc. Have ready about ½ pint of good white sauce, add to this the egg yolk(s), and pour it over the cauliflower mixture in the dish. Sprinkle the top with breadcrumbs and bake in a good oven till brown (15–20 minutes).

CAULIFLOWER SOUFFLE

1 cooked cauliflower
2 tomatoes
1 oz butter
1 oz flour
1½ teacups milk
2 eggs
1 tablespoon bread-
    crumbs
A small piece of butter
Salt/Pepper

The remains of any cold cooked cauliflower will do for this, but you should have a good breakfastcupful. *Method.* Break the cauliflower into small pieces, peel the tomatoes and cut them in very thin slices, and arrange them in layers in a greased pie or soufflé dish, seasoning them with pepper and salt. Make a good white sauce with the butter, flour and milk, then draw the pan off the heat, add the yolks of the eggs, and mix well. Beat the egg whites to a stiff froth, fold them lightly into the white sauce, and pour this mixture over the cauliflower. Sprinkle the top with breadcrumbs and dot with butter. Bake in a moderate oven until nicely browned and firm to the touch (about 20 minutes). Serve at once in the dish in which it was cooked.

A SALTSPOON of dry mustard sprinkled over cooked beetroot, then vinegar poured over in the usual way, helps to keep the beetroot fresh for a much longer time.

SWEET CORN COBS

Cobs of sweet corn
Sugar
Butter
Salt/Pepper

Young fresh cobs which are short and plump are the best to choose.

Method. Strip off the outer covering and all the silky fibres, and place the cobs in boiling water with sufficient sugar added to slightly sweeten the water. Boil gently until the grains are tender (8–12 minutes), but do not on any account overcook, or you will make them tough and destroy the flavour. Bite a grain between the teeth and when it feels tender and milky, it is ready. Serve very hot, and on a separate dish serve melted butter well-seasoned with pepper and salt.

BAKED EGG PLANT (Aubergine)

1 or 2 egg plants
Butter
Salt/Pepper

Method. Wipe or wash the egg plants and put in a fireproof dish or a baking tin with a small quantity of water. Cover with a greased paper or a lid, and bake in a moderate oven until tender. They can be cut open at the table and mashed up with a little butter, pepper and salt. This is one of the best ways of doing this vegetable as you keep in the full flavour.

If you prefer, you can peel them after baking, and serve in a vegetable dish with a good sauce poured over.

STUFFED EGG PLANT

2 egg plants
Seasoning

STUFFING

3 tablespoons bread-
crumbs
2 tablespoons chopped
ham or tongue
1 teaspoon chopped onion
1 teaspoon chopped
parsley
1 oz butter
1 dessertspoon chopped
mushrooms (if liked)
Grated lemon rind
Egg to bind

Method. Wipe the egg plants, and cut them in halves lengthwise. Scoop out the seeds, sprinkle the insides of the halves well with fine salt and let them lie with hollow sides downwards for 1 hour. Meantime prepare the stuffing by putting all the chopped ingredients into a basin. Season them nicely and bind all together with beaten egg. Drain and wipe the egg plant halves, and fill them with the stuffing, piling it fairly high. Spread a few crumbs on top and lay the stuffed halves on a greased baking dish. Cover with a butter paper and bake in a moderate oven till ready (about 1 hour). Serve hot with a paper doily under them.

NOTE. You can vary the stuffing to suit your taste, and if you do not like meat, chopped nuts can be used instead.

EGG PLANT WITH CREAM SAUCE

2 or 3 egg plants
2 oz butter
½ pint cream sauce
Seasoning

Method. Peel the egg plants and cut them in thin slices, sprinkle with salt and let them lie for ½ hour. Pour off the water which has been drawn from them and wipe the pieces with a clean cloth. Put them into a fireproof dish with the butter, cover and cook gently for ½ hour in the oven. Meanwhile make a good white sauce to which you have added two tablespoons of cream or top of milk. Pour this over the egg plant and cook for a few minutes longer. Season to taste and dish very carefully so as not to break the slices.

STEWED LEEKS

6 leeks
A small piece of butter
Some light stock
Seasoning

This is a very nourishing way to serve leeks, especially if there are any colds in the house, or any liver complaints.

Method. Trim off the roots, the green ends and the outer covering of the leeks, and split them down the middle. Wash thoroughly and let them lie in cold water with a little vinegar for about ½ hour. Drain them, and cut in suitable pieces and wash them again in fresh cold water. Put them into a saucepan with enough stock to cover, put the lid on and stew slowly until they are really tender (20–30 minutes). Reduce the stock until there is just enough to serve as a nice gravy. Season with salt and pepper, and add a little piece of butter just before serving.

NOTE. If you prefer it, you can cook the leeks in milk for the second half of the cooking time, and use this milk to make a rich white sauce instead of a gravy. Sprinkle with chopped parsley.

SAVOURY STUFFED MARROW

1 small vegetable marrow
2 tablespoons suet
1 teaspoon chopped parsley
1 egg
¼ lb sausage, mince or ham
4 tablespoons bread-crumbs
Salt/Pepper to taste

Method. Peel marrow with potato peeler. With a sharp knife, cut a wedge lengthways out of marrow, and scoop out the seeds. Mix meat, suet, crumbs, parsley, salt and pepper with the egg. Stuff the marrow and replace wedge. Stand in 2 inches of water in baking tin, and cover with another tin. Bake in a moderate oven till tender when tested, usually about 1 hour. Serve with gravy, or a white sauce made from the remaining water in the tin.

BAKED ONIONS

3 or 4 Spanish onions
½ pint milk
1/2 oz butter or dripping
Salt/Pepper

Method. Choose smallish onions of equal size. Cut off the roots and tops and all the brown outside skin, as usual. Throw them into a saucepan of boiling salted water, boil for 10 minutes, and drain. Then put the onions in a deep fireproof dish, just big enough to hold them, season well with pepper and salt, then heat the milk and pour it over them. Add the dripping or butter dotted in tiny pieces, cover with a greased paper and bake in a moderate oven until tender, basting occasionally if necessary, with the milk (1–1½ hours). When nearly ready you may add a little grated cheese. Serve very hot.

ONIONS AU GRATIN

3 or 4 cooked onions
½ pint white sauce
3 tablespoons grated
   cheese
1 dessertspoon bread-
   crumbs
A small piece of butter

Method. Break the onions in pieces, but do not chop them. Grate the cheese, and get ready about ½ pint of good white sauce, well-seasoned. Grease a fireproof dish and put in a layer of onion, then a layer of cheese, then some sauce, then onion, and so on until all is used up. Sprinkle some browned breadcrumbs on top, dot with butter, and bake in the oven until nicely browned. Serve in the same dish.
NOTE. If you like them, a few peeled, sliced tomatoes make a nice addition to this dish, mixed in with the onions.

GLAZED ONIONS

Small silver onions
Salad oil
Brown stock
Salt
Caster sugar

Method. Skin the onions and wipe them very dry with a cloth. Put a little salad oil into a shallow stewpan and heat it on the stove. Put in the onions, sprinkling them with caster sugar, and tossing them over and over until they are well-browned on all sides. Pour off any superfluous oil and pour in enough brown stock to barely cover the onions. Add a little salt if necessary and let the onions cook slowly on the stove or in the oven. When they are nearly ready, let the stock boil down quickly till it forms a glaze on the onions, turning them over gently till they are evenly coated.

These are a delicious garnish for all sorts of meat dishes.

LEEKS AND BACON

1 leek for each person
1 bacon rasher per person
A little olive oil

Method. Wrap each leek in a bacon rasher and brown in a little olive oil, then cover with water and cook for 15 minutes until tender. Serve with boiled potatoes and the gravy from the leeks.

VEGETABLE MARROW WITH CHEESE

1 small marrow
2 teacups milk
1 teacup water
2 or 3 cloves
Seasoning
1 oz butter
3 oz grated cheese
1 tablespoon cornflour

Method. Wash the marrow, cut it in quarters, remove the seeds and peel it thinly. Cut it into neat pieces and put in a saucepan. Pour the milk and water over the marrow and the onion stuck with the cloves. Cook slowly until it feels quite tender, then drain and keep the liquid for making the sauce.

Melt the butter in a small saucepan, add the cornflour, and blend smoothly. Then pour on the strained milk and water and stir till boiling. Cook for 2 or 3 minutes. Season to taste with a little white pepper, salt and made mustard. Add most of the cheese and mix it well in, but do not boil again. Lay the pieces of marrow in a greased fireproof dish, pour the sauce over, and sprinkle the rest of the cheese on top. Brown in the oven or under the grill. (Cooking time 20–30 minutes.)

STUFFED ONION SURPRISE

3 Spanish onions
3 sheep's kidneys
2 oz butter
1 tablespoon bread-
    crumbs
Pepper/Salt
1 teacup brown gravy

Method. Peel the onions and scald them in boiling salted water for a few minutes. Then cut off the tops and remove the centre part from each (you will find a potato peeler is excellent for this). Skin the kidneys, season with pepper and salt, and place one inside each onion. Sprinkle the breadcrumbs over and dot with some of the butter. Melt the rest of the butter in a baking tin or fireproof dish, lay the stuffed onions on it, and bake in a moderate oven for 1½–2 hours, basting frequently with the butter. When ready, lift on to a hot dish and pour a little brown gravy round.

ONIONS will not sprout when stored if the root end is held for a few moments over a flame or singed with a hot iron before being hung up.

IF YOU boil the marrow too much so that it breaks away when strained, it looks better and tastes grand if it is mashed with butter, pepper and salt. Drain away as much water as possible before mashing.

STUFFED ONIONS (1)

3 or 4 Spanish onions
1 or 2 oz butter or
  dripping
1 teacup brown stock

STUFFING

2 tablespoons cooked meat
2 tablespoons bread-
  crumbs
1 teaspoon chopped
  parsley
Salt/Pepper
3 or 4 button mushrooms
A pinch of nutmeg, if liked
1 tablespoon brown or
  tomato sauce

Method. Choose smallish Spanish onions of equal size. Cut off the root and top and remove all the brown skin, as usual. Put them in a saucepan of boiling salted water and boil them for 10 minutes, then strain and throw them into cold water. When they are cool enough to handle comfortably, remove one or two of the outer layers from the onions and scoop out the centres, leaving a hole big enough to take about a tablespoon of stuffing. Chop up these onion trimmings and put them into a casserole with the butter or dripping and the cup of stock, and let them get hot in the oven.

Now make the stuffing : Use chicken, tongue, ham or any nicely cooked meat, and chop up enough to make about 2 tablespoons. Put it into a bowl with the breadcrumbs, parsley, finely-chopped mushrooms (if desired) and seasonings, and add enough brown or tomato sauce to bind all together.

Fill the onion centres with this mixture, piling it quite high in the centre. Then put them in the casserole with the minced onion, cover with a greased paper, or a lid, and cook in the oven until the onions are completely tender (about 2 hours). Serve them in the casserole with the minced onion and gravy round.

NOTE. If this is wanted completely vegetarian, then use grated nuts instead of meat, and use vegetable stock instead of meat stock.

STUFFED ONIONS (2)

3 large onions
Bread as required
Pepper/Salt to taste
Parsley, chopped
A little butter
2 oz grated cheese
1 oz breadcrumbs
1 oz butter

Method. Boil the onions, then cut them in half cross-ways. Take out the centre carefully, chop it and mix with a little bread (which you have previously soaked in water till soft and squeezed dry), pepper and salt to taste, and chopped parsley. Fill the onions with this mixture and brown them slightly in a little butter on the underside. Then place them in a fireproof dish, sprinkle with grated cheese and breadcrumbs, dot with the oz of butter, and bake in a moderate oven till the top is golden and everything thoroughly heated through. Serve in the dish in which you have baked them.

GREEN PEA PUREE

Garden peas
Butter
Milk
Sugar
Seasoning

When the peas get too old for serving whole, you can very tastily make them into a purée.

Method. Boil the peas in salted water till they are tender, then drain and rub through a sieve. Put the sieved peas back into the saucepan with a good piece of butter or some bacon fat, and enough hot milk or top of milk to moisten. Season to taste, plus a very little sugar.

You can serve this separately with meat, or as a fancy border, or piped through a forcing bag as a decoration.

GREEN PEAS WITH CURRIED RICE

1 pint shelled peas
A sprig of mint
1 or 2 oz butter
Seasoning
Curried rice

CURRIED RICE
1 teacup Patna rice
1 onion
1 or 2 oz butter or dripping
1 tablespoon curry powder
1 pint light stock
Salt/Pepper
A pinch of sugar
1 teaspoon lemon juice

Method. First prepare the curried rice : Peel and thinly slice the onion, melt the butter or dripping in a saucepan, and cook the onion in it for a few minutes without browning it. Then add the rice, well-washed and drained, and the curry powder, and stir over the heat until the butter is absorbed. Add the stock, sugar and pepper and salt to taste, and cook over a gentle heat until the rice is tender, stirring occasionally. Add lemon juice last of all. ($\frac{1}{2}$-$\frac{3}{4}$ hour.)

While this is cooking, boil the peas with a sprig of mint. When tender, drain them well and then put them back in the saucepan with the butter and seasoning. Toss over the heat for a few minutes and serve piled on a hot dish with the curried rice in a border round them.

NOTE. The curried rice can be used as an accompaniment to all sorts of meat and vegetable dishes.

POTATO AND CHEESE BALLS

4 potatoes
$\frac{1}{4}$ lb grated cheese
2 egg yolks
Seasoning
A little flour
A little butter

Method. Choose large potatoes, and bake them in the oven. When ready, scoop out the pulp and rub it through a sieve. Mix it in a basin with most of the cheese and seasoning, then bind together with the egg yolks. Form into balls and roll lightly in flour. Melt some butter in a frying pan and when smoking hot put in the balls and fry them to a nice brown colour, turning round and round to brown evenly. Drain, serve with a paper doily underneath them, and sprinkle the rest of the cheese over the top.

SCALLOPED PARSNIPS

2 or 3 cooked parsnips
½ pint good white sauce
Seasoning
1 tablespoon chopped onion
2 tablespoons bread-crumbs

Method. Cut the cooked parsnips into small cubes or thin slices. Butter a fireproof baking dish and put a layer of good white sauce in the bottom, then a layer of the prepared parsnips, sprinkling them with a little chopped onion, pepper and salt. Repeat the layers until sauce and parsnip are used up, making the last layer sauce. Cover the surface with the breadcrumbs, dot with butter and brown in a quick oven.

NOTE. If you do not like the flavour, you can omit the onion, and a little grated cheese can be mixed with the sauce.

POTATO AND CHEESE MOULD

½ lb cooked potatoes
2 oz grated cheese
2 tablespoons top of milk
1 oz butter
2 eggs
Browned breadcrumbs
Pepper/Salt

Method. Sieve the potatoes and add to them the melted butter, egg yolks, cheese, seasoning and top of milk. Mix well together. Beat the whites to a stiff froth and fold them in lightly. Grease a plain mould or basin and coat it with browned breadcrumbs. Three parts fill it with the mixture and bake in a moderate oven for 30 minutes. Turn out on to a hot dish and serve immediately.

STUFFED POTATOES

4 or 5 potatoes
3 or 4 tablespoons cooked meat, finely-chopped
1 teaspoon chopped parsley
2 tablespoons sauce, or top of milk
Seasoning
A little butter
A few breadcrumbs

Method. Choose potatoes of equal size and good shape, scrub them clean and bake them in a moderate oven until soft—do not use too hot an oven or the skins will get hard and prevent proper cooking of the potatoes. Cut a piece from the end of each potato, and with a teaspoon scoop out the insides without damaging the skins. Mash this pulp and put it into a basin. Add to it the finely-chopped meat, seasonings and parsley, and bind all together with some good sauce, top of milk or beaten egg. Refill the skins with this mixture, piling it fairly high in the centre. Sprinkle a few breadcrumbs over the top and put a small piece of butter on top of each. Put the potatoes back in the oven and bake them until piping hot. Dish them on a folded napkin and decorate with a few sprigs of parsley.

NOTE. If you have no left-over meat, you can use grated cheese or finely-shredded fish for the stuffing.

PICNIC POTATO SALAD

1 lb diced cooked
    potatoes
6 oz diced luncheon meat
    or cooked sausage
4 oz diced tart apple
French dressing, salad
    cream or mayonnaise
Seasoning

DRESSING FOR POTATOES

3 tablespoons oil
1 dessertspoon vinegar or
    lemon juice

Method. Dress potatoes while they are still warm with the oily dressing. When they are cold, mix with diced cold meat or sausage and the apple, then dress salad again with dressing or mayonnaise, lightly seasoned with sugar, mustard, salt and pepper.

NOTE. This salad lends itself admirably to the addition of chunky pieces of cucumber, or some walnut halves, or a few chives or spring onions, chopped.

Carry it in a wide vacuum jar or in a covered basin, and serve on crisp lettuce leaves.

POTATO PUFFS

Left-over cold roast meat
Pepper/Salt to taste
Few pickles, cut up small
Potatoes
1 egg

Method. Cut the meat up very small, season with pepper and salt and a few chopped pickles if liked. Boil and mash enough potatoes as required, and make them into a paste with a beaten egg. Roll out on a floured board and dredge with flour to prevent sticking. Cut into fairly large rounds with a saucer, spread some of the seasoned meat on one half, and fold over the other half. Pinch neatly round, and fry gently in hot fat to a golden brown.

NOTE. If the potatoes are very creamy, you may have to add quite a lot of flour to these puffs, before you will get them to roll out without breaking. It is safer to be on the generous side with the flour as this will prevent puffs breaking in the fat.

STEAMED POTATOES

Potatoes
Salt
Butter
Parsley

Method. Scrub potatoes and take off a thin ring of skin round the outside edge of the potatoes. Put them in a steamer on top of the soup pot, and allow about 45 minutes to cook. Take potatoes off, put into hot dish and sprinkle with salt. Garnish with parsley and melted butter.

NOTE. This saves a pot as they can be cooked at the same time as soup.

LEMON juice added to the water in which rice is boiled keeps it a good colour.

POTATOES A LA DUCHESSE

¼ lb cooked potatoes
1 oz butter
1 egg yolk
1 or 2 tablespoons milk
A pinch of nutmeg
Salt/Pepper
Beaten egg

Method. Sieve the potatoes. Melt the butter in a saucepan and add the potatoes to it with the egg yolk, seasoning and enough milk to bind all together, but do not make it too moist. Beat well together and turn out on a slightly floured board. Form the mixture into small round cakes, or roll it out and cut in squares with a knife. Mark across in a lattice pattern with the back of a knife, and place on a greased baking tin. Brush them over with a little beaten egg and bake them in the oven until nicely browned.

NOTE. This way of serving potatoes is very attractive if the unexpected guest turns up and you want to make something a bit more substantial than sandwiches. They look very appetising served with cold meat, mixed salad, or any simple egg dish, such as scrambled egg, omelette or poached egg.

EMPIRE POTATOES

4 large potatoes
¼ lb minced meat
Little egg white and flour

Method. Wash the potatoes, cut off the tops and scoop out some of the inside. Fill the cavity with the meat, well-seasoned. Seal the tops on again with a little egg white and flour mixed to a paste, and bake the potatoes in a brisk oven for 30–40 minutes.

PORTUGUESE TOMATOES

6 tomatoes
1 oz butter
1 tablespoon chopped onion
Seasoning
3 oz rice
1 cup light stock
2 tablespoons grated cheese

Method. First prepare the rice mixture for the filling. Wash the rice and dry it well. Melt the butter in a saucepan, put in the chopped onion and fry it until lightly browned. Add the rice and cook for a few minutes, but do not let it colour. Then pour in the stock, season to taste, and cook with the lid on until the rice is tender and the stock absorbed.

Wipe the tomatoes, cut a slice off the stalk end of each and scoop out the soft inside. Fill up with the rice mixture, piling it high in the centre. Sprinkle with grated cheese, put a dot of butter on top of each tomato and cook in a moderate oven for about 15 minutes. Serve very hot, garnished with parsley.

If, like me, you do not want to waste anything, heat the soft inside and pour it round the tomatoes as a sauce.

STUFFED TOMATOES

5 medium-sized tomatoes
2 tablespoons bread-
    crumbs
2 tablespoons chopped
    ham or tongue
1 teaspoon chopped
    parsley
1 shallot or small onion
1 oz butter
Salt/Pepper
1 tablespoon sauce or
    gravy
A few browned bread-
    crumbs
5 rounds of fried bread

Method. Wipe the tomatoes, remove the stalk, and cut a round piece neatly off the top of each. With a teaspoon scoop out the soft part from the inside, and put it into a basin. Be careful not to leave the sides of the tomatoes too thin, or break the skins. Season the insides with pepper and salt and turn the tomatoes upside down on a plate to drain. Strain the soft part from the inside, or rub through a sieve, and use this for moistening the stuffing. Personally I used everything, seeds and all, but a lot of people do not like this so for them I recommend straining or sieving. The best meat to use for this stuffing is ham, tongue or chicken, but any nicely cooked meat will do. Melt the butter in a small saucepan, and put in the finely-chopped shallot or onion. Cook gently for a few minutes, then add the meat, the white breadcrumbs, and parsley. Mix well together, season to taste, and bind with the tomato liquid and a little good sauce or gravy if necessary. Cook over a gentle heat to swell the crumbs, then fill tomatoes with this stuffing, piling it quite high in the centre. Do not pack too tightly or they might burst during cooking. Sprinkle a few browned crumbs on top, and place the tomatoes on a greased baking tin. Cover with a buttered paper and bake in a moderate oven till tender but not broken (10-15 minutes). Have ready 5 rounds of fried bread and place a tomato on each, garnished with parsley. NOTE. You can vary the stuffing according to taste and left-overs. The meat can be left out, and a few chopped mushrooms or grated cheese added. Well-cooked rice or macaroni, cut small and mixed with a little sauce and well-seasoned can also be used. Any nicely cooked vegetable, such as green peas or cauliflower, mixed with tasty sauce and the yolk of an egg will make an alternative filling.

SCALLOPED TOMATOES

Tomatoes as required
Breadcrumbs
Salt/Pepper
Butter

Method. Grease a fireproof dish and put in alternate layers of tomatoes, breadcrumbs and salt and pepper, finishing with a layer of breadcrumbs. Dot with butter and bake in a moderate oven till brown and thoroughly cooked.

BRAISED SPROUTS

Remove withered leaves from sprouts and cut across stem end in the form of a cross. Allow to soak in salt water to remove dirt and insects. Put a dessertspoon dripping or butter in a stewpan and add sprouts to melted fat. Cook with the lid on and shake occasionally to prevent sticking. A tablespoon hot water may be added if necessary. Cook for 20 minutes.

BRUSSELS SPROUTS WITH CHEESE SAUCE

1 lb Brussels sprouts
1 oz butter
1 teacup white sauce
2 oz grated cheese
Seasonings
A potato border

This is a lovely vegetarian dish, or a very nourishing accompaniment if you have only a little meat.
Method. Prepare and cook sprouts in a little boiling salted water until tender, but do not let them get too soft. Drain well, then toss them in hot butter, seasoning with pepper and salt. Arrange a border of creamy mashed potatoes on a greased fireproof dish and put the sprouts in the centre. Add most of the cheese to the white sauce, season well and make it thoroughly hot. Pour the sauce over the sprouts only, not over the potatoes. Sprinkle the rest of the cheese over the top and brown under the grill or in the oven.

VEGETABLE CURRY (1)

Vegetables as required
Boiled rice
2 tablespoons olive oil or
    margarine
1 onion
½ apple
1 tablespoon flour
1 dessertspoon curry
    powder
A bay leaf
1 tomato
Tomato purée
Cinnamon
Chutney
Red currant jelly
Seasoning

Method. Simmer a chopped onion in olive oil or margarine, without browning it. After a couple of minutes, add sliced apple and cook for 5 minutes. Add flour and brown it very gently, then add curry powder and cook slowly for another few minutes. Add a bay leaf, and work in chopped tomato, tomato purée, a pinch of ground cinnamon, 2 tablespoons chutney, and, if liked, 2 teaspoons red currant jelly. Season to taste, adding a few grains cayenne pepper.

Remove from the heat and *very slowly* stir in ¾ pint of warm water. Simmer until the desired consistency is reached. Meantime, parboil a selection of any vegetables—the mixture as you please—such as French beans, diced carrots, sprigs of cauliflower, haricot or butter beans, new potatoes, and cucumber. Drain them, then strain the curry sauce over them and finish cooking in the curry sauce. Place the vegetable curry at one end of a hot plate, with dry boiled rice at the other end.

NOTE. This sauce is excellent and can be used for almost all curries.

VEGETABLE CURRY (2)

Cooked vegetables
Curry sauce
Boiled rice

CURRY SAUCE
1 oz butter or dripping
1 oz rice flour
3 teacups meat stock
1 onion
1 lump of sugar
1 teaspoon curry powder
1 teaspoon chutney
1 small apple (or rhubarb
   or a few gooseberries)
Pepper/Salt
Squeeze of lemon juice

Method. Any nicely cooked vegetable may be used for a curry, such as turnip, carrot, cauliflower, French beans, peas, potatoes, etc., or a mixture of vegetables, if you prefer this. The vegetables should be well-cooked but not too soft and pulpy, and cut in small pieces.

Now prepare the curry sauce : Peel and chop the apple, and skin and slice the onion very thinly. Melt the butter or dripping in a small saucepan, put in the apple and onion and fry them gently for a minute or two. Add the curry powder, rice flour and chutney, mix well together and fry for a minute or two. Add the meat stock (fish stock should be used for fish curry) and stir till boiling. Season to taste with pepper and salt, and let the sauce simmer for about ½ hour, or until apple and onion are quite soft. If a smooth sauce is wanted, rub through a sieve before using and return to the pan to reheat. Add lemon juice and the sugar just before serving.

Put the cooked vegetables into the sauce and allow to simmer for a few minutes until thoroughly heated and flavoured with the sauce. Serve on a hot dish with a border of rice, or the rice can be served on a separate dish.

NOTE. The amount of curry powder can be increased or reduced according to your own taste.

SAVOURY VEGETABLE PIE

½ lb parsnips
¼ lb carrots
1 onion
2 oz grated cheese
2 tomatoes, halved
Margarine

Method. Boil the parsnips, carrots and onion gently in very little water, or steam lightly. Remove the parsnip cores when cooked, and mash all the vegetables lightly with any water that is left in the pan. Add 1 oz of the grated cheese. Put half the mixture into a greased pie-dish, cover with the tomato halves, add the rest of the mixture, sprinkle the top with the other ounce of grated cheese, dot with margarine, and bake until lightly browned.

If you like the flavour, celery salt makes an excellent seasoning for this dish.

COOK sprouts in butter, with only a spoonful of water, and a tightly-fitting lid to the pan. Add a drop or two of water, if necessary, to prevent sticking.

NEW VEGETABLE HOT-POT

¼ lb butter or margarine
3 oz bacon
½ lb small new potatoes
½ lb small new carrots
2 cups shelled green peas
Salt/Pepper
1 teaspoon sugar
Few leaves of mint
Few lettuce leaves, or
   sprigs of watercress
6 spring onions
¼ pint stock or water

Method. Melt the fat in a saucepan, chop the bacon finely and add it. Cook it for a minute or two, then add the potatoes and carrots, sliced. Fry till golden brown, turning with a wooden spoon. Add the rest of the ingredients, cover with a tight-fitting lid and simmer steadily for about 20 minutes or until tender. When ready, all the liquid should be absorbed so do not strain.

Serve hot, with either hot or cold meat, or with grilled sausages.

OVEN VEGETABLES

1 oz dripping
Thinly-sliced vegetables
2 tablespoons water or
   stock

Method. Place ingredients in a pie-dish or fireproof dish with a lid and cook very slowly in the lowest part of the oven. This keeps in all the flavour of the vegetables, and is delicious by itself or with any cooked meat.

Puddings and Sweets

This covers a fairly wide range, from what we in Scotland call a dumpling and those in the South call a steamed pudding, to the lightest of caramel custards. This should give you a sweet for every season and for every type of weather and taste. For pies and tarts see Home Baking section, p. 162.

HOT PUDDINGS

APPLE AMBER PUDDING

1½ lbs apples
2 or 3 tablespoons sugar
1 lemon
1 oz butter
2 eggs
A little pastry
1 tablespoon caster sugar
Vanilla

Method. Peel and slice the apples and put them into a saucepan with the butter, sugar and grated lemon rind, and stew slowly till they are reduced to a pulp, stirring frequently. Beat with a wooden spoon until perfectly smooth and then add the egg yolks. Line a pie-dish with some good short crust or other pastry, and pour into this the apple mixture. Bake in a good oven till the pastry is cooked and the apple mixture set (about ½ hour). Beat up the egg whites to a stiff froth, fold in the caster sugar and a few drops of vanilla, and pile this meringue on top of the pudding. Return to a cool oven to set and brown lightly. A few pieces of cherry and angelica are nice dotted among the meringue before browning in the oven.

NOTE. Other fruits can be used but if you use a very juicy kind, you may have to add a few bread or cake crumbs to thicken it.

APPLE BALLS

6 apples
1½ oz brown sugar
1 oz butter
Grated rind of ½ lemon
Short crust pastry or any
    pastry scraps

Method. Roll out short crust pastry, cut out 6 rounds about 6″ in diameter. Wet round the edge of these rounds with cold water, and in the centre of each place an apple, peeled and cored. Mix the butter, sugar and grated lemon rind together and fill up the cores of the apples with this. Draw up the edges of the pastry to meet on top of the whole apple, and roll in the hands to make a good shape. Place the apple balls on a wetted baking tin with the join downwards, brush over with milk, dredge with sugar, and bake in a moderate oven till the apples are soft and the pastry nicely browned. Serve hot or cold, and dredge again with sugar.
NOTE. To vary the flavouring, you can use ground cloves, ginger or cinnamon instead of lemon rind.

BAKED APPLE SOUFFLE

3 large apples
2 eggs
2 oz caster sugar
½ oz butter
Grated rind of ¼ lemon

Method. Bake the apples in the oven till thoroughly cooked, then scoop out all the soft inside and rub this pulp through a hair sieve, or beat till light and fluffy. Put the sugar, lemon rind and egg yolks into a medium-sized basin and beat until of a light creamy consistency. Add the apple pulp and mix all together. Beat the egg whites to a stiff froth and fold them lightly in at the last. Pour the mixture into a greased fireproof soufflé or pie-dish, and bake in a moderate oven until well-risen and firm to the touch (about 20 minutes). Sprinkle with sugar and serve at once.

APPLE PANCAKES

2 apples
2 eggs
2 tablespoons sugar
2 tablespoons flour
Juice of ½ lemon

Method. Cream the sugar and the yolks of eggs together until light and creamy. Peel the apples, grate or chop them finely and add them to the egg mixture, along with the flour and lemon juice. Mix well together and then stir in the stiffly-beaten whites of eggs. Make small pancakes with this mixture, by pouring into the centre of your hot omelet pan (which has been greased with melted lard), enough of the mixture to spread to the size you wish. Cook for a few minutes until set and nicely browned on one side, then turn over and cook on the other side. Slip on to sugared paper, sprinkle with sugar and keep hot till all are cooked.

BAKED APPLES (1)

Apples
Sultanas
Golden syrup or black
   treacle
Cinnamon
A few cloves

Method. Core the apples and stuff with sultanas. Into each pour 1 teaspoon golden syrup or black treacle, according to your preference. Sprinkle some cinnamon on top, stick 2 or 3 cloves into the skin of each apple and place apples on a baking tin with a little water in the bottom to prevent sticking. Bake in a moderate oven until the skins are crinkly and the apples tender. Serve very hot, with some thin cream or top of milk, if possible.

BAKED APPLES (2)

Apples
Caster sugar
Butter
Lemon rind or cinnamon

Method. Peel and core the apples, roll them in caster sugar and place them in a fireproof baking dish. Fill up the hole in the centre of the apples with a small piece of butter mixed with sugar and grated lemon rind or ground cinnamon. Pour a little water round them and bake in a moderate oven, basting occasionally with the liquid.

FRENCH APPLE BATTER

1 lb cooking apples
Sugar to taste
2 tablespoons brandy

BATTER
½ lb flour
2 eggs
Pinch salt
3 tablespoons sugar
½ pint milk

Method. Peel and slice the apples, add sugar and brandy (if liked) and place in buttered casserole or pie-dish.

    Gradually combine ingredients to make batter, and when smooth, pour over the apples and bake for 45 minutes in a moderate oven.

APPLE MERINGUE

1 lb cooking apples
4 oz demerara sugar
2 eggs
3 oz caster sugar
1 eggcup milk
½ cup hot milk

Method. Stew the apples and the demerara sugar until tender and place in a fireproof dish or pie-dish. Beat the egg whites until stiff and fold in 2 oz of caster sugar. Pile on top of the apples and put into a cool oven to form the meringue.

Now make the custard : Whip the 2 egg yolks with an eggcupful of milk and 1 oz of caster sugar. Add to ½ cup of hot milk and stir until it comes to the boil, but do not cook too quickly or it may curdle. Pour over the apple-meringue mixture.

APPLE FRITTERS

Frying batter
2 or 3 apples
Sugar
Flavouring

Method. Make the usual pancake batter with flour, eggs, pinch of salt and a little melted butter or oil and let it stand as long as you can allow before using it. Choose firm ripe apples and peel and cut them in slices about ⅛" thick. Stamp out the cores with a small round cutter, sprinkle the rings with sugar and grated orange or lemon rind and, if liked, a few drops of any other flavouring. Let them stand for a minute or two, then dip an apple ring in the batter. Coat it well, lift out with a skewer, and drop into a pan of boiling fat. Repeat with the other rings, but do not put in more than six or seven pieces at a time as they swell quite a lot in the cooking. Turn over and let them fry on both sides to a nice golden brown. Lift out with a skewer or perforated spoon and dry on sugared paper in a moderate oven. Serve on a folded paper serviette, slices overlapping each other.

NOTE. You can use bananas this way too, cutting them in two lengthwise and then once across, making four pieces from each banana. Flavour them and finish off as for apple fritters.

BAKED APPLE BATTER

Apples
Syrup

BATTER
4 oz flour
3 oz sugar
1 egg
¼ pint milk, or milk and
  water

Method. Peel and core apples, but do not go right through with the corer. Fill a greased pie-dish with apples standing upright, and pour golden syrup into each.

Now make the batter : Beat all ingredients together and pour round the apples. Bake in a moderate oven for 1 hour. For a sugary top, sprinkle with a little sugar and bake for 5 minutes more.

FRENCH ROASTED APPLES

4/5 medium cooking
  apples
Nut of butter
2 tablespoons honey
Few snippets of lemon
  rind

Method. Peel and slice the apples and put them in a casserole or earthenware pot. Dot the top with the butter, and cover with the honey and the lemon rind. *No water or liquid at all is required.* Bake in a moderate oven for ½ hour, turning the apples occasionally so that they cook evenly. Serve very hot with a dollop of cream, or the top of the milk.

AMBER PUDDING

6 oz breadcrumbs
4 oz minced apple
2 oz sugar
2 oz flour
4 oz chopped suet
1 teaspoon baking powder
2 tablespoons syrup
2 eggs
Pinch of nutmeg or spice
A pinch of salt
Grated lemon rind

Method. Mix all the dry ingredients together in a basin and make a well in the centre. Add the syrup, slightly warmed, and the 2 eggs which have been well-beaten. Mix together, adding a little milk if necessary to make a dropping consistency.
Pour into a well-greased basin, cover with greased paper, and steam till thoroughly cooked (2–3 hours). Serve with lemon, orange or syrup sauce.

APPLE WHIRLIES

½ dozen apples
¼ lb sugar
Water
1 teaspoon baking powder
½ lb flour
2 oz butter
A pinch of salt
About ⅛ pint milk

Method. Peel and slice the apples and stew them with the sugar and enough water to cover, until nearly tender. Meantime sieve the flour, salt and baking powder into a basin, and rub in the butter till the mixture is like fine breadcrumbs. Add enough milk to form a dough. Roll out on a floured board to 1" thick and cut out in small rounds. Lay these on top of the hot apples, cover with a lid and simmer slowly till everything is cooked. Serve the apples in the centre of the dish and the dumplings round about. NOTE. You can use other fruit, or a mixture of fruit, this way.

FROSTED APPLES

2 baked apples
2 egg whites
Honey to taste

Method. Spoon out the pulp from the skin of the baked apples and mash well, then pile back into the skin. Beat the egg whites until stiff and sweeten with a small amount of honey. Spoon this mixture over the top of the apples, and bake in a moderate oven till the meringue is a pale golden brown.

ALSACE PUDDING

3 oz whole rice
1¼ pints milk
3 oz beef suet
2½ oz sugar
1 oz candied peel
6 oz sultanas
2 eggs

Method. Cook the rice in the milk till tender. Cool it a little, mix in the suet, finely-grated, then the sugar, peel, finely-chopped, sultanas and the well-beaten eggs. Pour into a buttered basin, cover with a grease-proof paper and a cloth, and steam for 2¼ hours. Serve with custard sauce flavoured with a little lemon.

BIRD'S NEST PUDDING

3 oz tapioca
1½ pints cold water
Sugar to taste
5 or 6 small apples
Flavouring

Method. Soak the tapioca in the water for at least
1 hour, then turn into a saucepan and cook until it
turns quite clear, stirring occasionally. Add sugar
and flavouring to taste (a little spice, or grated orange
or lemon rind and juice, according to your fancy).
Pare and core the apples, keeping them whole, and sit
them in a greased pie-dish. Pour the tapioca over
them and bake in a moderate oven till the apples are
soft but not broken (¾–1 hour). Sprinkle with sugar,
and serve milk or cream separately.

NOTE. Be sure the oven is not too hot and so overcook the apples, as the pudding is greatly enhanced if
the apples remain whole. Test with a skewer to make
sure apples are soft but not mushy.

STEAMED BREADCRUMB PUDDING

¼ lb breadcrumbs
1 pint milk
1 oz butter
2 oz sugar
Grated lemon rind
2 eggs

Method. Put the breadcrumbs and butter in a basin
and pour the milk, boiling hot, over them. Add the
sugar, the grated lemon rind, and the egg yolks.
Soak for a few minutes and lastly fold in the egg
whites, beaten to a stiff froth. Pour the mixture into
a well-greased pudding basin and steam very slowly
until firm to the touch. Turn out carefully and serve
with jam or custard sauce.

NOTE. You can bake this pudding instead of steaming
it, but less breadcrumbs will be required. Alternatively, you can use sponge-cake or biscuit crumbs
instead of breadcrumbs for a sweeter pudding.

BROWN BETTY

6 oz browned bread-
   crumbs
1½ lbs apples
2 oz butter
2 tablespoons golden
   syrup
¼ teaspoon cinnamon
1 teacup water

Method. Peel, core and slice the apples thinly and
put a layer of them into a greased pie-dish. Sprinkle
some of the breadcrumbs over, and dot with butter.
Add another layer of apples, one of breadcrumbs, and
so on until all are used up, the last layer being breadcrumbs. Mix the syrup, water and cinnamon
together, and pour over the top. Sprinkle with sugar
and dot with butter again. Sit the pie-dish in a baking
tin containing hot water, and bake in a moderate oven
until the apples are soft (about 1 hour). Serve with
cream or the top of the milk.

TO SET a jelly quickly in hot weather, add a pinch of baking soda. It sets in half the time.

STEAMED STALE BREAD PUDDING

3 teacups soaked bread
1 teacup sugar
1 teacup chopped suet
¼ teacup currants
¼ teacup raisins
1 teacup flour
1 or 2 eggs
1 teaspoon mixed spice
A little milk

Method. Any scraps of bread can be used for this. Put them into a basin, cover with cold water and soak until quite soft (if you can leave them all night, this is excellent). Strain off the water and squeeze as dry as possible. Measure the bread, put into a basin and beat with a fork until free from lumps. Prepare the fruit, chop the suet, and add them to the bread with the other dry ingredients. Mix well together, and moisten with beaten egg and a little milk. Put into a well-greased basin, cover with greased paper, and steam until firm to the touch and thoroughly cooked (2–3 hours). Serve plain, or with custard sauce.
NOTE. Figs and candied peel can be used instead of raisins.

BROWN BREAD PUDDING

¼ lb brown breadcrumbs
1 oz butter
A little grated lemon rind
2 oz brown sugar
1 teacup milk
2 oz glacé cherries
2 oz candied peel
2 eggs
1 teaspoon baking powder
A pinch of salt

Method. Rub some stale brown bread through a sieve to make the crumbs. Put them into a basin with the butter, sugar and grated lemon rind. Heat the milk almost to boiling point, pour it over these ingredients and soak for 10 minutes. Meantime prepare the fruit —cut the cherries in small pieces, shred and chop the peel. Add these to the mixture, then add the egg yolks and baking powder, and lastly fold in the egg whites beaten to a stiff froth with a pinch of salt. Do not beat after adding the baking powder. Pour into a well-greased basin and decorate with a few pieces of cherry. Cover with a greased paper and steam until well-risen and firm to the touch (about 1 hour). Serve with lemon or jam sauce.

BREAD AND BUTTER PUDDING

Slices of bread and butter
Sultanas
Currants
Lemon juice
Custard

Method. Line a buttered pie-dish with thin slices of bread and butter, sprinkle with sultanas and currants and a squeeze of lemon juice. Cover with more slices of thin bread and butter, and add more fruit and lemon juice, repeating till dish is filled. Cover with a thin custard sweetened with golden syrup and flavoured with vanilla. Bake for 15 minutes in a moderate oven. Can be served hot or cold.

A CLOTH wrung out in vinegar and wrapped round cheese, helps to keep it from going dry or mouldy.

APRICOT PUDDING

¼ lb dried apricots
Bread and butter
Sugar

Method. Soak the apricots overnight, then stew them until tender with a little sugar to sweeten. Butter a pie-dish, and fill it with alternate layers of apricots and thinly-sliced bread and butter, using up all the sweetened juice. Sprinkle the top with sugar and bake until nicely browned.

STEAMED APRICOT PUDDING

2 oz butter
2 oz caster sugar
2 oz flour
Rind and juice of ½ lemon
2 eggs
A pinch of cinnamon
¼ teaspoon baking powder
4/5 pieces tinned apricot

Method. Cream the butter and sugar, then add the flour and eggs by degrees. Beat well until light and frothy. Drain the pieces of fruit, cut them in small pieces and add them to the mixture with the cinnamon, lemon rind and juice, and lastly the baking powder. Do not beat after adding the fruit mixture, but mix well and pour into a greased basin. Cover with greased paper and steam steadily until well-risen and firm to the touch (about 1½ hours). Serve with apricot sauce.

CARAMEL CUSTARD

CARAMEL
3 oz loaf sugar
¼ teacup cold water
A squeeze of lemon juice

CUSTARD
2 eggs
½ pint milk
1 dessertspoon sugar
Vanilla flavouring
A pinch of salt

Method. Boil the loaf sugar in the lemon juice and cold water until it is a light toffee colour, but watch it carefully so that it does not burn. When it is the right toffee colour, pour it into a plain straight-sided fireproof soufflé dish (which you have slightly warmed) and run the toffee up the sides and over the flat top so that it coats it evenly. Let this become cold while you are making the custard.

To make the custard, put the eggs into a basin with the sugar, flavouring and a pinch of salt and mix to a cream with a wooden spoon. Heat the milk and pour it slowly on to the egg mixture, stirring all the time. Pour this into the prepared mould and cover with greased paper. Steam *very* slowly till the custard feels firm in the centre ; or bake in a moderate oven with some warm water round the mould, sitting in a baking tin. Stand for a few minutes before turning out and serve hot or cold. The pudding should have a glaze of caramel over the top and some will run round the sides to serve as a sauce.

NOTE. You must be careful to cook the custard really slowly, as it will curdle if it is allowed to boil.

CARAMEL CUSTARDS

SAUCE
2 tablespoons sugar
2 tablespoons cold water

CUSTARD
2 eggs
1 oz sugar
½ pint milk
Few drops vanilla

Method. Heat sugar and water together on medium gas and leave to come to boil without stirring. When mixture reaches medium brown shade, pour quickly into greased moulds, running it evenly round the sides.

Now make the custard: Beat sugar and eggs thoroughly until thick and creamy. Add warmed milk and vanilla, then pour into moulds on top of the caramel sauce. Place on baking tray containing a little water and bake in a very moderate oven for about ½ hour until custard is set. (Do not fill moulds completely.) Slide knife round edges of custard and turn out immediately on plates. Serve either hot or cold.

CORNFLOUR or ARROWROOT PUDDING

1½ oz cornflour or
   arrowroot
1½ pints milk
A pinch of salt
1 or 2 eggs
1 tablespoon sugar
A little flavouring

Method. Heat most of the milk in a saucepan. Mix the cornflour or arrowroot to a smooth paste with the rest of the milk, and stir it into the milk in the pan. Stir constantly until the mixture thickens and boils, then simmer at least 5 minutes. Remove the saucepan from the heat, and when the mixture has cooled a little, stir in the sugar, flavouring, egg yolk or yolks, and lastly fold in the white of egg(s) beaten to a stiff froth with a pinch of salt. Pour into a greased pie-dish and bake in a moderate oven till nicely browned and well-risen (about 20 minutes or so). Lift out, sprinkle with sugar and serve immediately.
NOTE. A small piece of butter added to the pudding is an improvement.

CLOVELLY PUDDING

8 oz flour
4 oz finely-chopped suet
1 tablespoon sugar
2 apples, peeled and cored

Method. Mix flour and suet and gradually stir in water, or milk and water mixed, to the consistency of a thick batter. Add the sugar. Cut the apples into very thin slices and mix with the batter, then turn into a well-greased pie-dish. Bake in a moderate oven until thoroughly cooked. Serve with cream or custard.

CAKES and puddings are lighter if a little hot water is added to the eggs before they are beaten and added to the mixture. The beating itself takes less time too.

CHELSEA PUDDING

¼ lb flour
¼ lb breadcrumbs
¼ lb suet
¼ lb raisins
A pinch of salt
¼ lb currants
1 teaspoon baking powder
1 teacup treacle
1 teacup milk

Method. Chop the suet finely and mix it in a basin with the breadcrumbs, flour, salt and baking powder. Mix well together with the fingertips, and add the currants and raisins, carefully prepared. Make a well in the centre and add the slightly warmed treacle, and then the milk by degrees. Beat all together and pour into a well-greased basin. Cover with a greased paper and steam for 3 hours.

FIG AND GINGER PUDDING

6–8 oz figs
¼ teaspoon ground ginger
8 oz flour
4 oz suet
½ teaspoon baking soda
4 oz golden syrup
½ pint milk
1 egg
4 oz brown sugar

Method. Soak the figs overnight, and next day cut them up and remove the stalks. Grease the pudding basin and warm the syrup before pouring into it. Mix all the dry ingredients, add the finely-shredded chopped suet, the figs, then the well-beaten egg, and mix thoroughly with the milk to a nice soft dropping consistency. Press the mixture into the basin and cover with a greaseproof paper. Steam for 2 hours.

EVE'S PUDDING

Method. Peel and cut up as many apples as desired and put them with sugar to taste in a greased pie-dish. Take the weight of 1 egg in butter, sugar and flour. Cream the butter and sugar, add beaten egg and flour very gradually, and a pinch of baking powder if desired. Pour this over the apples and bake in a brisk oven for ¾ hour.
NOTE. The apple is always associated with Eve, but I sometimes use rhubarb cut up small, and it makes an equally delicious pudding.

ECONOMICAL STEAMED PUDDING

4 oz flour
4 oz breadcrumbs
4 oz chopped suet
2 oz currants
1 oz raisins
1 tablespoon treacle
1 teaspoon baking powder
½ pint milk

Method. Mix all dry ingredients (ie. flour, breadcrumbs, suet, currants, raisins and baking powder) together in a basin. Melt the treacle by warming slightly in a pot and stir into the dry ingredients together with the milk. Beat well. Put into a greased bowl and steam for about 3 hours.

MARMALADE PUDDING

¼ lb flour
¼ lb breadcrumbs
¼ lb chopped suet
2 oz moist sugar
1 or 2 eggs
2 or 3 tablespoons
   marmalade
¼ teaspoon baking powder
Milk if necessary

Method. Mix all the dry ingredients together in a basin and make a well in the centre. Put in the marmalade and the well-beaten eggs and mix all together, using a little milk if necessary to make a dropping consistency, but do not get it too liquid. The amount of milk will depend on the amount of marmalade and eggs used. Pour into a greased basin, cover with a greased paper and steam for 2½–3 hours. Serve with lemon or marmalade sauce.

GOLDEN PUDDING

¼ lb flour
2 oz butter
2 oz caster sugar
1 teaspoon baking powder
A pinch of salt
1 teacup milk
1 egg
2 tablespoons golden
   syrup

Method. Grease a basin and pour in the warmed syrup and run it round the sides, coating it well. Sieve the flour, salt and baking powder into a basin, rub in the butter till it is like fine breadcrumbs, and add the sugar. Make a well in the centre, add the well-beaten egg and then the milk. Mix thoroughly and pour into the prepared basin. Cover with a greased paper and steam for about 2 hours.

MACGREGOR'S JAM ROLL PUDDING

8 tablespoons s.r. flour
¼ lb margarine
3 tablespoons sugar
1 egg
Milk
Jam

Method. Rub margarine into flour until it is like fine breadcrumbs. Add sugar, then beaten egg and milk, to make a stiff paste suitable for rolling out. Roll into an oblong and spread with jam, then roll up roly-poly fashion. Put in an ungreased pie-dish and over it pour a cup of milk. Bake in a moderate oven for 45 minutes.

LEMON PUDDING (1)

¼ lb breadcrumbs
¼ lb chopped suet
2 oz flour
3 oz caster sugar
A pinch of salt
2 oz rice flour
½ teaspoon baking powder
Rind and juice of 1 lemon
1 egg
A little milk

Method. Grate the rind off the lemon on top of the sugar. Mix all dry ingredients thoroughly together in a basin, and make a well in the centre. Add the lemon juice, strained, the well-beaten egg, and enough milk to make a softish consistency. Pour into a greased basin, cover with greased paper and steam for 2–3 hours. Serve with custard or lemon sauce.

LEMON PUDDING (2)

2 oz breadcrumbs
1 oz flour
1½ oz chopped suet
½ teaspoon baking powder
1½ oz sugar
Grated rind of 1 lemon
1 egg
Milk

SAUCE
½ oz butter
1 rounded teaspoon flour
1 gill water
1 teaspoon sugar
The juice of the lemon

Method. Put all the dry ingredients in a bowl and mix with beaten egg and sufficient milk to make a soft consistency. Put in a greased bowl, cover with grease-proof paper, tie down securely, and steam for about 1¼ hours. Serve with lemon butter sauce.

To make the sauce, first melt the butter. Take pan off fire and add flour. Add water, sugar and lemon juice. Return pan to fire and bring to boil, stirring all the time. Let sauce boil quickly till it coats the back of the spoon, when it is ready for pouring over the pudding.

MINCEMEAT TART

½ lb short crust pastry
2 tablespoons golden
   syrup
2 oz sultanas
2 oz currants
1 oz chopped candied peel
1 apple
1 oz almonds
A pinch grated nutmeg
A pinch of ginger
A pinch of allspice
Breadcrumbs

Method. Line an open tart tin or dish with the short crust pastry. Melt the syrup by warming slightly in a pot, peel and chop the apple and blanch and chop the almonds. To these add all the other ingredients and mix together in a basin. Add sufficient soft breadcrumbs to make a fairly thickish consistency which will spread easily.

Fill the tart with this and bake in a moderate oven until the pastry is golden brown and the fruit well-cooked (about 30 minutes).

PRESERVED GINGER PUDDING

2 eggs
3 oz butter
3 oz caster sugar
2 oz flour
2 oz rice flour
¼ lb preserved ginger
1 tablespoon ginger syrup
¼ teaspoon baking powder
¼ teaspoon ground ginger

Method. Cream the butter and sugar, then add the eggs and the two flours alternately, and beat well. Cut the ginger into small pieces and mix lightly in, then stir in the baking powder, ginger syrup and ground ginger. Pour into a well-greased basin and steam for 1½ hours. Serve with custard sauce.
NOTE. You can steam this mixture in small moulds, if preferred, and they will then only require 15–20 minutes.

WHEN making an apple tart, add a spoonful of raisins and a sprinkling of cinnamon. This makes a tasty additional flavour.

MILLIONAIRE'S DELIGHT

Apricot jam
1 lb cooking apples
Demerara sugar
1 clove
Sponge mixture

Method. Butter a pie-dish or fireproof dish, and spread a good layer of apricot jam on the bottom. Spread over the jam 1 tablespoon demerara sugar. Cut up the apples in thick slices and spread over the sugar. Cover with demerara sugar to taste. Add the clove.

Take the weight of 1 egg (or 2 eggs if you wish) in butter, sugar and flour. Make sponge mixture by creaming the butter and sugar and adding the flour and egg.

Spread the sponge mixture on top of the apple mixture, and bake in a fairly quick oven. This will deal with the sponge gently but very firmly.

LITTLE GINGER SOUFFLES

1 oz butter
½ oz cornflour
½ teacup milk
½ teacup ginger syrup
1 oz sugar
2 egg yolks
3 egg whites
2 oz preserved ginger

Method. Melt the butter in an enamelled saucepan, add the milk and the cornflour broken down in a little milk, and stir till thick and smooth. Remove the pan from the heat and add the sugar, ginger syrup, and ginger cut in tiny places. Mix well and add the egg yolks one at a time, beating well between each. Lastly, stir in the egg whites beaten to a stiff froth, mixing in as lightly as possible. Grease small moulds or paper soufflés, three-quarters fill them with the mixture and bake in a good oven till they are a nice brown colour and well risen (about 15 minutes). Sprinkle with sugar and serve at once.

NORMANDY PUDDING

4 oz rice
¾ pint water
1 oz butter
2 oz sugar
1 lemon
1 lb apples
Sugar to taste
Dots of butter

Method. Boil the rice in the water till tender, then add the butter and the sugar, and boil for 5 minutes, adding the juice of 1 lemon. Then draw aside to cool a little.

Put a layer of this into a greased pie-dish or fireproof dish and cover with a layer of peeled, sliced apples. Add sugar to taste, then more layers until all is used up. Cover finally with the grated lemon rind, dot with butter, and bake in a moderate oven for about ½ hour, or until apples are cooked and everything thoroughly blended.

PLUM SPONGE

½ lb plums
Sugar to taste

SPONGE MIXTURE
1 egg and its weight in
    butter, sugar and flour
½ teaspoon baking powder
A little milk

Method. Stew the plums with the sugar, removing the stones as they loosen, and then put the hot fruit into a greased pie-dish.

Now make the sponge : Cream the butter and sugar, add the flour and beaten egg alternately, and if too stiff, add a little warmed milk. Stir in the baking powder last of all.

Pour this over the hot fruit, and bake in a moderate to quick oven for ½ hour.

This is nicest served hot, but can also be eaten cold.

PARTY PUDDING

¼ lb breadcrumbs
2 oz suet
1½ oz candied peel
1½ oz sweet almonds
1 teacup milk
2 oz sugar
2 eggs
Rind of ½ lemon
Lemon sauce

Method. Put the breadcrumbs in a basin and pour boiling hot milk over them, leaving to soak for a few minutes. Now add the finely-chopped suet, the almonds, blanched and chopped, the lemon rind, grated, candied peel cut in small pieces, egg yolks, and sugar. Mix all together thoroughly, and lastly fold in the egg whites beaten to a stiff froth. Pour into a well-greased pudding basin, cover with greased paper and steam till firm to the touch (1½–2 hours). Serve with lemon, custard or any other preferred sauce.

BAKED RICE PUDDING

1 tablespoon rice
1 tablespoon sugar
¾ pint milk
Nutmeg
Pieces of butter

Method. Put rice, sugar and milk in buttered fireproof dish or casserole, sprinkle nutmeg on top, and dot with pieces of butter. Bake for at least 1 hour on bottom shelf of very moderate oven.

SWEDISH RICE

¼ lb rice
½ pint milk
4 apples
2 inches cinnamon stick
2 tablespoons sugar
Rind of 1 lemon
¼ lb raisins
1 glass sherry

Method. Wash the rice and put it into a lined saucepan with enough cold water to cover. Bring to the boil and cook for a minute or two, then pour off the water. Now add the milk, cinnamon stick, lemon rind and the apples, thinly sliced. Cook all slowly until the apples and rice are tender, then add the sugar, wine and raisins, carefully stoned and roughly chopped. Cook for a few minutes longer, remove the cinnamon, and serve hot or cold, either with or without milk as you prefer.

RICE SOUFFLE WITH PINEAPPLE

2 oz ground rice
1 pint milk
2 eggs
1 to 2 oz sugar
1 cup tinned pineapple
Pineapple sauce

Method. Heat the milk with the butter in a saucepan. Sprinkle in the ground rice and stir till the mixture is smooth and thick, then simmer for a few minutes until thoroughly cooked. Take the pan off the heat, and add about a cupful of small pineapple chunks. Add the egg yolks, one at a time, and sugar to taste. Beat the egg whites to a stiff froth and fold in lightly at the last. Pour into a well-greased soufflé dish or pie-dish, leaving room for it to rise, and bake in a moderate oven till well-risen and nicely browned (20–30 minutes). Serve with pineapple sauce made by boiling together some pineapple juice, water, sugar to taste, some colouring and a squeeze of lemon juice. You can stir in some tiny pieces of pineapple to the sauce if you like.

RICE PUDDING WITH EGGS

2 tablespoons rice
1 teacup water
1½ pints milk
A pinch of salt
1 or 2 eggs
2 tablespoons sugar
Grated lemon rind

Method. Wash the rice and put it into a lined saucepan with the water and boil till the water is absorbed. Add the milk, salt and a little grated lemon rind or other flavouring. Simmer slowly over a gentle heat, or by the side of the fire, till the rice is thoroughly cooked, stirring occasionally with a wooden spoon. When ready, take the saucepan off the heat, and cool slightly. Then stir in the sugar and egg yolks. Beat up the whites to a stiff froth and stir them in lightly at the last. Pour into a well-greased pie-dish and bake in a moderate oven till nicely browned. Sprinkle with sugar and serve with milk or cream.
NOTE. You can add a little butter to the mixture for extra richness if you like, and if you can spare it. Grannie made it this way when we were young. The more butter the better for " growing bones ", she said.

RICE PUDDING WITHOUT EGGS

1½ pints milk
1½ tablespoons rice
1 tablespoon sugar
1 tablespoon chopped suet
A pinch of salt
Nutmeg or any flavouring

Method. Wash the rice and put it into a well-greased pie-dish with the sugar, salt and a little grated nutmeg or other flavouring. Pour in the milk and sprinkle the suet, very finely shredded or chopped, over the top. Bake in a slow oven till the rice is quite soft (2–3 hours). The slower the cooking, the softer and creamier it will be. Serve with milk or cream.

GROUND RICE SOUFFLE

1 pint milk
1½ oz ground rice
A pinch of salt
1 tablespoon sugar
1½ oz butter
3 eggs
Vanilla essence

Method. Mix the ground rice with a little of the milk, and when the rest of the milk is hot, but not boiling, add this blended ground rice and stir over the heat till boiling. Add the sugar and butter and cook for about 10 minutes. Take the pan off the heat, stir in the egg yolks, and flavour with vanilla or any other preferred flavouring. Lastly, fold in the egg whites beaten to a stiff froth. Pour the mixture into a greased pie-dish or fireproof dish and bake in a moderate oven till well-risen and nicely browned. Sprinkle with sugar and serve at once. (Baking time—about 20 minutes.)

BAKED SEMOLINA PUDDING

2 oz semolina
1½ pints milk
A pinch of salt
1 tablespoon sugar
A little flavouring
1 egg

Method. Heat the milk in a lined saucepan, but do not let it boil. Sprinkle in the semolina, then simmer slowly until the semolina swells and thickens. Add the sugar and a little flavouring. Take the saucepan off the heat and when the contents have cooled a little, add the egg yolk, and lastly the white which has been beaten to a stiff froth with a pinch of salt. Pour into a well-greased pie-dish and bake in a moderate oven until brown and set. When ready, sprinkle with sugar and serve at once.
NOTE. If you want to make a little variety, some stewed fruit, such as apples, can be put at the bottom of the pie-dish before you pour in the semolina.

SEVEN-CUP DUMPLING

1 cup each :
   flour (plain or s.r.),
   breadcrumbs,
   chopped suet,
   currants,
   raisins,
   sultanas,
   sugar
1 level teaspoon mixed
   spice
1 egg
Milk

Method. Put the seven cupfuls in a basin. (A teacup or breakfast cup will do, to make a larger or smaller dumpling as required, so long as you keep to the same cup for everything.) Add 1 level teaspoon mixed spice, beaten egg and mix with milk to a soft consistency. You can also add a spoonful of syrup or treacle, if you wish. Put into a greased bowl, cover with a greased paper tied closely down and steam for 2–3 hours. Longer steaming is an advantage, for it makes it richer and darker, if you can spare the time.

   Alternatively, you can put it into a floured cloth and tie securely. Drop into boiling water and boil for about 2–3 hours. This is the "clooty" dumpling.

SAGO PUDDING

1½ tablespoons sago
1 pint milk
1 oz butter
Grated rind of ½ lemon
A pinch of spice
1 or 2 tablespoons sugar

Method. Wash the sago and put it at the bottom of a greased pie-dish. Sprinkle with the sugar, grated lemon rind and a good pinch of spice, and put in the butter, broken in small pieces. Pour the milk over and bake in a slow oven (2–3 hours). Stir it up once or twice at the beginning of the baking, to blend it properly.
NOTE. If you are using large sago, it is better to let it soak for an hour or so before baking.

SPONGE PUDDING

1 oz butter
1 tablespoon sugar
1 egg
3 oz flour
2 tablespoons jam
½ teacup milk
1 teaspoon baking powder
A pinch of salt

Method. First grease a basin and put the jam at the bottom. Then cream the butter and sugar, add to them the egg and half the flour and beat well. Add the milk with the rest of the flour, and mix to a batter the consistency of thick cream, which will just drop from the spoon. Beat again and finally stir in the salt and the baking powder. Put into the prepared basin, cover with a greased paper and steam till well-risen and firm to the touch (about 1 hour).
NOTE. You can leave out the jam if you like, and add any of your favourite flavourings.

TREACLE SPONGE

½ lb flour
6 oz suet
½ teaspoon ground cinnamon
1 teaspoon ground ginger
½ teaspoon baking soda
¾ teacup milk
¼ teacup treacle
1 egg
A pinch of salt

Method. Sieve the flour, salt and spices into a basin and add the finely-chopped suet. Mix all lightly together with fingertips till free from lumps, and make a well in the centre. Pour in the warmed treacle and the well-beaten egg. Heat the milk and add the soda to it. Then mix all together for a few minutes and pour the mixture into a well-greased basin, leaving room for the pudding to rise. Cover with greased paper and steam till the pudding is well-risen and firm to the touch (2–3 hours). Serve with custard or sweet white sauce.

USE a piece of elastic instead of string when tying on a pudding cloth. This can be slipped off easily when the pudding is ready and saves burnt fingers.

ALWAYS wash spinach in running water. A low-growing vegetable like this can become gritty and needs extra attention in cleansing.

SILVER AND GOLD PUDDING

1 heaped tablespoon
    butter
1 teacup caster sugar
2 eggs
2 heaped tablespoons
    flour (one s.r., one
    plain)
Rind of 1 lemon
Juice of 2 lemons
Pinch of salt

Method. Cream the butter till light and fluffy, add the sugar and beat well, then add the egg yolks one at a time and beat thoroughly. Add the finely-grated lemon rind and the juice. Sift in the flour and salt, and mix thoroughly but do not beat again after the flour is added. At the last, fold in the stiffly-beaten egg whites. Put the mixture in a well-greased fireproof dish, and stand this dish in a pan of cold water. Bake in a slow oven for ¾–1 hour, till risen and cooked through. If you can spare it, serve with whipped cream, otherwise with top of the milk.

TAPIOCA PUDDING

2 tablespoons tapioca
1 pint milk
½ pint water
A pinch of salt
1 or 2 eggs
1 tablespoon sugar
Flavouring

Method. Cover the tapioca with the water and let it soak for 1 hour. Then add the milk and bring slowly to the boil over a gentle heat. Simmer until it turns quite clear, stirring occasionally. (The time depends on the kind of tapioca used.) If it gets too thick, add a little more milk. When ready, take the pan off the heat and stir in the sugar, egg yolk(s) and flavouring. Lastly add the egg whites, beaten to a stiff froth. Pour into a greased pie-dish, and bake in a moderate oven till brown and set. Sprinkle with sugar and serve at once.

NOTE. If you are using fine tapioca, you will not require to soak it, and you can cook it in the same way as semolina. For flavouring, sometimes I use a few drops of almond or vanilla, another time grated lemon or orange rind and a few drops of the juice.

SPANISH PUDDING

¼ lb flour
½ lb minced suet
¾ lb breadcrumbs
1 cup milk
⅛ cup golden syrup
4 tablespoons orange
    marmalade
¼ teaspoon baking soda
2 eggs

Method. Butter a mould or a pudding basin. Sift flour, soda and breadcrumbs into your mixing bowl, and stir in minced suet, then well-beaten eggs diluted with milk, warmed syrup and marmalade. Pack into the basin or mould and cover with greaseproof paper and cloth firmly tied down. Steam for 3 hours. Serve with lemon custard sauce. *For 6 persons.*

A PINCH of bicarbonate of soda added to fruit that is to be stewed or made into a tart, takes away a great deal of the roughness and acidity.

SIMPLE XMAS PUDDING

1 lb breadcrumbs (or flour
    and breadcrumbs)
1 lb raisins
¼ lb sultanas
¼ currants
⅛ lb shredded suet
¼ lb lemon or mixed peel
¼ lb golden syrup
3 oz grated carrot
½ lb demerara sugar
1 teaspoon ground ginger
½ teaspoon salt
1 teaspoon mixed spice
2 tablespoons brandy or
    rum

Method. Dissolve syrup in 1 tablespoon of hot milk. Clean all fruit and mix all dry ingredients. Then add the syrup and hot milk, making a nice softish mixture. Fill the basin to the top. Cover, tie carefully, and boil for 8 hours. This quantity makes two moderately-sized puddings.

COLD SWEETS

APPLE FOAM

1 lb Bramley apples
2 oz demerara sugar
1 lemon
⅛ pint milk
¼ oz gelatine
2 oz caster sugar
2 eggs

Method. Peel, core and slice the apples and cook them to a soft pulp. Stir in the sugar and grated lemon rind. Separate the yolks from the whites of the eggs and use the yolks to make a custard with the milk in the usual way, sweetening to taste. Dissolve the gelatine in the warmed lemon juice and stir into the apple pulp. Whisk hard and leave to cool.

When partly set, stir in the custard and whisk well again. Beat up the egg whites stiffly, fold in the sugar and beat again. Fold the egg whites lightly into the apple mixture, pile into a glass dish or dishes and leave to get cold. Serve with sponge fingers.

NOTE. A little cochineal improves the look of the dish.

BANANA FLUFF

3 ripe bananas
3 tablespoons icing sugar
Pinch of salt
1 teaspoon vanilla or 1
    tablespoon lemon juice
1 cup cream
8 pairs sponge fingers

Method. Mash the bananas with a fork. Stir in the sugar, salt and flavouring. Whip the cream stiffly and fold in lightly. Arrange two pairs of cut sponge fingers in each of 4 tall glasses and heap the fluff lightly over them. Alternatively, make a ring of cut sponge fingers on a round plate and heap the fluff in the centre. Top with more sliced bananas.

APPLE SNOW

2 apples
Honey
White of egg

Method. Shred 2 medium-sized apples with a fine shredder (do not peel). Add a spoonful of honey or sugar and the white of an egg, and beat well together. Serve with or without cream, piled in long glasses.

BANANA TRIFLE

4 bananas
3 sponge cakes
2 tablespoons jam
1 glass sherry, or fruit juice
½ pint custard
2 or 3 macaroons
A few sweet almonds
1 small carton cream

Method. Split the sponge cakes and spread them with jam, then cut them in slices. Peel the bananas and cut them in four or six pieces. Arrange the sponge cakes and bananas in a glass dish, sprinkle them with the crushed macaroons and the sweet almonds, blanched and shredded. Pour the wine or fruit juice over and leave to soak for a short time. Then pour the custard over. Whip the cream, sweeten and flavour to taste, and decorate the top of the trifle with this. Decorate with a few pieces of cherry and angelica, or other glacé fruits. Serve very cold.

PARTY FRESH FRUIT SALAD

Packet lemon jelly
¼ pint hot water
½ pint fresh orange juice
Any fresh mixed fruit

Method. Make up a packet of lemon jelly with ¼ pint of hot water and ½ pint of strained fresh orange juice, and pour into ring mould. Chill till firm.

Make a special fruit salad of peeled orange cut into little chunks; fresh peeled, cored and diced pear; ½ lb washed mixed black and white grapes; fresh peeled, cored and diced apple; sliced banana with a squeeze of lemon juice to keep the colour; any other fruit you wish, diced or cut into chunks or sliced.

Unmould the jelly, pour the fruit salad in the centre of the ring of jelly, and top if you like with a blob of whipped cream.

BANANA WHIP

4 or 5 bananas
½ pint lemon jelly
Cream to decorate

Method. Choose nice ripe bananas. Peel them, cut in small pieces and rub through a sieve. Take ½ pint lemon or other clear jelly which is just beginning to set, and mix it with the banana pulp. Whip them together with a wire whisk until white and frothy, and pile up on a glass dish. Decorate with cream if you can spare this, but it is excellent served on its own.

CHRISTMAS FRUIT SALAD

2 grapefruit
4 oranges
Sugar to taste
Miniature bottle of liqueur

This is a delicious alternative for those who do not like Xmas pudding, or feel it is too heavy after the bird.

Method. Mix the flesh of the 2 grapefruit and the 4 oranges in a bowl, making sure you have got rid of all the pith. Then spoon it into a tall preserving jar with a layer of sugar between each layer of fruit. Put more sugar on top, and then gently pour over the contents of a miniature bottle of liqueur. Put the lid on and leave it aside to get everything thoroughly permeated with flavour, for 24 hours, turning the jar gently upside down once or twice to make sure the sugar and liqueur get completely blended. Turn into a nice glass serving bowl and serve with or without cream, just as you fancy.

NOTE. You can use any of the miniature liqueurs for this, choosing the flavour you prefer.

FRESH FRUIT SALAD (1)

½ pint cold water
4 oz loaf sugar
Rind of 1 lemon
A selection of fresh fruits

Method. Put the water, sugar and thinly-peeled lemon rind into a saucepan, bring to the boil and simmer for about 5 minutes.

Take a selection of fresh fruits—orange, apple, banana, pear, dessert gooseberries, currants, etc., and prepare them according to their type. Pour the strained sugar syrup over the fruit and let it get cold before serving.

FRESH FRUIT SALAD (2)

1 jaffa, peeled and cut up
1 large sweet apple, cut up
1 large sweet pear, cut up
2 small bananas, sliced
Lemon juice
Made-up syrup

Method. Mix together in a bowl all the cut-up fruit and squeeze some lemon juice over it.

Make up the syrup by boiling 4 oz loaf sugar in ½ pint of water with a little grated lemon rind added. Boil this for 5 minutes and then pour over the mixed fruit.

CHOCOLATE CREAM

2 oz grated chocolate
2 tablespoons water
1 small carton double cream

Method. Put the chocolate and water in a saucepan and stir over a gentle heat till dissolved. Cool slightly. Whip the cream till thick and fold in the chocolate, mixing thoroughly. Sweeten if necessary and serve piled up in a glass dish.

SIMPLE BANANA SWEET

Bananas
Icing sugar
Lemon juice

Method. Mash the bananas with icing sugar to taste and a squeeze of lemon juice. Pile into glass dishes, with a spot of cream on top.

GOOSEBERRY FOOL

1 lb gooseberries
¼ lb sugar
½ teacup water
¼ teacup custard
¼ teacup cream

Method. Top and tail the gooseberries, wash them and stew in the water and sugar until tender and really soft, then rub through a fine sieve. Mix the custard and cream with this purée, and serve in a glass bowl or in custard glasses with a spoonful of whipped cream on top.

NOTE. You can use all custard if you want a more economical dish, or all cream if you want an extravagant one. Other fruits can be used in the same way. This way of serving fruit is especially nice during a hot summer. It is also very welcome after a fairly rich main course, for it goes down very smoothly and happily after the richest meal, particularly if you use all custard and omit the cream.

DEVONSHIRE JUNKET

1 pint warm milk
1 teaspoon rennet
1 tablespoon brandy or rum
1 tablespoon caster sugar
¼ teaspoon cinnamon
Clotted cream

Method. Mix together in a deep dish the brandy, cinnamon and sugar. Pour on to these 1 pint of new milk or fresh milk heated to the temperature of new milk, and add the rennet. Stir it well and leave till set. Then spread some clotted cream on top and sprinkle with caster sugar. When it is well made, junket should cut into smooth shiny slices like jelly, but unlike jelly it will set better and more quickly in a room of ordinary temperature than in a cold larder.

LEMON FLUFF

1 cup caster sugar
2 cups water
2 eggs
1 heaped tablespoon cornflour
Juice and rind of 1 lemon

Method. Put sugar and water in pan and add the juice and rind of the lemon. With a spoonful of this liquid mix the cornflour and add to the pan. Then drop in egg yolks and stir well to break up thoroughly. Bring just to the boil, but do not allow to boil. Allow to cool, and add the two stiffly-beaten whites of egg. Put in glass dish. If you like, decorate with whipped cream.

COMPOTE OF PEARS

1½ lbs cooking pears
½ lb loaf sugar
A few drops of cochineal
1 inch of cinnamon stick
2 or 3 cloves
½ pint cold water
Juice of ½ lemon

Method. Put into a lined saucepan the sugar, water, lemon juice, cloves and cinnamon stick and bring to the boil, then boil for 10 minutes. Peel and quarter the pears, remove the cores, then stew them slowly in the syrup till tender (from ½–1½ hours depending on the size and quality of the fruit). When nearly ready, add the colouring. Serve in a glass dish, with the cooled, strained syrup poured over.
NOTE. If you have a drop of port handy, and you like the flavour, you can add 2 tablespoons of this when you add the colouring. This makes it more of a party sweet.

MARIE CREAMS

½ pint milk
1½ oz rice flour
1 oz sugar
2 egg yolks
1 tablespoon apricot purée
1 carton thick cream
Sugar
Flavouring
Pistachio nuts, chopped
Almonds, cut and
    browned

Method. Heat the milk and rice flour in a lined saucepan, stirring over a gentle heat till boiling, then simmer for 5 minutes, and remove from the heat. Add the sugar, egg yolks and apricot purée (tinned apricots or jam rubbed through a sieve). Cook a minute or two over the heat, then pour the mixture into small moulds and let them cool. Whip the cream, sweeten and flavour to taste, pile a little on top of the mixture in each case, and sprinkle with the almonds and pistachio nuts.

LEMON FOAM

Rind and juice of 2 lemons
2 oz sugar
2 egg whites
¼ oz gelatine
½ pint water
1 tablespoon sherry

Method. Wipe the lemons and peel off the rind as thinly as possible. Put rind into a saucepan with the gelatine, sugar and water and dissolve over a gentle heat, then strain into a basin and cool slightly. Strain in the lemon juice, add the whites of eggs and the sherry, and whisk all together until white and frothy. Put the mixture into a wet mould and leave in a cool place until firm.
NOTE. Half the mixture can be coloured pink with a few drops of cochineal and put into the mould in alternate spoonfuls. Or, instead of putting it into a mould at all, you can pile it up on a glass dish in a rocky style, and spear it here and there with small pieces of angelica.

QUICK PARTY SWEET

1 strawberry jelly (or any other preferred flavour)
1 family block ice-cream

Method. Mix jelly according to instructions on the packet, and let it get quite cold and almost set. When almost set, whip the ice-cream into it until it is light and frothy and pile into individual glasses. Serve it like this, or for variation decorate with sprinkling of coconut, tiny snippets of glacé cherries and little spears of angelica.

This is a delicious sweet, very easily made, and with something of the quality of a very light mousse.

SUMMER PUDDING

Slices of bread and butter
Raspberries (or any other soft fruit available)
Sugar

Method. Line a pint bowl with thin slices of bread and butter, buttery side inwards. Stew the raspberries with sugar to taste, for 1 minute, then fill into the centre of the bowl. Make a lid with another thin slice of bread and butter, cutting one or two little extra pieces to make an exact fit. Cover the lot with a plate and a weight and leave until next day. Turn out carefully, and serve with cream or the top of the milk.

MOCK MOUSSE

This is just like a mousse but much simpler to make. *Method*. Melt about ½ lb marshmallows in a saucepan together with about ½ pint black coffee. Leave to cool. Whip up ½ pint double cream in a bowl and fold into the cooled marshmallow mixture. Pile in glasses and chill before serving.

NOTE. Have the marshallow mixture really cool before adding the cream, or it will curdle. Merely fold the cream in very lightly to keep the mixture fluffy.

FRESH RASPBERRIES WITH RED CURRANTS

¼ lb raspberries
¼ lb red currants
Caster sugar to taste

Method. Wash and clean the fruit, then place a layer of raspberries, a layer of sugar, a layer of red currants, a layer of sugar, and so on until fruit and sugar are used up. Leave overnight to draw the juice. Give it a final stir up to mix in everything before serving it on your fruit plates, next day. Serve with thin cream.

WHEN peeling oranges for fruit salads, first soak the oranges in boiling water for 5 minutes or so. The white pithy part will peel off quite easily and leave the oranges clean for slicing.

EMPRESS RICE

1 lb of dark plums
¼ lb rice
Approx. 1 pint of milk
1 gill thick cream
1 gill thin cream
Sugar to taste

This is a good party sweet.
Method. Wash the rice and cover with cold water. Bring to the boil and boil for 10 minutes. Pour off any surplus water, cover with milk and bring to the boil again. This milk is soon absorbed, so cover again with milk and bring to the boil. Go on adding milk and boiling until the rice is soft and creamy and completely cooked. Then add sugar to taste and leave to get cold. Whip the thick and thin creams together until light and fluffy and fold through the cold rice. Line a glass dish with halved, stoned, dark plums, cut sides downwards, and cover with creamed rice. Decorate the top with a few of the halved plums which you have kept back and, if you like, add strips of sliced banana for further decoration. Dot with little blobs of the cream also kept back.

If you wish to make this dish less rich and less expensive, for everyday eating, use thin cream only or the top of the milk for folding through the cooking rice.

NOTE. Peaches or apricots or any similar fruit in season can be used if preferred, instead of plums.

STRAWBERRY RICE CREAM

Strawberries
Cream
Rice
Vanilla essence
Caster sugar

Method. Cook the rice in boiling water and cool it by straining under a running cold tap. Stir in thick, whipped cream, flavoured with vanilla and sweetened with caster sugar. Serve topped with strawberries.
NOTE. You will judge your own quantities, allowing 2 oz of rice for two people.

ORANGE WHIP

¾ pint milk
1 teacup water
Grated rind and juice of
 1 sweet orange
2 rounded tablespoons
 semolina or custard
1 level tablespoon sugar

Method. Heat the milk and water with the grated orange rind, then add semolina or custard powder blended with the juice. Stir over a gentle heat till boiling and thick. Add the sugar, cool, and whisk vigorously till fluffy, then pour into a glass dish.

TRY mixing the pulp of an orange with the apples next time you are stewing them and see what a new and delicious flavour it gives.

Cold Sweets

AMERICAN SEMOLINA

1 tablespoon semolina
1 oz butter
1 tablespoon sugar
2 tablespoons chopped
   almonds
1 pint milk
2 eggs
Flavouring
2 tablespoons red currant
   jelly

Method. Put the semolina, milk and butter in a saucepan and bring slowly to the boil, stirring occasionally. Cook for 5 to 10 minutes then take the pan off the heat. Add the sugar, almonds, egg yolks and flavouring and mix well together. Pour the mixture into a glass dish and let it cool. Beat up the egg whites and jelly to a stiff froth and pile it on top of the pudding. Serve cold.

Sauces, Dressings and Stuffings

These are a few basic recipes which might be useful for providing an extra " zing " to some dishes.

SWEET SAUCES

APPLE SAUCE

½ lb sharp green apples
1 oz butter
½ teacup water
1 tablespoon brown sugar
A pinch of nutmeg

Method. Wipe the apples, peel, core and slice them thinly and throw them into cold water until you have peeled them all. When they are all sliced, drain them and put in a lined saucepan with the water, sugar and nutmeg. Stew slowly until reduced to a pulp, stirring frequently with a wooden spoon (do not use a metal spoon as it spoils the colour). Lastly, add the butter and mash until smooth, or rub through a hair sieve for extra smoothness. Make thoroughly hot before serving with your roast pork, duck or goose.

ARROWROOT SAUCE

½ pint water
1 dessertspoon arrowroot
Lemon juice
1 dessertspoon sugar
¼ oz butter

Method. Put most of the water into a small lined saucepan and heat it. Mix the arrowroot with the rest of the water, blend it smoothly and add it to the saucepan. Stir till boiling and cook for at least 10 minutes, then add the sugar, lemon juice to taste and lastly the butter.

You can vary this by adding any other flavour you like, or a little wine or fruit syrup can be added, and you can colour it with a few drops of cochineal.

APRICOT SAUCE

1 teacup apricot purée
1 teacup water
1 teaspoon arrowroot or
    cornflour
1 dessertspoon sugar
1 tablespoon sherry or
    1 teaspoon maraschino
2 or 3 drops cochineal

Method. Make the purée from tinned apricots by rubbing 4 or 5 pieces through a hair sieve and making up the quantity with the syrup. Put this purée into a small lined saucepan, add to it the arrowroot broken up with the cold water, and stir over a gentle heat until it boils and thickens. Add the sugar, the flavouring (if you do not like sherry or maraschino, add any flavouring you prefer), and enough cochineal to make it a nice pink colour. Cook 2 or 3 minutes longer and serve.

NOTE. Apricot jam can be used instead of tinned fruit, although you will need a little water to thin it down while sieving.

COFFEE SAUCE

1 teacup black coffee
1 teacup milk
2 egg yolks
1 dessertspoon sugar

Method. Cream the egg yolks and the sugar in a basin. Heat the coffee and milk in a saucepan and pour slowly on to the creamed yolks, stirring all the time. Return to the saucepan and stir till the sauce thickens in the same way as a custard sauce, but be careful not to boil. Serve hot or cold.

Alternative recipe. Heat 1 teacup strong black coffee in a saucepan, add to it 1 teaspoon arrowroot mixed to a smooth paste with 1 tablespoon cold water, and boil for a few minutes. Add 1 dessertspoon each brandy and sugar. Make thoroughly hot and serve.

CORNFLOUR SAUCE

½ pint milk
1 heaped teaspoon corn-
    flour
1 dessertspoon sugar
Rind of ½ lemon

Method. Blend the cornflour smoothly with a little of the milk. Put the rest of the milk in a saucepan with the thinly peeled lemon rind, and heat gently until well-flavoured. Strain this flavoured milk on to the cornflour, mix and return all to the saucepan, and stir till boiling. Cook for 4 or 5 minutes, adding sugar to taste.

NOTE. If you do not like lemon flavour, leave out the rind, and add any flavouring you prefer. If you want a richer sauce, add 1 tablespoon cream or a small piece of fresh butter just before serving.

CHOCOLATE SAUCE (1)

1 teacup milk
1 oz chocolate
1 teaspoon sugar
1 egg yolk
4/5 drops vanilla essence

Method. Rinse out a small lined saucepan with cold water, and put in the milk and chocolate, either grated or shredded finely with a knife. Simmer until completely dissolved. Mix the egg yolk and sugar together in a basin, and pour the chocolate gradually over them. Return to the saucepan and stir over the fire until *almost* boiling. Remove at once and add the flavouring.

NOTE. If you want a plainer sauce, leave out the egg yolk, thicken with 1 teaspoon cornflour broken with a little cold water, and cook thoroughly in the sauce. On the richer side, you can add 1 teaspoon brandy or liqueur if you like.

CHOCOLATE SAUCE (2)

2 oz chocolate
⅛ pint water
1½ oz caster sugar
1 dessertspoon rice flour
1 teaspoon rum
Vanilla essence

Method. Grate or shred the chocolate and put in a saucepan with the sugar and half the water. Stir over a gentle heat till dissolved and perfectly smooth. Add the flour broken with the rest of the water and stir again till boiling. Simmer for a few minutes, add the rum and vanilla, and if too thick, thin down with a little more water. Strain before using.

BRANDY BUTTER

2 oz fresh butter
4 oz caster or icing sugar
½ teaspoon vanilla essence
1 dessertspoon brandy

Method. Beat the butter in a basin until light and creamy, then gradually add the sieved sugar, and beat until very light and frothy. Flavour with the brandy and vanilla, and set the sauce in a very cool place (or in the refrigerator or on ice) to harden. Serve piled up in a little fancy glass dish, lightly sprinkled with nutmeg.

CHERRY SAUCE

1 oz glacé cherries
2 oz loaf sugar
1 teacup water
Juice of ¼ lemon
2 or 3 drops cochineal
1 teaspoon brandy

Method. Put the sugar, water and strained juice of ½ lemon into a saucepan, bring to the boil and simmer slowly for 10 minutes. Add the cherries cut in small neat pieces, a little cochineal to colour, and the brandy (if used). Cook for a minute or two more, then turn into a basin to cool. Serve cold.

133

Sweet Sauces

CRANBERRY SAUCE

1 lb cranberries
¼ lb brown sugar
1 teacup water

Method. Pick and wash the cranberries and put them into an enamelled saucepan. Bruise them well with the back of a fork, then add the water and stew slowly until reduced to a pulp. If you want to sieve them, do it now, then add the sugar and reheat. If you are not sieving them, simply stir in the sugar, heat and serve. Serve with mutton, poultry or game.

NOTE. If you like, you can add a little port wine to this sauce, and sometimes 1 or 2 apples are preferred along with the cranberries.

CREAM SAUCE

2 oz butter
2 oz caster sugar
1 teacup double cream
Vanilla essence

Method. Beat the butter in a basin till creamy, add the sugar, finely-sifted, and beat again till soft and light. Then add the cream gradually, and flavour with vanilla or any other flavouring you prefer. Stand the basin over a saucepan of hot water and whisk lightly till smooth and frothy. Be very careful not to let the sauce boil or it will curdle.

JAM SAUCE

2 tablespoons red jam
1 teacup water
1 oz loaf sugar
A squeeze of lemon juice
2 or 3 drops cochineal

Method. Put the water, sugar and jam (raspberry or strawberry are best) into a small lined saucepan and let them boil quickly for a few minutes, skimming if necessary. Add the lemon juice and 2 or 3 drops of colouring. Strain before using.

CARAMEL SAUCE

2 tablespoons caster sugar
2 tablespoons water
½ pint custard sauce
Vanilla essence

Method. Put the sugar into a saucepan and stir until melted over a gentle heat, letting it get a nice brown colour. Then add 1 or 2 tablespoons water, mix until smooth, and pour this caramel into ½ pint custard sauce. Flavour with vanilla to taste.

CUSTARD SAUCE (1)

1 yolk of egg
1 dessertspoon caster sugar
1 gill milk
Vanilla essence

Method. Mix yolk with the sugar in a cup. Heat milk in a saucepan, then pour on to the sugar and egg. Return to the saucepan and cook over a gentle heat. Flavour and serve either hot or cold.

A SIMPLE CUSTARD SAUCE (2)

½ pint milk
1 teaspoon cornflour
1 egg
Sugar
Flavouring

Method. Put most of the milk into a saucepan and heat slowly. Mix the cornflour to a paste with the rest of the milk and add it to the saucepan, stirring it until boiling, and simmering slowly for 5–10 minutes to cook the cornflour. Take the saucepan off the heat and let the contents cool slightly. Beat up the egg and strain it into the sauce, blending all thoroughly, and reheat until the egg thickens but *do not boil again.* Sweeten and flavour to taste.

LEMON SAUCE

½ oz arrowroot
Rind and juice of ½ lemon
1 oz sugar
1½ teacups water
½ oz butter

Method. Grate the lemon rind on to the sugar and work them together in a basin until they are well blended. Blend the arrowroot with a little of the water, then stir into the rest of the water in a lined saucepan. Stir till boiling, then add the lemon-sugar, and the strained lemon juice, and cook for a minute or two. Break the butter in tiny pieces and stir it in just before serving.

MOCK CREAM

1 cup milk
1 tablespoon cornflour
2 oz margarine
1 tablespoon caster sugar
Vanilla essence

Method. Make a custard with the milk and cornflour, and allow to cool. Cream margarine and caster sugar till light and fluffy, and whip this into the cold custard, adding a few drops of vanilla essence. Beat until the mixture is smooth and like whipped cream.

ORANGE SAUCE

½ pint water
1 large orange
2 egg yolks
1 oz butter
½ oz flour
1 tablespoon sugar

Method. Grate orange rind and rub this into the sugar. Melt the butter in a saucepan, mix in the flour and blend smoothly, add water and stir till boiling. Then add the sugar with the rind, the strained juice of the orange and cook for 2 or 3 minutes. Take the saucepan off the fire, and when it is off the boil, stir in the egg yolks quickly and pour at once into a hot sauceboat.
NOTE. You can add a little sherry or brandy.

WHEN making an egg custard tart, if you heat the milk (not boil) before adding to the egg, the custard will set more quickly and ensure no overcooking of pastry.

MARMALADE SAUCE

2 tablespoons marmalade
¼ pint water
1 teaspoon arrowroot
1 teaspoon lemon juice
Sugar

Method. Put the marmalade and most of the water into a saucepan and bring them to the boil. Blend the arrowroot with the rest of the water, blend into the contents of the saucepan, and stir till boiling. Cook for a minute or two, sweeten to taste, and add the lemon juice.

SYRUP or TREACLE SAUCE

Method. Put 2 tablespoons syrup or treacle with 1 teacup water into a saucepan, and strain in 1 tablespoon lemon juice. Bring to the boil and boil for 10 minutes. If you like, you can add a little ginger or other spice for extra flavour. Pour over steamed puddings.

NOTE. North of the border syrup is always golden and treacle black, but in England "treacle" can mean golden syrup or black treacle so you must be careful.

SAVOURY SAUCES

SAUCE TARTARE

¼ pint mayonnaise
1 teaspoon chopped parsley
1 teaspoon chopped capers
1 teaspoon chopped gherkin
1 teaspoon each chopped tarragon and chervil
A pinch of sugar

Method. Put the mayonnaise in a basin, add to it the parsley, capers, gherkin and sugar, and tarragon and chervil if available. Keep in a cool place until required. If you like the flavour of garlic, rub round the basin with a small clove of this before putting in the mayonnaise.

MINT SAUCE

2 tablespoons chopped mint
1 tablespoon sugar
2 tablespoons boiling water
1 teacup brown vinegar

Method. Put the sugar (brown preferably) into a jug or sauceboat, pour over it the boiling water and let it stand until dissolved. Wash the mint, which should be young and fresh, pick it from the stalks, dry it and chop it finely. Mix all the ingredients together and stand for 2 or 3 hours before serving with your roast lamb.

BARBECUE SAUCE

1 tablespoon fat
1 onion, chopped finely
1 tablespoon flour
¼ cup vinegar
½ cup water
1 tablespoon Worcester
   sauce
½ cup tomato sauce
2 tablespoons sugar
1 tablespoon mustard
1 teaspoon salt
½ teaspoon pepper
1 thick slice lemon

Method. Melt the fat in a pan, add the chopped onion and fry until lightly brown. Stir in the flour slowly to make a smooth paste. Now add the liquid ingredients (vinegar, water and sauce). Stir till boiling, then add the sugar, mustard (mixed up with a little water), salt, pepper and the slice of lemon. Cover with a lid or plate and leave to simmer for 10 minutes. Remove the lemon before serving, and spoon this sauce sizzling hot on to the cooking meat.

CAPER SAUCE

¾ oz butter
¾ oz flour
½ pint meat liquor or fish
   stock
1 tablespoon capers
1 tablespoon vinegar
White pepper/Salt

Method. Melt the butter in a small saucepan, add the flour and blend smoothly. Cook for a minute or two, then take the saucepan off the heat and pour in the liquid. Return to the heat and stir constantly until boiling. Add the capers, cut in halves or roughly chopped, and season to taste with white pepper and salt. Boil for 2 or 3 minutes longer, then add the vinegar, using the caper vinegar if you can spare it. NOTE. If you are serving this sauce with any boiled meat, then use the water in which the meat was cooked. If you are serving it with fish, make it with fish stock. If you want to make it richer, you can add 1 tablespoon of cream, or 1 egg yolk, or an extra piece of butter after the saucepan is removed from the heat. Be sure to add these rich " extras " after the sauce is cooled a little or there is danger of curdling.

BREAD SAUCE

½ pint milk
2 oz breadcrumbs
¼ small onion
2 or 3 cloves
1 oz butter, or
   1 tablespoon cream
White pepper/Salt

Method. Rinse out a small lined saucepan with cold water and put into it the milk and the piece of onion stuck with the cloves. Simmer this very gently until the milk is well flavoured, then take out the onion and cloves, and add the breadcrumbs, which should be very fine. Stir over a gentle heat and cook slowly until the breadcrumbs swell and thicken the sauce. Add the butter or cream, and season to taste.

This is *the* sauce for serving with roast fowl and roast game.

CHESTNUT SAUCE

½ lb chestnuts
3 teacups white stock
Rind of ⅛ lemon
1 bay leaf
2 tablespoons cream or
 top of milk
Seasoning

Method. Take off the brown outside skin from the chestnuts and throw them into a saucepan of boiling water. Let them boil for a minute or two, then drain and peel off the inside skin. Put them back into the saucepan with the stock, bay leaf and thinly-peeled lemon rind, and simmer slowly for 1 hour or more until the chestnuts are really soft and pulpy. Rub them and the stock through a hair sieve with a wooden spoon, and return again to the saucepan. Add the cream or top of milk, season to taste, and stir till almost at boiling point. Serve very hot.

NOTE. If you have no cream or top of milk, you can use milk instead, but you will have to thicken with 1 teaspoon cornflour and cook it for a minute or two to cook the cornflour.

MUSTARD SAUCE

1 oz butter
1 teaspoon flour
1 teaspoon dry mustard
Pinch of salt
2 teaspoons white vinegar
1 teacup water or fish
 stock

Method. Melt the butter in a small saucepan, but do not let it colour. Stir in the flour and mustard and blend till smooth. Then add the water or fish stock, stir till boiling and cook for 2 or 3 minutes. Add the vinegar and salt and serve hot. If you like, and can spare it, a spoonful of cream can be added at the last minute.

This is excellent with grilled fish.

EGG SAUCE

¼ pint good white sauce
A squeeze of lemon juice
1 or 2 hard-boiled eggs
½ oz butter

Method. If this sauce is to be served with fish, the foundation sauce should be made with some of the liquid in which the fish has been cooked, otherwise use white stock or milk. When the sauce is hot, add a squeeze of lemon juice and season to taste. Then add the chopped hard-boiled egg and heat all thoroughly. Take the saucepan off the heat and stir in the butter just before serving.

NOTE. If you have the time and want to make a really good-looking sauce, you can sieve the yolks and shred the whites very finely before adding to the white sauce. It is also most attractive to keep back a little of the sieved yolk for decorating whatever the sauce is poured over.

MAITRE D'HOTEL BUTTER

1 oz butter
1 teaspoon chopped
   parsley
1 teaspoon lemon juice

Method. Put all the ingredients on to a plate, and with a knife work them well together to form a neat pat. Stand the plate slightly on end so that the lemon juice can run out of the butter again, and set in a cool place or on ice until wanted. The parsley should be very green and very finely chopped to make this butter look well. This is a very tasty and dressy-looking accompaniment to all sorts of dishes—poached eggs, steamed fish, baked fish, etc.

NOTE. You can stamp out individual pieces of butter with a fancy butter-cutter and place a piece in the middle of a fish fillet, on top of a poached egg, etc.

ORANGE SAUCE

1 large orange
Gravy
Cornflour
Seasoning

This is a very easily made orange sauce for serving with duck.

Method. Pour off as much as possible of the fat from the pan in which the duck has been roasted, leaving some gravy which you can thicken with a little cornflour. Add the warmed juice from the large orange and the finely grated rind, and scrape round the pan well to get a good mixture. Add a pinch of sugar if you like and otherwise season to taste. Keep it hot, but do not let it simmer (just hot enough to let the rind soften a little). Serve in a sauce boat.

SALAD DRESSING (no oil)

Hard-boiled egg
2 tablespoons cream or
   milk
1 teaspoon sugar
1 tablespoon vinegar or
   lemon juice
¼ teaspoon mustard
¼ teaspoon salt
⅛ teaspoon pepper

Method. Remove shell, separate yolk from white of egg. Put yolk into a basin and bruise it with the back of a wooden spoon. Mix with mustard, sugar and seasoning. Add cream or milk and mix smoothly. Add vinegar or lemon juice, stirring very carefully. Serve separately or pour over salad immediately before serving.

If you like, white of egg may be chopped finely and stirred into the dressing.

IF THE mayonnaise sauce curdles, put another egg yolk into a clean basin, and gradually add the curdled sauce to it, being careful to stir all the time.

LEMON juice makes a grand substitute for vinegar in making mint sauce or salad dressings.

SALAD DRESSING FOR KEEPING

1 egg
1 teaspoon sugar
1 teaspoon salt
1 teaspoon dry mustard
1½ teaspoons flour
1 small teacup milk
1 small teacup vinegar
1 dessertspoon margarine

Method. Beat the egg and add to the dry ingredients. Mix together in a basin. Stir in the liquids very gradually, beating well till all is worked in. Melt margarine in saucepan. Add the mixture and stir over a gentle heat till boiling point is reached, then cook gently until thick. Cool, then bottle and cork. (Will keep about 1 month.)

STUFFINGS

CHESTNUT STUFFING

1 lb chestnuts
2 oz butter
3 oz breadcrumbs
Seasoning
½ lb sausage meat
Milk or stock

Method. To shell the chestnuts, make a small slit in the rounded side of each with the point of a knife. Cover them with cold water in a saucepan, bring them to the boil and boil for 2 or 3 minutes. Keeping them warm, skin them a few at a time, as they are more easily shelled while they are hot. Take the point of the knife and remove the two skins. Use an old pan, as the chestnuts are inclined to discolour the inside of it.

Having shelled them, put them into a saucepan with milk or stock to cover and simmer them slowly until tender and the liquid absorbed. Rub through a sieve, or mash until smooth. Add the butter and breadcrumbs, mix with the sausage meat and season to taste.

NOTE. The sausage meat can be left out, and egg yolk used to bind the stuffing.

FORCEMEAT FOR PIGEON

2 or 3 pigeon livers
3 tablespoons bread-
    crumbs
2 oz fat bacon
1 teaspoon chopped
    shallot or onion
Pepper/Salt
Pinch of nutmeg
1 egg yolk

Method. Put the livers of the pigeons into a pan of water and parboil them, then chop them finely. Chop the bacon and mix with the liver together with the chopped shallot or onion and the breadcrumbs. Season with pepper and salt to taste, add a pinch of nutmeg, and bind with the egg yolk. If it feels too stiff, you may add a little stock or milk to moisten.

MUSHROOM STUFFING

¼ lb mushrooms
¼ lb breadcrumbs
1 oz butter
1 egg
Pepper/Salt

Method. Wash and dry the mushrooms and chop them up, stalks and everything. Melt the butter in a small saucepan and cook the mushrooms in this over a gentle heat for 6 or 7 minutes, stirring them about. Put the breadcrumbs in a basin, add the mushrooms and season with pepper and salt to taste. Mix together and bind with a beaten egg.

This makes a very tasty stuffing for small birds.

POTATO AND CELERY STUFFING

½ lb cooked potatoes
1 cup finely chopped celery
2 oz butter or dripping
1 onion
Pepper/Salt
1 egg to mix

Method. The potatoes should be dry and mealy. Mash them up with a fork or rub them through a sieve. Melt the dripping or butter in a saucepan and cook the finely chopped onion in it for 5–10 minutes, but do not let it brown. Then add it to the potato and celery, season well, and add a well-beaten egg to bind. Mix all together.

This is a grand stuffing for goose.

SPECIAL POTATO STUFFING

4 large potatoes
2 oz butter
Salt/Pepper
Few breadcrumbs
½ dozen olives (optional)
Stock or gravy
Liver from the fowl

Method. Boil the potatoes, peel and break into pieces while still hot. Add the butter, salt and pepper, the breadcrumbs, and the olives, stoned and chopped very fine. Moisten with a little stock or gravy, and if you are using it, the liver minced. Mix all thoroughly and use for stuffing fowls.

SAGE AND ONION STUFFING

4 large onions
½ lb breadcrumbs
1 teaspoon powdered sage
1 oz butter
Salt/Pepper
Pinch of nutmeg
Pinch of caster sugar

Method. Slice the onions thickly and put them into a saucepan with a good sprinkling of salt, cover with hot water, bring to the boil, cook for 5 minutes, and strain off this water. Cover again with hot water and boil slowly for ½ hour, or until the onions are half-cooked. Then drain, press the onions as dry as possible, chop them finely, and put them in a basin with the breadcrumbs, sage, seasoning, and the butter, melted. Mix thoroughly together and use for stuffing roast goose, duck or pork.

SAUSAGE STUFFING

¼ lb sausage meat
¼ lb stale bread
A little hot milk or water
2 tablespoons chopped
  onion
1 oz butter or dripping
Seasoning
1 dessertspoon chopped
  parsley
1 egg

Method. Soak the bread in the milk or water until soft, and then squeeze it as dry as possible. Melt the butter or dripping in a small saucepan, put in the chopped onion and cook for 5 or 10 minutes without browning. Then mix all the ingredients together in a basin, binding with the well-beaten egg.

NOTE. If you do not want the onion flavour, you can omit the onion and the butter in which it would be cooked, and mix everything else in a basin as indicated.

STUFFING FOR TURKEY

FRONT

1 part sausages
½ part white breadcrumbs
¼ part dried apricots, cut
  and soaked
¼ part dried prunes, cut
  and soaked
A few boiled, skinned,
  chopped chestnuts
A little boiled ham
A grating of lemon peel
A sliced pickled walnut
Pepper/Salt to taste
Beaten egg

Method. With a fork mix together lightly all the ingredients for the front stuffing and pack tightly into the front end of the turkey.

Repeat the same process with the other list of ingredients to stuff the back end of the turkey.

BACK

1 part hot mashed
  potatoes
¼ part soft white
  breadcrumbs
¼ part diced celery
A little chopped onion
A small pinch of sage
Some fat salt chopped
  pork, lightly diced
Melted butter
Beaten egg

Home Baking

The number of recipes in this section may strike you as being particularly numerous, but this is because we in Scotland follow the custom of having high tea instead of evening dinner, and we have developed a very sweet tooth for all sorts of cakes and fancies, which are a delight to the visitor from the South. I hope you will be tempted to try some of our Scottish specialities.

CAKES AND BUNS

ALMOND ROCK CAKES

½ lb flour
2 oz sugar
2 oz butter
2 oz almonds
Pinch of salt
2 or 3 drops almond
    essence
1 egg
1 teaspoon baking powder
A little milk

Method. Blanch and chop the almonds finely, and dry them in the oven, but do not let them brown. Then sieve the flour, sugar and baking powder into a basin, and rub in the butter until free from lumps. Add the almonds, and make a well in the centre of these dry ingredients. Add the well-beaten egg, flavouring and enough milk to bind into a dough stiff enough to hold the spoon upright. Grease and flour a baking tin, and lay the mixture on it in small heaps (about 1 teaspoonful in each heap), and a little distance apart. Sprinkle the cakes with sugar, or with ground almonds and sugar mixed, and bake in a quick oven till brown and firm to the touch (12–15 minutes).

Cakes and Buns

ALMOND SLICES (1)

¼ lb butter
¼ lb caster sugar
¼ lb almonds
7 oz flour
¼ teaspoon baking powder
3 eggs
Few drops of almond
    essence

Method. Beat the butter and sugar until light and fluffy, then add the flour gradually. Drop in the eggs and beat until the mixture looks light and full of air bubbles. Add most of the almonds, blanched and finely shredded, the baking powder and flavouring, and pour out into a shallow tin that has been lined with greaseproof paper. Sprinkle the rest of the almonds over the top and bake in a moderate oven till brown and firm to the touch (about 20 minutes). When ready, turn out on to a sheet of sugared paper, and when cold cut in neat slices with a very sharp knife.

NOTE. Do not beat again after the flour has been well beaten in.

ALMOND SLICES (2)

2 teacups flour
1 teaspoon baking powder
4 oz butter or margarine
2 tablespoons caster sugar
1 yolk of egg
A little apricot jam

ICING

1 white of egg
3 tablespoons icing sugar
3 oz almonds

Method. Sieve flour and baking powder into basin and rub in butter or margarine. Add sugar, and bind all to a stiff paste with the beaten egg yolk. Turn on to a lightly-floured board. Knead well, and roll out in a long strip about ¼″ thick. Prick with a fork and pinch the sides.

Place paste on a greased and papered baking sheet or tin, and spread with jam. Make the icing by beating the egg white till frothy but not stiff, and gradually stir in the sieved icing sugar. Spread this mixture over the jam, sprinkle with the blanched and chopped almonds, and bake in a moderate oven for 45 minutes. When crisp and brown, cut into fingers and cool on a wire tray.

CHEESE TARTLETS

7 or 8 small pastry cases
½ oz butter
1 teaspoon cornflour
¼ teacup milk
2 tablespoons grated
    cheese
1 egg
Cayenne pepper

Method. Make the pastry cases from ordinary short crust pastry, and if you like you can work a little cheese into this before you roll it out. For the filling, melt the butter in a small saucepan, add the cornflour, and blend smoothly together. Stir in the cheese, egg yolk and seasoning, and lastly fold in the egg white, beaten to a stiff froth. Line the cases with the pastry, fill with the mixture, sprinkle a little grated cheese on top and bake in a good oven till nicely browned and well risen. Serve at once.

BANBURY PUFFS

1 oz butter
2 oz sugar
1½ oz flour
1 oz candied peel
Grated rind of ½ lemon
3 oz currants
Pinch of cinnamon
Pinch of allspice
1 egg
1 dessertspoon sherry
Puff or flaky pastry

Method. Cream the butter and sugar, add grated lemon rind and spices, and then the egg yolk and flour. Clean the currants, shred the candied peel very finely, and add to the other mixture. Moisten with the sherry (optional). Let this mixture stand for a little while before you use it.

Roll out some puff or flaky pastry, to a little less than ¼″ thick, and cut it in pieces about 6″ square. Wet round the edges with slightly beaten egg white, and put a good teaspoonful of the mixture in the centre. Fold over two sides of the pastry, overlapping them in the middle, then pinch the two ends together and draw out like a little bolster. Make two or three slits in the top with the knife, paint over with white of egg, dredge with sugar and bake in a good oven till they are nicely browned and the pastry thoroughly cooked. Sprinkle again with sugar and serve hot (20 minutes to bake).

BEER CAKE

8 oz flour
3 oz butter
3 oz moist brown sugar
3 oz currants
1 egg
¼ pint beer
¼ teaspoon baking soda

Method. Cream the butter till light and fluffy, then add the flour, sugar and currants. Beat up the egg with the beer, and dissolve the soda in it. Add to the mixture and mix all together thoroughly. Place in a well-greased cake tin and bake for 1 hour in a moderate oven, till well risen and firm to the touch.

CHERRY CAKE

½ lb flour
5 oz butter or margarine
5 oz caster sugar
A little grated lemon rind
3 eggs
1 teaspoon baking powder
4 oz glacé cherries

Method. Sieve the flour. Beat butter and sugar to a cream, and add lemon rind. Beat in flour and eggs alternately, by degrees, adding the baking powder with the last spoonful of flour. Finally stir in the cherries, cut in quarters or even smaller if preferred. Turn mixture into greased and papered tin, and bake steadily for 1½ hours. Have oven hot for the first 10-15 minutes (No. 6 or 7), then moderate (No. 4 or 5), depending on gas pressure, or the equivalent on an electric stove.

NOTE. Cherries should *not* be washed as dampness makes them fall to bottom of cake; and they should always be cut rather small so that they will mix well and not sink.

145

CHOCOLATE CAKE

4 oz self-raising flour
3 oz margarine
3 oz sugar
2 eggs
2 level tablespoons cocoa
½ teaspoon vanilla essence
2 or 3 tablespoons milk
1 teaspoon baking powder

ICING
8 level tablespoons icing
   sugar
1 level tablespoon cocoa

Method. Cream margarine and sugar very thoroughly until light and fluffy. Add flour and beaten eggs alternately, very gradually. Add cocoa and vanilla. Add milk to make a mixture like stiff cream. Add baking powder last of all, folding it in. Grease and flour two 7″ sandwich tins and bake in a hot oven for 20 minutes.

Make the icing by sifting together the icing sugar and cocoa and adding boiling water to make a thickish paste. When the cake is cold put icing in the middle and stick together, then use the remainder of the icing for the top and spread with a warm knife.

CANADIAN CAKE

½ lb short crust pastry
Filling

Method. Line pastry tin with good short crust pastry. For the filling, cream ½ oz butter and ¾ cup sugar, add 1 beaten egg, 1½ oz chopped walnuts, ½ teaspoon vanilla essence and 1 cup currants, then spread over the short crust pastry in the case. Bake for ½ hour in a moderate oven, or until the pastry and filling are entirely cooked.

NOTE. The size of egg used will affect the consistency of the filling. If you feel that it is too dry, you can add a little more softened butter. If you use a square baking tin, you can mark it out into neat squares for a professional finish.

CHOCOLATE TARTLETS

3 macaroon biscuits
2 tablespoons grated
   chocolate
½ pint milk
2 egg yolks
Caster sugar
A few drops of vanilla
Pastry

Method. Line about a dozen tartlet tins with pastry, but do not bake them. Melt the chocolate in a small quantity of the milk till it is perfectly smooth, then add the rest of the milk with the biscuit crumbs and simmer them for about 10 minutes over a gentle heat. Remove the pan from the heat and add sugar to taste, vanilla to flavour, and the egg yolks. Mix well and fill the little pastry cases with this mixture. Lay some narrow strips of pastry in a trellis pattern over the top, wetting one edge of pastry wherever a join is made. Bake in a good oven till the mixture feels firm to the touch and the pastry is thoroughly cooked (about 20 minutes).

CHOCOLATE TEA CAKE

4 oz butter
3 oz caster sugar
3 oz grated chocolate
1 oz ground almonds
Grated rind of ½ lemon
4 oz flour
1 teaspoon baking powder
Pinch of ground cinnamon
Pinch of nutmeg
3 small eggs

Method. Beat the butter to a soft cream, then sieve the sugar, almonds, cinnamon, chocolate and nutmeg on top and beat well in. Add the eggs and flour by degrees, beating and mixing well between the addition of each egg. Flavour to taste and lastly fold in the baking powder, but do not beat after this is added. If you do not like the grated lemon rind as flavouring, leave it out or substitute anything you prefer. Pour into a tin that has been greased and dusted out with a mixture of flour and sugar, and bake in a moderate oven until well risen and firm (about 1 hour). Test with a skewer to make sure it is really dry and cooked through.

When cold, you can decorate it with chocolate glacé icing, and add any fancy trimmings you prefer, such as a dusting of coconut, some split almonds, or angelica leaves.

COFFEE CAKE

¾ lb flour
2 eggs
¼ lb brown sugar
2/3 oz butter
2 tablespoons syrup
2 tablespoons coffee
   essence
1 teaspoon mixed spice
¼ lb currants
¼ lb sultanas
1 teaspoon baking soda
1 teacup warm milk

Method. Sieve the flour and spice into a basin, then rub in the butter (or margarine) until free from lumps. Add the sugar and the carefully prepared fruit. Mix together and make a well in the centre. Add the well-beaten eggs, the syrup, the coffee, and lastly the soda dissolved in the warm milk. Stir together until thoroughly mixed, then beat for a minute or two. Bake in a tin lined with greased paper till firm and well risen (about 1 hour).

CHOCOLATE WALNUT CAKES

1½ tablespoons butter
1 tablespoon grated
   unsweetened chocolate
¼ teaspoon baking powder
1 egg
1½ tablespoons sugar
1½ tablespoons flour
½ teaspoon vanilla essence
½ oz chopped walnuts

Method. Cream the butter and sugar till light and fluffy. Beat up the egg and add this. Mix the flour with the chocolate, the vanilla essence and the baking powder, and stir these in, but do not beat once you have added the baking powder. Put the mixture into small buttered tins. Sprinkle some of the walnuts on top of each, and bake in a moderate oven till risen and firm to the touch. When the cakes are almost done, brush them over with a little beaten egg.

CHERRY or PLUM TARTLETS

1 lb cherries or small
   plums
¼ lb sugar
1 teacup water
Juice of ½ lemon
1 teaspoon cornflour or
   potato flour
2 or 3 drops cochineal
A little butter
Short crust pastry

Method. Line about a dozen small tins with short crust pastry, and bake them "blind" to a golden brown. Put the sugar, water and lemon juice into a small saucepan and let it boil for a few minutes. Then lay in the fruit carefully, picked and wiped, and simmer slowly until tender. When ready strain the fruit, return the liquid to the saucepan and add to it the cornflour or potato flour mixed with a little cold water to blend. Stir till boiling, add the butter and enough cochineal to make the syrup a nice pink colour, and then reduce if necessary. Fill up the tartlets with the cooled fruits, and when the syrup has cooled, pour it over them. Serve hot or cold.

NOTE. It is an improvement if you can find time to stone the fruit, and if you are feeling extravagant or are having a party, you can add a few drops of brandy or liqueur to the syrup.

COCONUT CAKE

½ lb butter or margarine
6 oz caster sugar
1 lb flour
3 eggs
½ lb desiccated coconut
1 teaspoon baking powder
About 1 teacup milk

Method. Beat the butter and sugar to a cream, add the coconut and the well-beaten eggs. Sieve in the flour with the baking powder and stir in carefully, a little at a time, adding enough milk to make the mixture just soft enough to drop from the spoon (a cake mixed with milk should never be too moist). Pour the mixture into a lined cake tin and bake in a moderate oven until nicely risen and firm to the touch (1½–2 hours).

NOTE. If you want to make it a bit fancier, you can ice it when it is cold, and add a sprinkling of coconut over the top. For festive occasions, I like to decorate this by putting pieces of cherry round the edge, one piece in the centre, and strips of angelica forming narrow spokes from the centre.

COFFEE DROPS

6 oz self-raising flour
3 oz butter or margarine
2 oz sugar
1 dessertspoon coffee
   essence
1 egg to mix

Method. Beat the butter and sugar till light and creamy, then beat in the well-beaten egg mixed with the coffee essence. Add the flour and beat well. Place small spoonfuls on a greased baking tin and bake for 7 or 8 minutes in a hot oven.

CORNFLOUR CAKES

6 oz butter
4 oz sugar
2 eggs
4 oz cornflour
1 teaspoon baking powder

Method. Beat the butter to a cream, then add the beaten egg yolks, the sugar, cornflour and baking powder. Mix all thoroughly together, but do not beat after you have added the baking powder. Add the egg whites whipped to a stiff froth, folding them in gently. Bake in small buttered tins in a moderate oven till risen and firm to the touch.

DOUGHNUTS

2 cups self-raising flour
3 dessertspoons sugar
2 oz lard or margarine
1 egg
Milk to mix

Method. Mix flour and sugar, rub in fat, add beaten egg, and then sufficient milk to make a softish dough. Shape out dough with top of cup or cutter to required size. Shape out centre of doughnut with a thimble, twisting it sharply to form tiny hole in centre.

Prepare a pan of deep fat, lard if possible, and get it hot but not too fiercely smoking, otherwise doughnuts will burn. Drop a small piece of dough in to test and if it sizzles the fat is correct. Drop in doughnuts one at a time until pan surface is bobbing with them. Cook until one side is golden brown, turn over quickly with a long thin utensil and cook the other side. Have ready a bag with sugar, drop each doughnut inside and shake it to coat with sugar, then cool on wire tray. Serve as soon as possible.

AMERICAN DOUGHNUTS

2 eggs
4 tablespoons melted butter
4 to 6 oz caster sugar
¼ teaspoon salt
½ pint milk
¼ teaspoon ground cinnamon
1 teaspoon baking powder
Flour to make a soft dough

Method. Beat the sugar and eggs till light and creamy, then add the melted butter, cinnamon, salt, baking powder and milk. Sieve in, by degrees, enough flour to make a soft light dough, and knead very gently for a few minutes. Roll out on a floured board and cut out in circles, with a tiny piece removed from the centre of the circle to make a dough-ring; or the dough can be rolled out a little thinner and two rounds put together with a spoonful of jam in between, the edges wet and pressed together to form a puffed-out ball when they are cooked. Fry in boiling deep fat until they are well puffed out and golden brown, but once they are in the fat do not cook too quickly. Drain on kitchen paper, and roll in caster sugar while they are still warm.

EASTER CAKES

½ lb flour
¼ lb butter or margarine
¼ lb sugar
2 oz currants
2 egg yolks
1 teaspoon brandy
   (optional)

Method. Cream the butter and sugar till light and creamy, then beat in the egg yolks, the brandy if used, and mix well together. Work in the flour gradually, and add a little milk if necessary. Lastly mix in the currants, well cleaned. When smooth and free from cracks, cover the paste over and let it stand in a cool place for at least 1 hour. Then roll out on a floured board to a little less than ¼″ thick, and cut in rounds about 5″ in diameter. Lay them on a greased tin and bake in a moderate oven till brown and crisp. When nearly ready, brush over with slightly beaten egg white, and dredge with caster or icing sugar, then finish them off in the oven. Cool on a wire tray.

NOTE. In the old days, these were given as an Easter present, about ½ dozen being tied together with narrow coloured ribbon.

DUNDEE CAKE

6 oz butter
6 oz sugar
4 eggs
10 oz flour
6 oz sultanas
2 oz mixed peel
6 oz currants
Grated rind of 1 lemon
Pinch salt
1 heaped teaspoon baking
   powder
2 oz almonds

Method. Cream the butter with the sugar until it is light and fluffy. Beat up the eggs and sift the flour. Add the beaten eggs and sifted flour and salt alternately to the butter-sugar mixture. Roll the fruit in flour to prevent sinking in the cake and stir in along with the peel and lemon rind. Lastly stir in the baking powder and bake in a moderate oven for 1½–2 hours. After cake has been in the oven for 20 minutes, put the almonds, blanched and halved, on top.

ITALIAN BUNS

6 tablespoons flour
3 tablespoons sugar
Pinch of salt
1 oz shredded candied peel
2 eggs

Method. Put the dry ingredients on a pastry board, and make a little well in the centre. Beat the eggs, pour into the well, a little at a time. With the hands draw in the dry ingredients a little at a time, then more eggs, until, only using your hands, you have a nice well-blended mixture. Divide into buns, marking a line across each with the back of the knife. Brush over with a little of the egg white which you have kept back, and bake for 20 minutes in a moderate oven.

FANCHONETTES

Puff pastry
3 egg yolks
3 oz caster sugar
1 teaspoon vanilla
   essence
1½ teacups milk

MERINGUE
3 egg whites
Sugar
Lemon juice

Method. Line about a dozen tartlet tins with puff pastry and bake " blind " in a good oven till golden brown. For the filling, put the sugar, egg yolks, milk and vanilla into a small saucepan and stir very carefully over a very gentle heat until the consistency of thick cream. When the pastry cases are ready, fill them with this mixture, place them on a wire tray and let them cool gradually.

To make the meringue : Whisk the egg whites to a stiff froth, fold in a little sugar and a squeeze of lemon juice. Spread this on top, piling it fairly high, dust lightly with sugar, and return to a cool oven for a few minutes to set the meringue and colour it faintly brown. Serve cold.

GINGER CAKES

4 oz flour
4 oz butter or margarine
4 oz sugar
½ teaspoon ground ginger
2 eggs
Few drops of ginger
   essence
½ teaspoon baking powder
1 oz candied lemon peel

Method. Cream the butter and sugar till light and fluffy, beat in the ground ginger, ginger essence (if available) and the lemon peel, chopped finely, and mix well. Then add 1 egg and half the flour, beat well, then the other egg and the rest of the flour and beat again. When the mixture looks light and frothy, mix in the baking powder, but do not beat again. Half fill small prepared tins with the mixture, place on a baking tray and bake in a moderate oven till firm to the touch and nicely browned (about 15–20 minutes).

ORANGE CAKE (1)

¼ lb butter
¼ lb caster sugar
5 oz plain flour
1 teaspoon baking powder
Rind and juice of 1 orange
2 eggs
3 tablespoons icing sugar

Method. Cream butter and sugar till light and fluffy. Add sieved flour and beaten eggs alternately, then baking powder and lastly the juice and rind of the orange (remembering to keep back a little of both juice and rind for icing). Bake in a hot oven for 10 minutes, then lower the heat and finish off in a moderate-to-slow oven for 30 minutes, or until risen and firm to the touch.

Mix sifted icing sugar with some orange juice and rind to a smooth icing, and spread over the cake when cold, using a knife dipped in hot water to give a glossy finish.

151

ORANGE CAKE (2)

6 oz flour
Grated rind of 1 orange
3 eggs
1 teaspoon baking powder
5 oz caster sugar

ICING
½ lb icing sugar
Juice of 1 orange

Method. Sieve the sugar into a basin, grate the orange rind on top and rub together till thoroughly blended. Add the eggs and whisk until light and creamy. Then add the flour, sifted, and the baking powder and mix in very lightly—do not beat after the baking powder is added. Pour into a tin greased and dusted with flour, and bake in a quick oven till lightly browned and firm to the touch (20–30 minutes).

For the icing, sieve the icing sugar into a basin and gradually add enough strained orange juice to make just soft enough to spread smoothly over the top of the cake. You can add any extras you fancy, in the way of chopped nuts, or small pieces of preserved fruits.

GENOA CAKE

10 oz flour
¼ lb butter or margarine
¼ lb caster sugar
4 eggs
¾ lb sultanas
1 lb currants
10 oz candied peel,
    chopped or shredded
4 oz sweet almonds,
    blanched and chopped
1 teaspoon baking powder
Grated rind of 1 lemon

Method. First prepare the fruit and line a cake tin with greaseproof paper, ready for the cake. Beat the butter and sugar to a light fluffy creamy consistency, then add the flour and eggs alternately, gradually, beating between each addition, and beat all together till light and fluffy. Add the fruit, tossed lightly in a little flour to keep it from sticking together (keep back a few of the almonds), then the baking powder and grated lemon rind, mix lightly but do not beat again. Pour into the prepared tin and bake in a moderate oven for 1½–2 hours. When cooked, brush the top over with white of egg, sprinkle with the rest of the almonds and return to the oven for a few minutes to brown the almonds. Let the cake stay in the tin for a few minutes before turning it out, then cool on a wire tray.

MADEIRA CAKE

6 oz sugar
6 oz margarine
2 eggs
7 oz plain flour
1 oz rice flour
2 level teaspoons baking
    powder

Method. Cream the butter and sugar, then add eggs alternately with the flour, and lastly stir in the baking powder. Bake in a round tin for 1½ hours. Put in a hot oven for the first 5 minutes, then lower the heat to very moderate for the remainder of the time.

JAM SANDWICH

3 eggs, and their weight in
  butter, flour and
  sugar
Few drops vanilla or other
  flavouring
2 or 3 tablespoons jam

Method. Put butter and sugar in a warm basin, and beat till light and creamy. The success of the cake depends on this good beating. Add 1 egg and a little flour, and beat them in lightly. Then add the second egg and some more flour, and beat again. Lastly add the third egg and the rest of the flour with the flavouring. When all is blended thoroughly, pour into 2 sandwich tins that have been greased and lined with paper, and bake in a good oven for 15 to 10 minutes. When they are nicely browned and cooked through, turn them out on a sheet of sugared paper, and when cool spread one with jam and lay the other on top. NOTE. You can vary the filling by putting a butter icing between the sponges or lemon curd or fresh fruit and caster sugar. You can, of course, ice and decorate the top.

LEMON CHEESE CAKES

2 eggs, and their weight in
  butter, flour and
  caster sugar
1 lemon
½ teaspoon baking powder
Short crust pastry

Method. Line about a dozen small patty tins with short crust, but do not bake them. For the filling, beat the butter to a light creamy consistency. Grate the lemon rind over the sugar and mix to a well-blended yellow colour, then add this to the butter, beating it well in. Add the eggs and flour by degrees and beat until the mixture is light and full of air bubbles. Stir in the baking powder at the very last. Put a spoonful of the mixture into each tart case, and bake in a moderate oven till nicely browned and firm to the touch (about 20 minutes).

MACAROON CHEESE CAKES

6 oz caster sugar
3 oz sweet ground almonds
3 egg whites
Squeeze of lemon juice
Jam
Pastry

Method. Line about a dozen patty tins with pastry, but do not bake. Mix the sugar, almonds and lemon juice together. Beat the egg whites till frothy, then blend everything together to a nice creamy consistency. Put a little jam in the bottom of each pastry case, fill up with the almond mixture, and lay two thin strips of pastry across the top. Dredge the tartlets with sugar, which gives them a nice cracked appearance when they are baked. Bake in a moderate oven till the pastry is cooked and the mixture feels firm to the touch (about ½ hour).

MOFFAT GINGERBREAD

4 oz butter
4 oz sugar
4 eggs
4 oz treacle
1 teaspoon baking soda
14 oz flour
¼ teaspoon ginger
¼ teaspoon allspice
¼ teaspoon caraway seeds

Method. Beat the butter and sugar to a cream, then add the spices and beat well. Add the flour and eggs alternately, beating well with each. Warm the treacle and mix with the baking soda and stir in, blending everything thoroughly. Mix with your warm hand for a few minutes to make sure everything is properly and smoothly mixed. Pour into a well-greased and lined cake tin, and bake in a moderate-to-slow oven for 1 hour.

SCOTCH SEED CAKE (1)

¼ lb butter
¼ lb caster sugar
7 oz flour
3 eggs
¼ lb candied peel
2 oz sweet almonds
¼ teaspoon baking powder
A little grated lemon rind
Some caraway seeds

Method. When you have shredded the candied peel finely and blanched and chopped the almonds, mix them with about 1 tablespoon flour or just enough to prevent them clotting together. Then make the cake mixture. Put the butter in a large basin and beat it till light and creamy, then sieve the sugar on top and beat well together. Add the eggs, one at a time, with a little flour, and beat well until very light and all the flour is used up. Then mix in the fruit, baking powder and a little grated lemon rind or other flavouring, but do not beat again—just blend in thoroughly. Pour into a greased and papered cake tin, and put some caraway seeds (sugared if possible) on the top, if available. Bake in a moderate oven for 2–2½ hours.

SEED CAKE (2)

½ lb flour
¼ lb sugar
6 oz butter
1 dessertspoon caraway seeds
3 eggs
¼ teaspoon baking powder
1 or 2 oz orange peel

Method. Mix the finely-shredded peel with a little of the flour to prevent clotting. Beat the butter to a cream, sieve the sugar on top, and beat well together. Add 1 egg and a little of the flour, and mix well for a few minutes. Add the second egg and a little more flour, and so on, repeating until all eggs and flour have been added. Beat all well together, making it as light as possible. Mix in the seeds, peel and baking powder at the last, and do not beat after this is added, but blend everything thoroughly. Pour the mixture into a lined cake tin, and bake in a moderate oven until cooked and nicely browned. When ready, remove cake from the oven, let it stand for a few minutes, then turn on to a wire tray to cool (about 2 hours baking).

154

ORANGE SANDWICH CAKE

6 oz flour
1 or 2 oz butter or
    margarine
¼ lb sugar
2 eggs
1 teacup milk
2 teaspoons baking powder
1 tablespoon orange juice
Grated rind of ½ orange

FILLING

1 teacup orange juice
Grated rind of ½ orange
Juice of ½ lemon
1 dessertspoon cornflour
1 tablespoon caster sugar

Method. Cream the butter, sugar and grated orange rind together till light and fluffy, then add the well-beaten eggs and the orange juice, beating well. Sieve the flour and baking powder, and add them gradually to the mixture, along with the milk. Mix lightly. Spread on a flat tin lined with paper and bake in a moderate oven for 15–20 minutes. When ready, remove the cake from the tin and let it cool on a wire tray, then split and spread with the orange filling. Now make the filling : Mix the cornflour smoothly with the lemon juice, sugar and grated orange rind. Add the orange juice and turn all into a saucepan. Stir over a gentle heat till boiling and simmer slowly for 5 or 6 minutes, then turn the mixture on to a plate to cool, and use it when cold.

RAISIN CAKE

1 lb flour
3 oz butter
3 oz lard
6 oz sugar
¼ lb raisins
¼ lb currants
1 oz baking powder
Rind of ½ lemon
2 eggs
1½ teacups milk

Method. Sieve the flour into a large basin and rub in the butter and the lard till free from lumps and like fine breadcrumbs. Then add the carefully prepared fruit, the grated lemon rind, sugar and baking powder. Mix all together, make a well in the centre, and pour in the well-beaten eggs and the milk and mix again from the centre outwards. Bake in a papered, greased tin till well risen and firm to the touch (about 1½ hours).

STRAWBERRY SPONGE

4 oz butter or margarine
4 oz caster sugar
2 eggs
4 oz self-raising flour
Pinch of salt
1 tablespoon hot water
Strawberries, sweetened
Cream, if possible

Method. Cream together the butter and sugar until light in texture and colour. Beat in two eggs, one at a time with 1 oz of the flour, and the salt. Mix in, without too much beating, the rest of the flour and 1 tablespoon hot water. Turn into two 7″ greased and floured tins and bake for 12–15 minutes in brisk oven. Remove and turn out on to wire tray to cool.

Meantime mash 4–6 oz strawberries with caster sugar to taste, and fold in ½ gill of double cream whipped till thick. Spread over one half of the sponge and lay the other on top.

If cream is not available, the centre filling can consist of sweetened strawberries alone.

SWEDISH LEMON RING MADEIRA

¼ lb margarine or butter
2 eggs
6 oz caster sugar
Rind and juice of 1 lemon
4 oz plain flour
1 teaspoon baking powder
Pinch of salt
Icing sugar
Blanched almonds

Method. Melt the margarine in a saucepan and let it cool slightly while you get on with the rest of the cooking. Beat the eggs and sugar together, then add the rind and lemon juice. Sift the dry ingredients together and beat into the egg-sugar mixture. Stir in the melted margarine and blend thoroughly. If it is a little stiff, you can add a spoonful or so of the top of the milk, but do not get it too soft—just soft enough that you have to shake the spoon to drop it off. Have a baking ring well greased and line it lightly, if possible with very fine breadcrumbs to prevent sticking. Put the madeira mixture in carefully, to within ½″ of the top of the ring, and bake in a moderate oven for 40–45 minutes, till firm and well risen. Let it cool for a minute or two, then turn out carefully.

NOTE. It can be served plain, but is greatly improved if you ice it when cold, with a mixture of icing sugar, lemon juice and water, then sprinkle with blanched, shredded and toasted almonds. 2 oz almonds are sufficient to sprinkle the icing thickly, and they should be toasted lightly in the oven to bring out the full flavour.

RICE BUNS

4 oz butter or margarine
4 oz sugar
4 oz ground rice
1 tablespoon flour
¼ teaspoon baking powder
¼ teaspoon cinnamon
2 eggs
Pinch of salt

Method. Beat the butter or margarine to a cream, then beat in the sugar, cinnamon and salt and get it light and fluffy. Beat in eggs. Mix the flour, ground rice and baking powder, fold these in and blend well but do not beat after adding the baking powder. Half fill well-greased tins and bake in a moderate oven for about 20 minutes, or until well-risen and firm to the touch.

SPICED APPLE CAKE

3 oz butter
½ cup sugar
1 egg
1 cup flour
1 teaspoon cinnamon
¼ lb stewed apples,
    drained dry and cold

Method. Beat the butter and sugar to a cream, add the beaten egg alternately with the flour and cinnamon, very gradually. Put half the mixture into a 7″ sand-wich tin, and spread it evenly and thinly. Spread the apples over, then the other half of sponge, and bake in a brisk oven for ½ hour.

This can be used as a pudding and served with pouring custard, but also makes a lovely cake.

SWISS ROLL

2 eggs
2 oz caster sugar
2 oz self-raising flour
1 tablespoon hot water
½ oz melted butter or
    margarine

Method. Whisk the eggs and sugar in a large basin, until thick and really creamy. Fold in the flour (no more beating), then add the hot water and melted butter and fold all together. Pour this soft mixture into an oblong baking tin (about 10″×8″), which you have lined with greased and floured paper.

Bake for 7–10 minutes on the top shelf of a very hot oven. (Look in after 7 minutes, very carefully.) The sponge should be firm to the touch. Turn it out on to a sugared greaseproof paper. Spread the sponge with warmed jam, and roll the sugared paper swiftly away from you, when the sponge will roll up. Keep it tightly rolled with the help of the paper until cold.

XMAS CAKE

9 oz self-raising flour
1 teaspoon mixed spice
6 oz butter or margarine
6 oz soft brown sugar
1 lb currants
¼ lb sultanas
2 oz chopped raisins
1 oz glacé cherries
¼ lb candied peel
1 small tablespoon syrup
3 eggs
½ gill milk
Grated rind of ½ lemon
A little apricot jam
Almond paste
White glacé icing
Fruits or decorations to
    taste

As this is a rich cake, it should be baked in a strong tin to prevent burning. Line the tin with *two* thicknesses of greaseproof paper. Cut two rounds for the bottom of the tin slightly larger than the tin itself, then line the sides.

Method. Add a pinch of salt to the flour and sieve it. Get fruit and peel ready and grate the lemon rind. As you beat the butter or margarine to a cream with the sugar, add the spice (cinnamon and ginger in equal quantities will do) and grated lemon rind. Whisk up the eggs well and beat them gradually into the butter-sugar-spice mixture. Beat all together. Now sift in the flour, a little at a time, and continue to beat till all is used up. Warm the syrup and stir in. Roll fruit and shredded candied peel in flour very lightly, then stir this in, but do not beat again after adding the fruit. Stir well till all is mixed, but if the mixture is too stiff add the ½ gill of milk. It must be stiff but not too dry. Put into the prepared tin, smoothing the top with a knife, and set in a moderately hot oven. As soon as it begins to brown (about 30 minutes), cover with a round of greaseproof paper, reduce the heat in the oven, and bake for 3 hours in a slow oven. When cooked, turn out the cake and leave to cool on a wire tray. When cold, trim off any rough edges. Cover with almond paste and ice.

ROYAL ICING

2 lb icing sugar
3 to 4 egg whites
¼ teaspoon acetic acid, or
   a little lemon juice

This quantity is sufficient to cover and decorate simply a 9" or 10" cake.

Method. Sieve the icing sugar several times until smooth and entirely free from lumps. Lightly beat the egg whites. Make a well in the centre of the icing sugar and add the acid or lemon juice and egg whites, stirring well. Add only enough of egg whites to give a stiff but beatable mixture. Beat thoroughly until the icing is quite smooth and glossy. Put some of the well-beaten icing on top of the prepared cake, keeping the rest in the bowl covered with a damp cloth. Cover the cake roughly with icing, using a long-bladed knife dipped in hot water to smooth it over the cake, turning cake round and round as you work. Add all the icing, using the knife with long sweeping strokes, and dipping frequently in the water. To make a rough snow icing, cover in the usual way and then, using a small knife or a fork, work into points. Do not worry if it is too soft at first—go on working until it gets firmer.

ALMOND PASTE

6 oz ground almonds
5 oz icing sugar
4 oz caster sugar
A little lemon juice
½ egg
¼ teaspoon vanilla essence

Method. Sieve sugars to remove any lumps, then mix with the ground almonds. Stir the essence and lemon juice into the beaten egg. Work this into the dry ingredients, making a stiff paste. If too dry, add a little more lemon juice. If too moist, work in a little more icing sugar.

Paint the apricot jam over the cake a week before you wish to use it, and, having formed the marzipan into a round, press this firmly on top of the jammed surface of the cake.

NOTE. You can then cover the entire cake with a simple water icing, or a Royal Icing as you choose, having allowed the marzipan to dry out so that no stain shows through the white of your icing.

ICING BAG. The silver foil wrapping on butter or margarine, complete with its paper lining, makes a grand icing bag. Just twist it into a cone, snip off a tiny piece at the point, and there is your icing bag.

CREAM will be lighter and go much further if you add a tablespoon of sifted icing sugar and stiffly beaten egg white (fold in the egg white) to each gill of double cream.

SYRUP GINGERBREAD

½ lb self-raising flour
5 to 6 rounded tablespoons
    syrup
1 rounded teaspoon each :
    ginger,
    baking soda
1 teacup tepid water
A good handful currants
    or sultanas, or mixture
    of both

Method. Mix flour and syrup together. Mix ginger and soda in the tepid water, and then blend the two mixtures, having a very moist consistency. Stir in the cleaned fruit, beat mixture well and turn into a greased tin dusted lightly with flour. Bake for 1 hour in a moderate oven. (Regulo 4 to 5, or even less if the pressure is strong.) Cake should be well risen and firm to the touch. Remove from oven and leave to cool for a few minutes before turning out on to a wire tray. Mixed spice can be added if liked.

VIENNESE CAKE

4 oz butter or margarine
4 oz caster sugar
3 eggs
6 oz flour
1 teaspoon baking powder
2 oz blanched almonds
2 oz sultanas

Method. Beat the butter and sugar till light and fluffy, then add the egg yolks, one at a time, mixing well with each one. Mix in the flour and the baking powder, blending well, but do not beat after adding the baking powder. Beat the egg whites to a stiff froth and fold lightly into the mixture. Grease a flat tin with sides, and put in the mixture. Halve the blanched almonds and sprinkle them with the sultanas over the top and bake in a moderate to brisk oven till well risen and firm to the touch (about 45 minutes).

PASTRY

ROUGH PUFF PASTRY (1)

1 lb flour
10 oz fat (lard, or
    margarine, or mixture)
½ teaspoon salt
Cold water to mix

Method. If using two kinds of fats, blend together before adding to the flour and salt. Cut the fat into the flour in pieces about the size of a pea, using a knife and not your fingers. Add sufficient cold water to mix to a slightly stiff paste. Turn on to a lightly floured board, and roll into an oblong. Fold into three, and seal all the edges by pressing lightly with the rolling-pin, to keep in the air. Give pastry a half-turn, roll out again, again fold into three and seal. Repeat this process three times, and set pastry aside till ready to use. All pastry is improved if allowed to "rest" before using, and, if possible, leave it in the cold larder or the refrigerator for ½ day before using.

If necessary, however, it can be used immediately. Bake in a hot oven.

ROUGH PUFF PASTRY (2)

¼ lb flour
¼ lb butter or margarine
Pinch of salt
Squeeze of lemon juice
Cold water

Method. Have the butter or margarine as cold as possible. Sieve the flour and salt into a clean, dry basin and add the lemon juice (optional). Put the butter into the basin, cover it well over with the flour and break it into pieces the size of a hazelnut. Have some very cold water in a jug ready for mixing, and make a well in the centre of the flour. Mix very lightly with a knife, pour the water in very gradually until you have formed a stiffish dough. Turn on to a floured baking board and roll into a long strip, rolling always with short, quick strokes away from you. Fold it in three, press down edges with rolling-pin and turn the pastry half round, bringing the joins to the right-hand side. Roll again the same way, fold again in three, and give it a half turn once more. Repeat until the pastry has had three rolls and three folds. The fourth time, roll to size and shape required for use.

NOTE. This pastry is improved by being kept for an hour or two before using, and in cold weather it will keep for several days if kept wrapped in a piece of greased paper. You can use half lard and half butter if you prefer.

RAISED PIE CRUST

½ lb flour
2 oz lard
About 1 teacup milk or
    water
¼ teaspoon salt

Method. Put the lard and water or milk into a small saucepan, bring to the boil but do not let them reduce in quantity. Sieve the flour and salt into a clean, dry basin and make a well in the centre. Pour in the hot liquid, mixing first with a spoon or knife as it is fairly hot, then taking the hand and mixing quickly until all is formed into one lump. Turn out on a floured board and knead lightly until free from cracks. Use warm and as directed for any raised pies.

TO BAKE "BLIND"

Press pastry well into the sides of the tin to form a neat case. Trim round the edges with scissors, letting the pastry stand a little way above the tin. Prick the bottom to prevent it rising during baking, and line the case with greaseproof paper and crusts, beans or rice to hold it down. Remove beans or other filling and paper for last few minutes before taking from the oven, to let the pastry brown and dry on the bottom.

CHEESE PASTRY

¼ lb flour
1 oz butter
Pinch of cayenne
2 tablespoons grated
    Parmesan
Egg yolk
Cold water

Method. This pastry is used for making little biscuits or pastry cases for savoury mixtures. Mix the flour, cheese and cayenne in a basin, rub in the butter and bind into a paste with a little egg yolk mixed with water. Knead slightly, then roll out once and bake in a moderate oven until brown and cooked. They can be stamped out with a cutter to form little biscuits, or used to line small tins and baked "blind" for use with fillings.

SHORT CRUST PASTRY

8 oz flour
6 oz margarine
1 dessertspoon sugar
¼ teaspoon baking powder
Pinch of salt
1 egg

Method. Put the flour, sugar, baking powder and salt into a basin, and rub in the margarine with the finger-tips until the mixture is like fine breadcrumbs. Add the beaten egg and form into a stiff dough, kneading and blending with the hands. Roll out and use as required.

This is a rich excellent pastry for any sort of tarts or dessert pies.

SUET PASTRY

½ lb flour
¼ lb suet
¼ teaspoon baking powder
Cold water
¼ teaspoon salt

Method. Sieve flour, salt and baking powder into a clean basin. Skin the suet with a sharp knife and chop it very finely on a floured board. Then mix with the flour, rubbing all ingredients together with the finger-tips. Add cold water very gradually, mixing with a knife to a smooth soft dough. Turn out on to a floured board and roll out as required. Do not use too much flour when you are rolling the pastry out, or you will make it hard—just enough to prevent it sticking to the board.

Note. If you want to make a lighter pastry, you can use half breadcrumbs and half flour. If you want a richer pastry, you can use a larger proportion of suet.

HERE is a nice filling for tartlets: ¼ *lb butter, mixed with a small cup of shredded coconut, a well-beaten egg, sugar to taste, and a little lemon juice. Stir over the fire till thick, put into short crust pastry cases, and finish off in the oven for a few minutes. The pastry cases are baked " blind," of course, first.*

OVER-RIPE tomatoes can be helped towards firmness by leaving them for about 20 minutes in a basin of cold salted water. Wipe them dry before using.

PIES AND TARTS

ALMOND TART

Puff pastry
2 oz ground almonds
2 oz caster sugar
1 oz butter
2 egg yolks
Rum or other flavouring

Method. Make about ¼ lb puff pastry and roll it into two rounds for top and bottom of the tart. Line a 7″ tin with one of the rounds. For the filling, beat the almonds well with the butter, egg yolks and sugar, and flavour with about a teaspoonful of rum or any other flavouring preferred. Spread it over the bottom round of pastry, wet the edges of this, and press the other piece on top, sticking the edges firmly together. Mark round with the back of the knife, then mark the top too, making curved lines from the centre, but do not press too heavily with the knife. This makes a nice ornamental top. Brush over with beaten egg or milk, and bake in a good oven (20–30 minutes). When ready, dredge lightly with caster sugar and return to the oven for a minute or two to glaze.
NOTE. You can bake this on a flat plate if you prefer.

APPLE AND RAISIN PIE

8 oz pastry (any kind)
1 lb apples
3 oz raisins
¼ teaspoon cinnamon
Rind and juice of
    1 lemon
4 oz demerara sugar

Method. Peel and grate the apples. Stone and chop the raisins. Add the rind and juice of the lemon, sugar and cinnamon and mix well together. Cut the pastry in half and roll out to a round to fit a plate or pastry tin. Fill with the mixture and damp the edges. Cover with the second round of pastry. Brush over the top with water and sprinkle lightly with caster sugar. Bake for 40 minutes in a hot oven.

CHEESE TART

¼ lb short crust pastry
1 oz butter
1½ oz flour
1 teacup milk
¼ lb grated cheese
Seasoning
1 egg
1 or 2 tablespoons top
    of milk (or cream)

Method. Line a greased 7″ tin with good short crust pastry and bake it " blind " till it is crisp and a pale golden colour. Meantime prepare the filling. Make a nice thick sauce with the butter, flour and milk, and cook it thoroughly. Add the grated cheese, top of milk (or cream) and well-beaten egg, season to taste and mix thoroughly. Fill the pastry case with the cheese mixture and bake again till the mixture is nicely browned and feels firm to the touch.

CUSTARD TART (1)

8 oz short crust pastry
1 large egg
¼ pint milk
¼ teaspoon vanilla essence
½ oz sugar
Grated nutmeg

Method. Line a greased baking tin with good short crust pastry and prick the bottom well, ready to receive the custard. Now make the filling: Warm the milk slightly. Beat egg and sugar together and stir in the milk and essence. Pour into the short crust case, sprinkle a little nutmeg on top and bake in a moderate oven for ¾–1 hour, until set.

CUSTARD TART (2)

1 pint milk
1 tablespoon cornflour
1 or 2 tablespoons sugar
3 egg yolks and 1 egg white
Flavouring
Short crust pastry

Method. Make the custard for the filling first, so that it can be cooling while you make the pastry. Put the milk (keeping back 2 tablespoons) into a saucepan and heat it gently. Mix the cornflour smoothly with the 2 tablespoons milk and add it to the hot milk, stirring over a gentle heat till boiling. Cook for a few minutes. Put egg yolks and white into a basin with the sugar and beat well together with a wooden spoon until light and creamy. Then pour the milk and cornflour slowly on to this mixture, stirring all the time. Flavour with lemon, almond, vanilla or any other preferred flavouring, and stir occasionally until it gets cold. Make a good short crust pastry and line a 7" greased tin, pricking well at the bottom with a fork. Fill up with the custard and bake in a moderate oven until the pastry is thoroughly cooked and the custard lightly browned. When ready sprinkle with sugar, and serve either hot or cold. (½ hour baking time.) NOTE. This may be found an easier method, as I have had many letters from listeners who could not make a success of a custard tart when pouring the uncooked mixture into the pastry case.

BAKEWELL TART

Short crust pastry
Jam

FILLING
1 cup ground rice
½ cup sugar
½ cup desiccated coconut
1 level teaspoon baking powder
1 egg

Method. Line an 8" tin with short crust pastry, and spread it lightly with jam. Now make the filling by mixing together all the dry ingredients. Drop in the egg and mix to a softish consistency. If the mixture seems too dry, add a little milk. Spread this mixture over the jammy pastry and bake in a hot oven for about 20 minutes.

FLAN OF APRICOTS

Short crust pastry
Tinned apricots
Sugar
2 whites of eggs
Cherries and angelica

Method. Make a flan with good short crust pastry and bake it " blind." When ready, fill the case with tinned apricots which have been well drained from their syrup and dredge them with caster sugar. Whip up the egg whites to a very stiff froth and fold in 2 tablespoons caster sugar. Pile this meringue on top of the apricots, decorate with small pieces of cherry and angelica (can be omitted), dredge with sugar and place the tart in a cool oven till the meringue is dry and palely browned. Serve hot or cold.

FLAN OF RASPBERRIES WITH CREAM

Short crust pastry
1 lb raspberries
2 tablespoons cake or
    macaroon crumbs
Sugar
2 tablespoons red currant
    or gooseberry jelly
1 gill double cream
Angelica
Vanilla essence

Method. Line a greased 7″ tin with good short crust pastry, prick it well, bake it " blind " and let it cool. Pick the raspberries, put aside a few of the best for decoration, and sprinkle the rest with sugar and, if liked, a tablespoonful of liqueur. Leave in a cool place for ½ hour. Sprinkle the bottom of the baked flan with macaroon or cake crumbs, arrange the raspberries on top, and coat them over with the jelly. Whip the cream, add a little sugar, and flavour with a few drops of vanilla. Cover the whole top with this cream, either through a forcing bag, or spooned over and peaked up with a fork. Decorate with the raspberries you kept aside, and a little angelica cut in decorative shapes (if liked).

NOTE. You can do the strawberry flan this way too, if you prefer it, instead of baking them with the pastry.

FRESH COCONUT TART

¼ lb short crust pastry
A little jam
4 oz grated coconut
4 oz caster sugar
1 level tablespoon self-
    raising flour
1 beaten egg
A little coconut milk

Method. Line an 8″ tin with the short crust pastry and spread a thin layer of jam over the bottom. For the filling, mix the coconut, sugar, flour and beaten egg, and sufficient coconut milk to form a soft wettish mixture, like a thick porridge, and spread this over the jam. Bake in a moderate oven for 35 minutes, or until the top is crisp and brown. This timing gives a crisp outside and a softish inside, but if you like it crisp all the way through (more like a biscuit), then leave it in the oven until it is crisp and firm when you touch it with your fingers.

CORNISH APPLE AND SPICE PIE

½ lb short pastry
1 lb cooking apples
4 oz sugar
½ lb currants
1 heaped teaspoon mixed
   spice
1 oz lemon peel

Method. Roll out half the pastry and line a greased tin with it. Cut up the apples and spread over the pastry. Cover with sugar, add the currants, spice and finely-chopped peel. Roll out the other piece of pastry and place on the mixture. Press the edges of the two pastries together, having moistened the under pastry with cold water, and crimp with a fork. Bake in a moderate oven till golden brown (about 30–35 minutes).

OPEN STRAWBERRY TART

Short crust pastry
1 lb strawberries
2 oz caster sugar
Juice of ½ lemon
2 whites of eggs
2 tablespoons caster sugar

Method. Line an 8″ tin with good short crust pastry and prick over with a fork. Pick and wash the strawberries and arrange them closely on the pastry. Sprinkle with sugar and squeeze lemon juice over. Bake in a moderate oven until the pastry is brown and crisp. Then beat up the egg whites to a stiff froth, fold in 2 tablespoons of caster sugar, and pile this meringue on top of the strawberries. Dredge with sugar and return the tart to a cool oven to dry and slightly brown the meringue. Serve hot or cold.
NOTE. If you want to be very extravagant, a jug of cream is delicious with this.

LEMON MERINGUE PIE

¼ lb short crust pastry

FILLING

1 egg
1 tablespoon cornflour
1 teacup sugar
2 lemons
1 teacup boiling water

Method. Line an 8″ pastry tin with the short crust pastry and bake " blind." Let it cool a little, then take carefully out of tin and place on a wire tray.

For the filling, separate the yolk from the white of the egg, and beat yolk until light, then add it to the cornflour which has been dissolved in a little milk in a cup.

Now into a saucepan put the sugar and over it put the grated rind and juice of the lemons. Add the egg-cornflour mixture, then the boiling water, and stir over a lowish heat until thick. When the mixture cools, spread it into the pastry case, and cover with a meringue made by beating the egg white until stiff and folding in two tablespoons caster sugar. Put pie into a very cool oven until the meringue hardens and turns a pale golden brown.

PASTRY CUSTARD

½ pint milk
2 egg yolks and 1 egg white
1 oz sugar
½ oz cornflour
A little vanilla essence

Method. Heat the milk. Mix in a basin the cornflour, eggs, sugar and flavouring, and pour the hot milk on to them. Return to the saucepan and stir over a gentle heat until boiling. Let this custard cool and use it for filling any little pastry cases or éclairs.

GROUND RICE TART

Short crust pastry
2 oz butter
2 oz caster sugar
2 oz ground rice
1 egg
A little milk
Vanilla
½ teaspoon baking powder
2 tablespoons jam

Method. Line a greased 8″ tin with a good short crust pastry, rolled fairly thin, and put aside. For the mixture, cream the butter in a basin till it is soft and light. Add the sugar and the egg, and beat again for a few minutes. Sprinkle in the ground rice, and add enough milk to make the mixture of a dropping consistency. Add a few drops of vanilla or any preferred flavouring, and stir in the baking powder at the very last. Do not beat after this is added. Spread the pastry with some nice jam and put the mixture on top. Bake in a good oven till the pastry is brown and crisp and the mixture firm to the touch. Sprinkle with sugar and serve hot or cold (½ hour to bake).

ITALIAN PASTRY SWEET

8 oz puff pastry
3 oz sultanas
3 oz raisins
3 oz chopped nuts
2 oz mixed candied peel
Squeeze lemon juice
2 oz caster sugar
1 egg
½ oz butter

Method. Roll pastry into a long narrow strip ½″ thick. Beat the egg with the butter until smooth. Mix this in with all the fruit and chopped peel and spread over the pastry. If liked, sprinkle with a little ground cinnamon. Cover the pastry with this mixture and bake in a hot oven for 10–15 minutes until golden. Can be eaten hot or cold, but must be very fresh.

MIXED FRUIT TART (Summer)

Take equal quantities of strawberries, raspberries and red currants and pick them all carefully. Mix them together and arrange them in a pie-dish, adding white sugar to taste. Cover with a good short crust pastry and bake in a moderate oven until crisp and golden. Take it from the oven, sprinkle the top with caster sugar and serve either hot or cold. It can be served as it is, or with a jug of custard or cream for pouring over.

MIXED FRUIT TART (Winter)

¼ lb cranberries
2 or 3 apples
¼ lb prunes
¼ lb sugar
½ pint water
Short crust pastry

Method. Wash the prunes and soak them for some time in the water. Pick and wash the cranberries, and peel and slice the apples thinly. Put the three fruits into a lined stewpan with the water and stew slowly for ½ hour. Add the sugar and stew for another ½ hour, breaking down the cranberries with the back of a wooden spoon. Pour into a pie-dish just large enough to hold the mixture, remove stones from the prunes and let it all cool. Cover with short crust pastry and bake in a moderate oven until crisp and golden. When baked take it out, sprinkle the top with caster sugar, and serve with a jug of custard or cream, either hot or cold.

ORANGE TART

Rough puff pastry
2 large oranges
2 eggs
2 oz butter
2 oz sugar
2 oz biscuit crumbs

Method. Line a greased 7″ tin with the pastry and prick the pastry with a fork. For the mixture, wipe the oranges, grate off the rind and rub it into the sugar. Cream the butter and sugar together, add the egg yolks and then the biscuit crumbs and strained orange juice. Lastly, stir in the whites beaten to a stiff froth and pour the mixture into the pastry. Bake in a moderate oven till the pastry is brown and crisp and the mixture feels firm to the touch (about ½ hour). Sprinkle with sugar and serve hot.

RASPBERRY BAKEWELL TART

½ lb short crust pastry
Raspberry jam
4 oz ground rice
1 dessertspoon desiccated coconut
1 dessertspoon caster sugar
4 oz butter or margarine
1 egg
1 teaspoon baking powder

Method. Line the baking tin with short crust pastry and cover with a good layer of raspberry jam. For the filling, beat the butter to a cream with the sugar, beat in the egg, stir in the other dry ingredients and mix well, but do not beat after adding the baking powder. Cover the raspberry jam with this mixture and smooth it evenly over. Bake in a moderate oven till firm to the touch and a nice golden brown (about 30–40 minutes).

THE BEST way to stew damsons is to put them in an earthenware jar with sugar to taste and water to cover, and stew slowly in the oven.

ALWAYS use olive oil to paint loaf tins—there is no moisture in this oil and so the yeasty dough will not stick to the sides of the tins.

STRAWBERRY FLAN

6 oz short crust pastry
Strawberries
Sugar
Red currant jelly
1 teaspoon arrowroot

Method. Line a flan tin with the short crust pastry and bake it " blind."

Prepare strawberries, washing and hulling them, and pack closely in circles in the baked flan. Take some red currant jelly and dilute a little, making a good cupful in all, and bring to the boil. Stir in a teaspoon of arrowroot blended with a little water, which will clear the sauce immediately. Pour it over the strawberries to set and, if you like, when cold dot with little blobs of whipped cream.

SWISS APPLE TART

PASTRY

2 oz flour
2 oz cornflour
2 oz butter or margarine
1 oz sugar
¼ teaspoon mixed spice (optional)
1 egg yolk

FILLING

4 or 5 apples
1 oz butter
2 or 3 oz sugar
Rind of ½ lemon
Some cake crumbs
1 gill double cream
Sugar
Flavouring

Method. Make short crust pastry with the ingredients listed, roll it out fairly thinly, and line a 7″ or 8″ tin with it. Prick the bottom of the pastry with a fork, line with greased paper, fill up with crusts or beans and bake " blind " in the usual way, till the pastry is brown and thoroughly cooked. Do not forget to remove crusts and paper for the last few minutes to let the bottom dry out and colour.

For the filling, peel, core and slice the apples very thinly, and put them in a saucepan with the sugar, butter, thinly-peeled lemon rind, and a very little cold water. Stew carefully till the apples are a pulp, then beat them up for a minute or two to make sure they are really soft and velvety and let the mixture cool. Put the tart case on a plate, sprinkle some cake crumbs on the bottom of the tart and fill up with apple pulp. Whisk the cream until thick, sweeten it with caster sugar, flavour with a drop or two of vanilla or almond, or any preferred flavouring, pile this on top of the tart, and decorate (optional) with small pieces of preserved fruit or chopped nuts.

NOTE. Another way is to make half as much pastry again, line the tin with it, fill up with the mixture, put on another round of pastry on top, and bake in a moderate oven for 1 hour. When cool, coat the top with a thin layer of glacé icing (just icing sugar and water) and sprinkle with coloured sugar or chopped nuts. This is not so expensive as the cream top, but be sure you let the apple pulp mixture cool before you use it or the pastry will be soggy.

SYRUP or TREACLE TART

Short crust pastry
2 tablespoons syrup or
    treacle
2 tablespoons oatmeal or
    breadcrumbs
Flavouring

Method. Line a greased 7″ tin with short crust pastry and prick over with a fork. Put the syrup or treacle in a basin and thicken it with the oatmeal or breadcrumbs. Flavour with a little lemon or orange juice, or a little ground ginger or spice if preferred. Cover the pastry with this mixture and bake in a moderate oven till the pastry is crisp and nicely browned.

BISCUITS AND SHORTBREAD

AYRSHIRE SHORTBREAD BISCUITS

¼ lb flour
½ lb rice flour
¼ lb butter
4 oz caster sugar
1 egg
1 or 2 tablespoons top
    of milk

Method. Sieve the two kinds of flour and the sugar into a basin, and rub the butter into them. Beat up the egg in a small basin and add a little of the top of the milk to it. Pour this into the centre of the dry ingredients and mix all into a paste with the hand, turning it over and over, and adding a drop more of the top of the milk if necessary, but it must be kept to a stiffish paste. Turn out on to a floured board and knead lightly until free from cracks. Flour a rolling-pin and roll out the paste to about ½″ thick. Stamp it out in small rounds with a cutter and place the biscuits on a greased, floured tin. Roll the scraps again and cut out more biscuits until all is used, then bake in a moderate oven until a nice golden brown. Sprinkle them well with sugar while they are still hot and lift them on to a wire tray to cool. (They will take about 10–15 minutes to bake.)

CHEESE STRAWS

3 oz flour
2 oz butter
2 oz grated Parmesan
½ egg yolk
Pinch of salt
Pinch of cayenne
A little water

Method. Rub the butter lightly into the flour. Add the grated cheese and seasonings, and mix to a paste with the ½ egg yolk beaten with a little water. Have the pastry fairly stiff and work with the hands until it is free from cracks. Roll out on a floured board into a strip about 4″ wide and cut in thin strips, like straws. Bake in a good oven until lightly browned and firm to the touch. Watch them carefully as they burn very easily. You can serve these either hot or cold, and they are nice for savouries or with soup.

Biscuits and Shortbread

ALMOND BISCUITS

¼ lb flour
2 oz butter
1 egg yolk
1½ oz sugar
1 or 2 tablespoons top
of milk
3 or 4 drops almond
essence
A few skinned almonds

Method. Sieve the flour and sugar, and rub the butter into them till free from lumps. Mix the egg yolk with a tablespoon of milk and the almond essence, and pour this into the centre of the dry ingredients. Work up with the hand into a stiffish paste, adding more top of the milk if necessary. Roll out on a floured board fairly thinly and cut in fancy shapes. Bake on a greased and floured tin until golden brown (10 minutes). Let the biscuits cool on the tin, then brush them over with egg white and sugar mixed, and sprinkle with chopped and browned almonds. Return to the oven for a few minutes to dry.

ALMOND SHORTBREAD BISCUITS

3 oz caster sugar
5 oz butter or margarine
¼ lb flour
Almonds, blanched

Method. Beat the sugar and butter or margarine to a cream, then work in the flour till you have formed a well-blended stiffish dough. Roll out on a lightly floured board to ¼″ thick, then stamp out with a cutter and cover with the chopped almonds. Bake in a moderate oven till pale golden brown (about 20–30 minutes), and cool on a wire tray.

COFFEE BUNS

¼ lb margarine
1 egg
1½ teaspoons cream of
tartar
2 dessertspoons coffee
essence
¼ lb demerara sugar
2 teacups flour
¾ teaspoon baking soda
¼ teacup currants

Method. Beat the margarine and sugar to a cream, then add the beaten egg. Mix thoroughly. Add the dry ingredients (sugar, flour, baking soda, and cream of tartar), keeping the currants to the last. Stir in the coffee essence. Roll the mixture into balls the size of a walnut. Place them on a greased tin, flatten on top and bake in a moderate oven for 20 minutes.

COCONUT MACAROONS

2 oz desiccated coconut
2 oz caster sugar
1 white of egg
1 teaspoon flour
Wafer paper

Method. Mix dry ingredients. Whip white of egg until stiff and fold it into the mixture. Put wafer paper on a dry tin. Drop a teaspoonful of the mixture at intervals all over the paper, with a space between for tearing, and bake in a very slow oven till firm and pale golden. Cool on a wire tray, and tear off the wafer paper if it projects beyond the macaroon.

COCONUT BISCUITS

3 oz cooking fat
2 oz syrup
6 oz self-raising flour
¼ teaspoon vanilla essence
Desiccated coconut
Cherries (glacé)

Method. Cream the fat and syrup, and work in the flour. Add the vanilla essence and mix all to a stiff paste. Cut off small portions and roll into balls. Toss these in a little desiccated coconut till well covered, and place on a greased tin. Flatten slightly and top with a tiny piece of glacé cherry. Bake in a moderate oven for 15 minutes. Cool slightly, then remove to wire tray to get completely cold and crisp.

COCONUT SHORTBREAD

6 oz flour
3 oz margarine
1½ oz caster sugar
1 egg
A little water
2 oz desiccated coconut

Method. Sieve flour, rub in margarine, then add sugar. Bind to a stiff mixture with the beaten yolk and a very little water mixed together. Roll into an oblong about ¼″ thick, and prick with a fork. Brush over with the slightly beaten egg white, sprinkle with coconut and cut into equal-sized fingers. Place on a greased tray and bake in a moderate oven till crisp and golden (about 15–20 minutes). Cool on a wire tray and store.

EASTER BISCUITS

3 oz margarine
3 oz sugar
1 egg yolk
½ oz chopped mixed peel
1 oz currants
¼ teaspoon mixed spice
6 oz flour
Pinch of salt
Icing

Method. Cream the fat and the sugar, then beat in the egg, and add alternately the peel and the fruit and dry ingredients. Mix to a stiff dough, using a little milk if mixture is too dry, but do not get it too sticky. Roll out on a floured board. Prick with a fork and cut out with a cutter or tumbler. Bake on greased tin in a moderate oven for about 20 minutes until they are lightly coloured. Cool on a wire tray and store in tightly fitting tin when cold.

EMPIRE BISCUITS

4 oz flour
1 oz butter
1 oz caster sugar
Pinch of salt
1 egg
Pinch cinnamon
    (optional)

Method. Rub butter into flour and mix with egg and other ingredients to a stiff dough. Roll out, cut into rounds and prick over with a fork. Bake in a moderate oven till pale golden and leave on wire tray to cool (about 15 minutes baking time). When cold, spread one biscuit with jam, place another biscuit on top, spread with water icing and decorate if liked, with tiny pieces of cherry.

BRANDY SNAPS

¼ lb butter
¼ lb caster sugar
¼ lb flour
¼ lb golden syrup
½ teaspoon ground ginger
Few drops of vanilla

Method. Melt the butter, sugar and syrup in a saucepan over a gentle heat. Take the pan off the fire, sieve the flour in and mix gradually, then add the ginger and flavour with vanilla. When all is thoroughly mixed, pour in small rounds on to one or two well-greased tins, and bake in a moderate oven (10 minutes or so). When ready, remove the snaps from the tins with a palette knife, and twist round the handle of a wooden spoon to form a roll, or round cornet moulds if you have them, and remove when cold.

NOTE. If you turn off the oven, leave the door open, and lift out the snaps one by one to deal with them, they will not all cool before you can twist them.

FROSTED FINGERS

2 oz caster sugar
4 oz margarine
1 teacup self-raising flour
½ teacup fine coconut
Icing

Method. Work margarine and sugar together until creamy, then work in the flour and coconut, making a stiff dough. Roll out into a thin strip or square. Do not prick over or pinch the edges. Bake in a moderate oven.

Put 2 or 3 tablespoons sifted icing sugar into a cup, and add sufficient milk to make a thin icing. Spread this on the cooked pastry and sprinkle thickly with coconut. Return to oven until the icing has set. Cut into fingers while still hot.

GINGER CRUNCHIES

6 oz self-raising flour
¼ teaspoon ground ginger
½ teaspoon baking soda
2 oz margarine
2 oz sugar
4 oz syrup

Method. Sift flour, ginger and soda together. Rub in margarine and stir in sugar. Add warmed syrup, mixing all well together. Knead into a soft dough. If it is too dry, you may add a little warm water. Put dessertspoon heaps on greased baking trays, placed well apart, and flatten lightly into rounded shapes. Bake in a moderate oven for 15 minutes. Leave to cool and remove carefully on to a wire tray to get thoroughly cold. Store in biscuit tin with close-fitting lid.

IF YOU do not like peel in cake, use a large tablespoon of orange marmalade instead, and you will have the lovely flavour without any hard pieces of peel.

NEVER catch a falling knife—let it go to avoid greater damage to precious hands.

GINGER CRUNCHIES (with oatmeal)

3 oz margarine
4 oz demerara sugar
¼ teaspoon baking soda
2 teaspoons powdered
    ginger
2 teacups oatmeal

Method. Melt sugar and margarine in a saucepan. When boiling, remove from the heat and stir in ginger and baking soda. Pour this mixture over the oats and mix together thoroughly. Put into a Swiss roll baking tray, well-greased, and bake in a moderate oven for 20 minutes. Cut into fingers while hot and leave on the tray to cool. Store in tightly fitting tin when cold.

GINGERBREAD NUTS

¼ lb flour
3 oz sugar
3 oz lard
2 tablespoons treacle or
    syrup
1 teaspoon lemon juice
1 teaspoon ground ginger
¼ teaspoon baking soda
Grated rind of ½ lemon

Method. Put the fat, treacle and sugar into a saucepan and melt them over a gentle heat. Put the flour, ginger, lemon rind and juice into a basin. Add the soda to the hot mixture in the saucepan and pour all into the centre of the dry ingredients. Mix all together to a smooth paste, form into small balls the size of a marble, and place them on a tin lined with greaseproof paper. Let them stand for ½ hour, then bake in a moderate oven for about 15 minutes.

SHORTBREAD

4 oz flour
2 oz caster sugar
2 oz rice flour
4 oz butter

Method. Sieve dry ingredients together. Add the butter and knead this well into the flour until it is all absorbed. Do not add any liquid. Form into a ball, and press into an 8″ baking tin, spreading and flattening into a cake until it fills the tin. Prick all over with a fork and pinch the edges into a pattern. Bake in a steady oven, moderate to slow, until it begins to colour. Reduce heat and allow to bake for about 1 hour altogether.

SWISS HAZELNUT BISCUITS

¼ lb hazelnuts, minced
2 oz butter
2 oz caster sugar
Little grated lemon rind
Flour as necessary

Method. Beat the minced nuts, butter and sugar together, and add the lemon rind, if used. Knead in enough flour to make a stiffish mixture which will roll out smoothly and easily. Roll out to about ¼″ thick, and stamp out in rounds or fancy shapes as desired. Bake on a greased tin in a moderate oven for 10–15 minutes, or until a pale golden brown and cooked through. Remove from the oven, dredge with caster sugar and cool on a wire tray.

OATCAKES

4 oz fine oatmeal
A pinch of baking soda
½ teaspoon salt
1 tablespoon melted bacon
    fat or dripping
Hot water to mix

Method. Mix dry ingredients then pour melted fat in the centre. Mix to a soft consistency with the hot water. Knead lightly on a floured board and roll out as thinly as possible. Cut into triangles and cook on a hot girdle until the edges curl, then toast them lightly in the oven or before the fire, as is convenient.

PITCAITHLY BANNOCK

½ lb butter
¾ lb flour
¼ lb rice flour
2 oz sweet almonds,
    blanched and chopped
2 oz candied orange peel,
    finely shredded
¼ oz caster sugar
A little flavouring

Method. Warm the butter very slightly, then beat it to a cream. Mix all the other ingredients with the creamed butter and knead into one lump with the hands. This takes a little time, for no liquid must be used. Form into a round flat cake about 1½ inches thick, and prick all over with a fork. Place on a baking tin and tie a double band of paper round it, then bake in a moderate oven till the cake feels firm and is a nice golden brown. Let it cool on the tin before removing it, and take off the band of paper. When it is cool this cake should be rolled in paper and kept in an air-tight tin, then broken in pieces when you want it.

RICE BISCUITS

2 eggs
3 oz caster sugar
2 oz butter
½ lb rice flour
1 oz cleaned currants

Method. Beat the eggs and sugar together with the butter till light and fluffy. Mix the flour and currants, and add gradually to the rest, and beat well. Roll out on a floured board and cut into any shapes liked, place on a greased floured tin and bake in a slow oven till cooked and pale golden.

SHORTBREAD BISCUITS

¼ lb butter
2 oz sugar
½ lb flour

Method. Cream the butter and sugar till light and fluffy, then slowly add to this the flour. Mix well, kneading thoroughly with the hand, then turn on to a floured board, flatten and cut out in any preferred shapes. Prick all over with a fork, and bake on a greased tin till a pale gold, in a moderate oven.

ALWAYS leave your cakes and loaves to shrink for a little in their tins when you remove them from the oven, and then they can be easily slipped out to cool on the wire tray.

THIN SHORTBREAD

5 oz plain flour
1½ oz ground rice
1½ oz caster sugar
¼ lb butter

Method. Rub and knead butter into other ingredients until you form a smooth firm mixture. Roll out very thinly into two 8″ sandwich tins. Bake for 20 to 30 minutes in a moderate oven. Remove from oven, sprinkle the top lightly with caster sugar and mark into thin strips.

VANILLA NUT BISCUITS

4 oz margarine
2½ oz brown sugar
3 oz flour
Pinch of salt
½ teaspoon vanilla essence
1 oz chopped nuts

Method. Cream the fat and sugar until light and fluffy. Add the sifted flour, salt and vanilla essence. Drop small teaspoonfuls of the mixture into the chopped nuts, roll into balls and place on a greased baking tray. Flatten a little, and bake for 15 minutes in a moderate oven. This quantity makes 22 biscuits.

SCONES

RICH OVEN SCONES

8 oz plain flour
½ teaspoon baking soda
1 teaspoon cream of tartar
Pinch of salt
4 or 5 dessertspoons sugar
1½ oz margarine
1 beaten egg
Milk to mix

Method. Keep back a little of the egg for painting the tops of the scones to give a rich golden brown colour.

Mix all dry ingredients together. Rub in the margarine with the fingertips. Mix to a soft dough with the egg and milk. Roll out lightly and cut into rounds with cutter or top of small cup and bake in a very hot oven for 7–10 minutes.

OATMEAL SCONES

1 teacup oatmeal
1 teacup flour
½ teaspoon baking soda
1 teaspoon cream of tartar
½ teaspoon salt
About 1 oz butter
Milk as required

Method. Mix dry ingredients in a basin, then rub in the butter. Add enough milk to form a soft dough. Knead and roll out into a thick round. Place on a floured tray, mark across in four or eight sections and bake in a hot oven for 15–20 minutes. When ready, break into scones, and wrap in a clean towel till required.

HERE is an old-fashioned hint to help children over the effects of a heavy cold. Stir a teaspoon of fresh chopped suet in a cup of hot milk and give it to the children to sip at bedtime.

SPICED SCONES

2 teacups flour
1 teaspoon cream of tartar
1 teaspoon ginger
1 dessertspoon sugar
Buttermilk or plain milk
1 teaspoon baking soda
1 oz butter
1 teaspoon ground
    cinnamon
1 tablespoon treacle

Method. Mix together all the dry ingredients (flour, cream of tartar, ginger, sugar, baking soda and cinnamon). Warm the butter and treacle together in a pan and add to the dry ingredients. Add sufficient milk to make a soft dough, then turn out on to a floured board and knead lightly. Roll out to a thickness of about ½″, cut in rounds and bake on a hot girdle.

PANCAKES

½ lb flour
1 pint milk
2 eggs
A pinch of salt
A little lard for frying
Caster sugar
Lemon or orange juice

Method. Sieve the flour and salt into a basin and make a well in the centre. Drop in the 2 egg yolks and with a wooden spoon mix a little of the flour gradually into them. Then add about half the milk very gradually, mixing in the flour by degrees from the sides of the basin. Keep the batter thick enough to allow all lumps to be rubbed smooth, then beat well until the mixture is full of air bubbles. Add the rest of the milk, and if possible let the batter stand for an hour at least before using it. Just at the last, fold in quickly and lightly the egg whites beaten to a stiff froth. Melt some lard in a saucepan and let it stand by the heat to keep warm. Pour a little of this into a small frying or omelet pan and make it smoking hot. Then pour quickly into the centre of the pan half a cup or so of batter. If the fat is hot enough the batter will run all over the pan at once, whereas if it has not quite reached the necessary heat the pan may have to be tilted slightly to get the batter to cover it properly. Let it rest for a minute or two until set and nicely browned on the under side, then slip a broad-bladed knife round the edges, and either toss the pancake over or turn it with the knife. Brown on the other side, then slip on to a sugared paper, sprinkle sugar over it, then lemon or orange juice, and roll up. Keep this pancake hot on a plate placed over hot water till the others are cooked. Each pancake will need a little fresh fat added to the pan. Serve very hot and as quickly as possible, and send the cut lemon or orange to the table with them.

IF YOU yourself wilt too much in hot weather, drink a glass of water with a teaspoonful of salt in it. This is an instant refresher.

SCOTCH PANCAKES or DROPPED SCONES

2 teacups plain flour
2 tablespoons sugar
½ teaspoon baking soda
1 teaspoon cream of tartar
1 egg
A little milk
About 1 teaspoon melted
    butter

Method. Put dry ingredients into a bowl and mix lightly. Drop egg into centre and gradually draw in the flour, etc., from the sides until all is beaten in. Add milk and melted butter and continue beating until the mixture forms bubbles on the top. Cover with a cloth and leave for an hour or two, or as long as you can afford. Beat again just before using and bake on a hot girdle, greasing lightly between each batch of pancakes, to prevent sticking. When the bubbles which have formed on top of each pancake burst into tiny holes, it is ready for turning. Cook the other side till firm to the touch. Keep warm in a cloth, and serve with hot golden syrup, lemon juice and sugar, or hot jam.

NOTE. Scotch pancakes should be small and spongy, so do not pour too much batter into each one. An ordinary girdle can bake up to ½ dozen at once.

GIRDLE SCONES

2½ teacups s.r. flour
A pinch of salt
1½ oz margarine
Milk to mix

Method. Rub the margarine into flour and salt, and add milk to make a stiff dough. Roll out lightly and cut into triangles. Cook on a hot girdle or frying pan until risen and firm to the touch.

OVEN SCONES

2½ teacups s.r. flour
A pinch of salt
2 oz margarine
A little milk

Method. Rub the margarine into flour and salt, add milk to make a stiff dough and roll out lightly.

Cut into rounds with cutter or top of small cup, and bake for about 20 minutes in greased trays in moderate oven. If you like them a good golden brown, paint the tops with milk before putting in the oven.

WHEATEN SCONES

½ lb wheaten flour
½ lb plain flour
2 oz butter or margarine
1 teaspoon cream of tartar
1 teaspoon baking soda
1 teaspoon salt
Sour milk

Method. Rub butter into flour. Mix in rest of dry ingredients. Add sour milk and mix to an elastic consistency. Knead lightly and roll out to ¾″ thick. Cut into rounds and put in greased, floured tin. Bake in a hot oven for 10 to 15 minutes. Cool on a wire tray.

NOTE. If sweet milk is used, double the amount of cream of tartar.

177

SCOTTISH POTATO SCONES

½ lb cooked potatoes
2 oz flour, approx.
½ oz butter
Salt

Method. Boil the potatoes and mash them up with the butter in a bowl. Add salt to taste. Turn out on to a well-floured board, and have the flour in top right-hand corner of board. Proceed to rub in as much flour as the potato will absorb, and work it all into a pliable dough. Roll out as thinly as possible, cut in triangles or circles and bake on a hot girdle. After placing scone on girdle, prick all over with a fork. This lets the steam out and prevents toughness. Cook for 3 minutes on each side. Allow to cool by wrapping in a clean cloth.

NOTE. If any are left over, they are delicious fried with the breakfast bacon, but when eaten fresh they should be spread with butter, as lavishly as possible.

BREAD AND ROLLS

Nothing equals the flavour of home-made bread, and the recipe I have given for wholemeal bread is very simple to follow and well worth while trying. Once you have tasted home-made bread it will be difficult to go back to shop bread. The sweet loaves make nourishing and satisfying fare at teatime and are more substantial to many palates than richer cakes.

BOSTON BROWN BREAD

1 lb black treacle
1 lb wholemeal flour
1 teaspoon baking soda
1 teacup of warm milk

Method. Warm the treacle. Mix with the flour. Add the baking soda to the teacup of warm milk and stir into the treacle and flour. Mix well. Pour into loaf tin and cook in a moderate oven until ready (approx. ¾–1 hour). Cut into slices and spread with butter.

BUTTERMILK BREAD or SODA LOAF

4 teacups flour
1 teaspoon baking soda
1 teaspoon cream of tartar
Pinch of salt
Small tablespoon sugar
1 oz butter
Buttermilk or sour milk

Method. Rub butter into flour, add other dry ingredients, and make into a soft dough with about ½ pint of buttermilk or thick sour milk. Put into a floured, greased tin and bake in a moderate oven for ¾ hour, or until ready.

DATE LOAF

A ½-lb packet of dates
1 teaspoon baking soda
1 tablespoon margarine
¾ teacup sugar
1 teacup boiling water
1 egg
2 teacups self-raising flour

Method. Put dates (cut into small pieces), baking soda, margarine and sugar in basin and pour the boiling water over. Add the well-beaten egg and the flour, and mix well to form a softish consistency. Put into an oblong loaf tin and bake in a moderate oven for up to 1½ hours. Leave to cool a little before turning out to cool thoroughly on a wire tray.

EASTER BREAD

8 oz flour
1 level teaspoon mixed spice
3 oz lard
2 oz chopped dates
1 egg
2 teaspoons baking powder
¼ level teaspoon cinnamon
3 oz caster sugar
2 oz sultanas
Approx. 6 tablespoons milk

Method. Sieve the flour, baking powder and spices into a bowl and rub in the lard. Add the sugar and fruit and mix to a soft dropping consistency with the beaten egg and the milk.

Turn into a well-greased 2 lb loaf tin and bake for 45 minutes in a moderate to strong oven, then lower the heat to moderate and give it another 30 minutes. Test with a skewer. Leave in tin for a few minutes, then turn on to wire tray to cool. Cut into slices and serve buttered.

FRUIT LOAF

1 lb self-raising flour
1 oz butter
3 oz currants
3 oz sultanas
½ teaspoon salt
¼ pint milk and water

Method. Add the salt to the flour, rub in the butter, add the cleaned prepared fruit, and mix to a soft dough with the milk and water. Bake in a greased tin in a moderate oven for about 1 hour. Test with a skewer. Let it cool in the tin for a few minutes, then turn out on to a wire tray.

MALT LOAF

6 oz flour
3 oz chopped dates
1 level tablespoon syrup
1 level dessertspoon malt
1 oz margarine
1 teaspoon mixed spice
¼ teaspoon baking soda
2–3 tablespoons milk
1 oz sugar

Method. Gently heat the malt with the milk. Rub margarine into flour, add other dry ingredients, then warmed syrup, and heated malt and milk. Mix all together thoroughly. Bake in well-greased loaf tin in moderate oven for 1½ hours. Cool a little, then turn on to a wire tray to get cold.
NOTE. Malt can be bought from the chemist.

SULTANA BREAD

1 lb flour
1 oz butter
1 teaspoon salt
¼ lb sultanas
½ pint warm milk
½ oz yeast
1 teaspoon caster sugar

Method. Sieve the flour and salt into a basin, rub in the butter until free from lumps, and add the sultanas carefully picked. Make a well in the centre. Cream the yeast in a smaller basin with the sugar, add the warm milk, and strain all into the centre of the flour mixture. Mix in a little of the dry mixture from the sides until a thickish batter is formed, then cover the basin and stand it in a warm place for about ¾ hour (a warming drawer or the top of the stove is fine).

Then mix into a soft dough, turn out on a floured board and knead for a few minutes. Put the dough into a greased and floured tin and leave it in a warm place to rise. When it is well risen, bake in a hot oven (1–1½ hours).

MILK BREAKFAST ROLLS

⅓ lb flour
1 oz butter
¼ teaspoon salt
1 teaspoon baking powder
About ¼ pint milk

Method. Sieve the flour, salt and baking powder into a basin, and rub in the butter as lightly as possible. Make a well in the centre and add enough milk to make a softish dough. Mix quickly and lightly, then turn out on to a floured board and form into small rolls. Lay them on a greased and floured baking tin and bake in a quick oven for about 15–20 minutes, but the time all depends on the size of the rolls. When brown and crisp, brush over with a little milk or melted butter to glaze them.

NOTE. Speed is essential for these rolls, and they must be put in a good oven at once.

MORNING ROLLS

4 oz flour
½ oz butter
½ teaspoon baking powder
¼ teaspoon salt
A little milk or milk and water

Method. Mix flour and butter together, rubbing with the fingertips. Mix in salt and baking powder. Make a well in the centre and pour in the milk or milk and water. Mix to a firm paste, which leaves the side of the bowl without sticking. Turn out on to a lightly floured board and shape as desired. Cut into several pieces and shape perhaps into a knot ; or roll out and cut into three and plait together ; or pull round into a horse-shoe shape. Whatever the shape, brush the top with egg or milk, and put on a greased floured tin. Bake in a hot oven for 15 minutes.

WHOLEMEAL ROLLS

¼ lb wholemeal flour
¼ lb ordinary flour
½ teaspoon salt
½ teaspoon caster sugar
1 teaspoon baking powder
1 oz butter
About ¼ pint milk

Method. Put all the dry ingredients into a basin and mix together, then rub in the butter with the finger-tips, and make a well in the centre. Add the milk gradually until you have a softish dough, then turn on to a floured board and knead lightly until free from cracks. Divide into about 6 equal portions and form into little rolls. Lay them on a greased and floured baking tin, brush over with beaten egg or milk and bake in a good oven till brown and well risen (about 20 minutes).

WHOLEMEAL BREAD

3 lbs wholemeal flour
2 dessertspoons salt
2 dessertspoons soft
   brown sugar
1 oz yeast
1 oz margarine
2 pints lukewarm water

Method. Put the yeast, with the sugar, into a teacup and pour over this ¼ pint of the lukewarm water. Leave to "prove" for about 10 minutes or until it bubbles up. Meanwhile light your oven at No. 4 (moderate heat, so you can make it the suitable heat if your oven is electric), and grease three loaf tins with *olive oil* to prevent bread sticking.

Put the flour in a basin, add the salt and rub in the margarine. Stir in the water with a wooden spoon, and lastly the yeast-sugar mixture. Finally, when it is all thoroughly mixed, mix with your hand for about 3 minutes to make sure it is all blended.

Divide the mixture into the three tins, bringing the dough half-way up the tins. Put the tins on the shelf above the oven where it will get a little heat. Cover with a clean cloth and leave for about 1 hour, or until the dough has doubled itself and is at the top of the tins. Put it into the oven and bake for about 1 hour. Sometimes it requires a little longer if the yeast is less spongy than at other times, but test with a skewer to make sure the bread is cooked right through. Turn out on to a wire tray to cool.

NOTE. If you wish to use half quantities, this works perfectly. Just halve everything, except the margarine. Put the whole oz of margarine in, as it will do no harm, and it helps to keep the bread soft. Bake in one oblong loaf tin, and a small round tin, to give a 1-lb loaf and a ½-lb loaf.

A LITTLE vinegar added to stewing prunes greatly improves the flavour and, surprisingly enough, lessens the quantity of sugar required when cooking them.

Bread and Rolls

RAISIN AND WALNUT LOAF

2 cups flour
1 egg
1 cup milk
½ cup brown sugar
2 teaspoons baking powder
½ teaspoon salt
¼ cup shelled walnuts
¼ cup raisins

Method. Mix beaten egg and sugar together thoroughly. Mix dry ingredients together, keeping walnuts apart. Add walnuts (chopped) and flour mixture alternately to the egg and sugar and mix well together. Turn into a well-buttered loaf tin and allow to stand for 20 minutes, to rise a little. Bake in a moderate oven for 1¼ hours. Test with a skewer and leave to cool, then turn on to a wire tray to get cold.

Breakfast and Supper Dishes

I have been asked more for this type of dish than for any other in my large correspondence with listeners to " Shopping Flash," and I have tried to be as varied and as appetising as I can in this section, so I hope there will be new ideas for you here, old ideas remembered again, and plenty of variety to suit all tastes and purses.

BACON AND EGG PIE

¼ lb short crust pastry
¼ lb streaky rashers, cut into smallish pieces
1 large onion
1 oz butter
1 egg for each person
2 oz thinly-sliced mushrooms
¼ lb tomatoes
Pepper

Method. Line a pie plate or a tin with the short crust pastry and cover the bottom with half of the cut-up bacon. Add a layer of onion rings, then a few dots of butter to keep it all moist. Now break over them as many eggs as you have people (one for each) and put a layer of the mushrooms, thinly-sliced, on top, then a layer of sliced skinned tomatoes, and season with pepper. No salt is necessary for bacon will add sufficient salt. Finish with another layer of cut-up bacon. Put the whole thing, pie and plate, inside greaseproof paper, just like a parcel, and bake for 40–50 minutes in a moderate oven. This is delicious hot or cold, and if cold, serve with plain tomato and lettuce or watercress salad, and no dressing at all.

BACON AND FISH ROLLS (from Shetland)

Small fillets of plaice or sole
Bacon slices

Method. Wrap the small fillets in slices of bacon, place in a buttered casserole with a tiny drop of water or stock, and bake in a brisk oven for ½ hour.

AFRICAN BAKED BEANS

¼ lb haricot beans
2 or 3 oz bacon
1 tablespoon golden syrup
Salt/Pepper

Method. Soak the beans overnight to soften, then cook in the usual way until very tender. Cut the bacon in small thin slices. Grease a fireproof dish or a pie-dish and lay the beans and bacon in layers, seasoning them with pepper, and salt if necessary, keeping back a few pieces of the bacon. Pour the syrup over, lay the last pieces of bacon on top, stand for a few minutes to let the syrup trickle through, and bake in a moderate oven for 20–30 minutes.

BACON-EGG-POTATO MERINGUES (from Glasgow)

Strips of bacon
Chopped tomato
Chopped cold potato
Eggs

Method. Line small individual ramekin dishes or patty tins with strips of bacon. Add a layer of chopped tomato and a layer of chopped cooked cold potato. Separate yolks from whites of eggs and drop an egg yolk in each container. Season and bake in a moderate oven until the yolk is set. Beat the egg whites until stiff and cover the egg mixture with this. Return to the oven for a few minutes to harden the meringue. Serve with buttered toast.

BAKED EGGS AND MASH, WITH VEGETABLES

Mashed potatoes
Eggs
Vegetables
Butter

Method. Whip mashed boiled potatoes with hot milk and butter, and make a wide border of them on a large shallow oven dish. Make little hollows with a tablespoon all the way round and brush the whole surface with beaten egg yolk. Into each hollow drop a raw egg and bake in a hot oven for 15 minutes, to brown the potatoes and cook the eggs. Remove from oven, and into the centre of the dish pour cooked diced carrots and peas which have been tossed in a little melted butter after boiling.

BAKED STUFFED TOMATOES

4 to 6 tomatoes
3 tablespoons ham or bacon
2–3 tablespoons bread-crumbs
1 onion
1 oz butter
Seasoning

Method. Chop up the ham or bacon and fry in the butter along with the breadcrumbs and chopped onion. Season to taste. Scoop out the centres of the tomatoes and add to the ham mixture. Refill the centres of the tomatoes with this mixture and bake for 10 minutes in a moderate oven.

BAKED TOMATO OMELETTE

4 oz breadcrumbs
4 onions
1 lb tomatoes
1 oz butter
3 eggs
½ pint milk

Method. Cook the onions and chop finely. Skin and pulp the tomatoes. Mix all these together with the milk, beaten eggs and crumbs. Season to taste and pour into a greased fireproof dish. Sprinkle a few breadcrumbs on top, then dot with tiny pieces of butter and bake in a moderate oven till a nice golden brown.

BEAN AND BACON PIE

1 medium-sized tin of beans in tomato sauce
3 or 4 tomatoes
A few rashers streaky bacon
4–6 oz short crust pastry

Method. Put alternate layers of beans and sauce, skinned and sliced tomatoes, and bacon rashers into a pie-dish. Cover in the usual way with the pastry and bake in a hot oven for about 30 minutes. Serve very hot.

BIRD'S NEST

½ lb streaky bacon rashers
6–8 eggs

Method. Cut the rashers into long strips and twine or plait them together to form a rough strip about 3″ wide, and long enough to wind round your upturned cake tin or soufflé dish. Skewer the ends firmly with an orange stick, stand on a baking sheet, and cook gently in a very moderate oven until the bacon is crisp but not brittle (about ½ hour). Slip the bacon off the tin gently, when it should stand by itself, ready to be filled with the scrambled eggs. *For 6 persons.*

BLOATER or KIPPER TOAST

1 cooked kipper or bloater
1 teaspoon chopped parsley
¼ teaspoon anchovy essence
1 tablespoon top of milk, or white sauce
Seasoning
Hot buttered toast
Grated cheese

Method. Remove all the flesh from a cooked kipper or bloater and chop it very finely. Put it into a saucepan with the chopped parsley, the essence, and a good pinch of pepper. Moisten with a little white sauce or top of the milk, and make all thoroughly hot. Pile the mixture on finger-shaped pieces of hot buttered toast, sprinkle with a little grated cheese and brown in the oven or under the grill. This makes a very tasty little supper dish.

IF YOUR eggs crack in the boiling, try a few drops of vinegar in the water and see how it helps to prevent the contents spilling out through the crack in the shell.

BREAKFAST CORN CAKES

2 corn cobs
1 egg
2 tablespoons s.r. flour
Seasoning

Method. Boil the cobs for 10 minutes. Cut off kernels with a sharp knife and beat into them an egg yolk and the flour and seasoning. Fold in the stiffly beaten egg white, drop in tablespoons on to a greased frying pan, and brown both sides.

BREAKFAST "JOCK" CAKES

2 oz self-raising flour
4 oz medium oatmeal
1 gill milk
Salt/Pepper

Method. Mix the dry ingredients together and gradually add the milk, beating until a fairly thin batter is obtained. Fry spoonfuls in hot fat (preferably bacon fat), turning once. Serve at once with the bacon.

CHEESE FONDUE (simple)

1 oz butter
3 oz grated Parmesan
1½ oz breadcrumbs
A little made mustard
1 teacup milk
2 eggs
Pepper/Salt
Pinch of cayenne

Method. Put the breadcrumbs and butter into a basin and pour the boiling milk over them. Add the cheese (keeping back about 1 dessertspoonful), the yolks of eggs and seasonings, and mix well. Beat the egg whites to a stiff froth and fold in lightly at the last. Pour the mixture into a greased pie-dish or fireproof dish and sprinkle the remainder of the cheese over the top. Bake in a good oven for about 20 minutes, or until nicely browned and well-risen.

CAPRI PANCAKES WITH CHEESE

Pancake batter (based on flour, milk and egg)

FILLING
White sauce
Yolk of egg
4 different kinds of cheese
Tiny piece of raw ham
Chopped parsley
Pinch of nutmeg

Method. Make one big pancake with a batter from flour, milk and one egg, in the usual way. Fry very lightly in butter and place it on a marble slab or any very cool surface to cool.

Now make the filling: Make a good white sauce with melted butter, flour stirred in, pinch of salt, and milk. Let it cool off, then add the yolk of an egg. Add pieces of four different kinds of cheese—Parmesan, Dutch, Gruyère, Cheddar—or any variety you prefer, and a few snippets of any good raw ham, a little chopped parsley and a pinch of grated nutmeg.

Turn this mixture on to the pancake, roll it up, cut into four pieces, and put it into a casserole or pie-dish with melted butter, topped with a little more butter, and grated cheese over the top. Cook in a medium-hot oven for about 15 minutes.

CHEESE AND TOMATO PUDDING

½ lb tomatoes
6 oz grated cheese
3 oz breadcrumbs
1 egg
Milk
Pepper/Salt

Method. Skin and slice tomatoes thickly, and place in layers at the bottom of a greased fireproof dish. Mix cheese and breadcrumbs in a basin, then add egg beaten until frothy, and a gill of milk to make a nice thick batter. Season carefully and pour mixture over the tomatoes. Bake in a moderate oven till well set, puffed up and golden brown. Serve at once.

CHEESE AND TOMATO RAREBIT

¼ lb Cheddar cheese
1 teacup tomato purée
2 tablespoons bread-
    crumbs
A pinch of cayenne
½ teaspoon made mustard
Hot buttered toast

Method. Grate or shred the cheese finely and put into a saucepan with a pinch of cayenne and the mustard. Add the breadcrumbs and 1 teacup fresh or tinned tomatoes rubbed through a fine sieve. Stir over a gentle heat until hot and smooth but do not let it boil. Cut the toast in pieces, arrange on a hot dish and pour the cheese and tomato mixture over.

CHEESE EGGS

Thin slices of cheese
Eggs
Seasoning
Grated cheese

Method. Line a well-buttered fireproof dish with the thin cheese slices. Break the required number of eggs on top and sprinkle with seasoning and grated cheese. Dot with butter and bake in a hot oven for 15 minutes.

CHEESE FRITTERS

1 oz butter
¼ pint water
1½ oz flour
1½ oz grated cheese
1 egg
Pepper/Salt/Cayenne
A little grated celery

Method. Bring water and butter to boil. Add flour all at once. Stir well, and beat till smooth. Season, then add cheese and beaten egg. Drop spoonfuls into hot fat and fry till golden brown. Drain well and serve piping hot.

CHEESE PANCAKES

1 teacup flour
Pinch of salt
1 egg
½ pint milk
2 tablespoons grated
    cheese

Method. Sieve flour and salt into a basin, drop in the egg and a little of the milk. Mix well and beat until lumps disappear. Gradually stir in the rest of the milk. Add most of the cheese, cover the basin and leave to soak for 1 hour. Fry mixture in spoonfuls, in a little fat, as for ordinary pancakes. Sprinkle with grated cheese, roll up and serve piping hot.

CHEESE POTATOES

Potatoes
Milk
Grated cheese
Salt/Pepper

Method. Scrub 1 potato for each person, make a cross slit in the top, and bake in a moderate oven until soft (about 1–1½ hours). With a teaspoon hollow out the centre of the potato, leaving only a thick case. Mash the removed potato and add grated cheese, salt and pepper, and a little milk to make a creamy mixture. Restuff the potato cases and heat through in a hot oven for another 5–10 minutes.

CHEESE PUFFS (1)

1 breakfastcup grated
    cheese
2 egg whites
Salt/Pepper to taste

Method. Beat the egg whites till very stiff, then fold lightly into the grated cheese. Season to taste. Heap up in a fireproof dish, bake for about 10 minutes in a quick oven and serve at once.

NOTE. This is a good way to use the whites of eggs, if the yolks are used in other ways, and they are left over.

CHEESE PUFFS (2)

3 oz Cheddar cheese
1 oz butter
1 hard-boiled egg
Cayenne pepper/Salt
A little made mustard
Flaky pastry
A little beaten egg or milk

Method. Roll out some flaky pastry rather thinly and cut it in pieces about 4" square. Melt the butter in a saucepan, and put in the cheese, finely chopped or grated, the chopped hard-boiled egg and the seasonings. Heat slowly over a gentle heat till thick but do not let it boil. Cool it down, then put a little of this mixture in the centre of each pastry square, and bring two opposite corners together so as to make triangular-shaped puffs, moistening the edges and pressing well together. Mark round the edges with the back of the knife, paint over with beaten egg or milk, and bake in a good oven until nicely browned. Serve hot on a paper doily.

CHICKEN LIVERS WITH BACON

Chicken livers
Butter
Bacon

Some grocers sell chicken livers, and this is a very tasty way of serving them.

Method. Slice the livers and fry lightly in butter. Roll each in a thin slice of bacon and put on a skewer. Cook under the grill till the bacon is as you like it, and serve on fried bread or toast, garnished with parsley.

188

CHEESE TOAST WITH BACON

1 oz butter
1 oz flour
1–1¼ teacups milk
3–4 oz grated cheese
Seasoning
Hot buttered toast
Rolls of bacon

Method. Melt the butter, stir in the flour and cook together for a minute or two. Draw the saucepan off the heat and gradually stir in the milk. Return to the heat, stir till boiling, and cook for 2 or 3 minutes longer. Now add the cheese and season with cayenne, a little mustard and salt if necessary. Let the cheese melt but not boil, and if it is too thick, add a little more milk. Spread the mixture on neat pieces of hot buttered toast and lay some rolls of bacon on the top. A quick easy way to do the bacon rolls is to roll thin slices up, put several on the same skewer, and cook them either on the roasting tin in the oven if you have anything cooking and the heat is on, or under the grill.

CORNISH EGGS

3–4 eggs
2 tomatoes
1 oz dripping
2 tablespoons browned
  breadcrumbs
Seasoning
A little mango chutney

Method. Thickly grease a fireproof dish and dust with a good layer of crumbs. Dip the tomatoes in boiling water and skin them carefully, then slice and lay in the bottom of the dish over the crumbs. Spread on these a little chopped mango chutney. Then break the eggs carefully on top and shake more crumbs over them. Dot with dripping and bake in a quick oven till the eggs are set. Serve very hot.

CURRIED EGG TOAST

3 eggs
1 small onion
1 teaspoon curry powder
¼ pint milk
Salt to taste

Method. Cut up onion and fry in butter till golden brown. Add curry powder and fry for a minute, stirring to prevent sticking, then add milk and salt, stirring well. Beat up the eggs and add them. Cook for 5 minutes, stirring all the time, then serve on thick slices of hot buttered toast. Serve very hot.

EGGS AND CREAMED POTATOES

Cooked potatoes
Grated cheese
Margarine
Eggs
Milk
Salt/Pepper

Method. Take as much creamy mashed potato as you wish, and spread in a greased pie-dish or fireproof dish. Make impressions in the potato with a cup bottom or a tumbler, and drop an egg into each little hollow. Grate cheese thickly over and bake in a moderate oven until the eggs are set (about 15–20 minutes). Serve at once, piping hot.

Breakfast and Supper Dishes

EGG BREAD

1 egg
Slices of stale bread
2 tablespoons milk
Salt/Pepper

Method. Mix beaten egg with milk, salt and pepper. Soak slices of bread in this until they absorb it. Fry in hot fat in pan till golden brown both sides. Serve at once cut in fingers.

CURRIED EGGS

4 hard-boiled eggs
1 oz butter
1 onion
1 dessertspoon curry powder
1 teaspoon flour
Salt/Pepper
1 teaspoon chutney
1 teacup stock
A squeeze of lemon juice
Boiled rice

Method. Melt the butter in a saucepan and add the onion, very thinly sliced. Cook slowly for a minute or two until the onion begins to colour. Then add the curry powder, flour, chutney, pepper and salt, and cook for a few minutes longer, stirring all round about. Pour in the stock and stir until boiling, then let it simmer slowly for 15–20 minutes. Add 2 of the eggs cut in small pieces, and a squeeze of lemon juice. When thoroughly hot put this mixture in the centre of a dish, with a border of boiled dry rice round. Then cut the other 2 eggs in six pieces lengthwise, cut a small piece from the end of each, and stand them round the dish between the curry and the rice.

EGGS WITH SPAGHETTI

¼ lb spaghetti
1 oz butter
A pinch of nutmeg
Seasoning
3 hard-boiled eggs
2 or 3 tablespoons grated cheese
1 teacup white sauce

Method. Cook the spaghetti in boiling water till tender. Drain it well and toss it in the butter, seasoning with pepper, salt and a pinch of nutmeg. Cut the eggs in slices, and make about a teacup of good white sauce. Grease a fireproof dish and arrange the spaghetti and eggs in it in layers. Sprinkle half the grated cheese over, pour the sauce on top, then the rest of the cheese. Dot with butter and brown in a quick oven, or under the grill.

EGGS MORNAY

Hard-boiled eggs as required
White sauce
3 oz grated cheese
2 tablespoons bread-crumbs
Butter

Method. Put halved or whole shelled hard-boiled eggs in a shallow greased dish. Make a good white sauce, and add grated cheese and breadcrumbs fried for a few minutes in butter, and pour this mixture over the eggs. Heat in the oven for about 15–20 minutes. NOTE. If you wish any extras with this dish, you could serve with spinach or grilled mushrooms; or you could mix prawns, shrimps, or flaked haddock with the sauce.

EGGS IN TOMATOES

6 tomatoes
6 eggs
1 dessertspoon chopped
    parsley
1 teaspoon chopped onion
Salt/Pepper
1 oz butter
Some breadcrumbs

Method. Choose large firm round tomatoes, wipe them, cut a slice off the stalk end of each, and scoop out the soft inside. Mix the parsley and onion together with a little pepper and salt, and sprinkle a little of the mixture inside each tomato. Then break a small fresh egg into the centre of each, cover with breadcrumbs, sprinkle with a little melted butter, and bake in a moderate oven for 10–15 minutes, basting once or twice with the butter.

NOTE. As you may not want to waste anything, you may like to heat the soft insides of the tomatoes and pour this round as a sauce when serving.

INDIAN SANDWICH

Rounds of bread
Melted butter
Grated Parmesan
Left-over cooked chicken
    and ham
Chopped pickles
Curry powder
Worcester sauce

Method. Cut some thin rounds of white bread, dip them in melted butter, and then in grated Parmesan. Chop some cooked chicken and ham very finely, mix with some chopped pickles, curry powder and a little Worcester sauce, and put some of this mixture between two rounds of bread. Brown in the oven, or fry in melted butter, turning them over and over until they are heated right through. This is a delicious way of using left-overs.

NOTE. Use this recipe as a basic one and vary the fillings to suit your own taste. Sometimes I put left-over fish in the middle, sometimes a little scrambled egg. You can omit or add any of the pickles, curry powder or sauce as used in the true Indian sandwich, and improvise entirely as you desire. It is fun to experiment with the sort of foods you like and invent your own " family " recipes.

MUSHROOM TOAST

2 oz mushroom stalks
1 oz butter
Salt/Pepper
Lemon juice
1 tablespoon brown or
    tomato sauce
1 egg yolk
1 tablespoon top of milk
6 or 7 rounds of bread

Method. Chop the stalks rather coarsely and cook them slowly in the butter and seasoning for about 10 minutes. Add the sauce, which must be thick and well-flavoured, and the egg yolk and top of milk. Stir over a gentle heat until thoroughly hot, then pile the mixture neatly on small rounds of fried bread or hot buttered toast, and decorate with small sprigs of parsley and tiny pieces of lemon (if available). Serve very hot.

HAM TOAST

3 oz lean cooked ham
1 oz butter
2 eggs
A little made mustard
Pepper
2 slices toast
A little parsley

Method. Trim off all skin and gristle from the ham or bacon, and chop it finely. Put it into a saucepan with the butter and seasonings, and add the two eggs well beaten. Stir over a gentle heat till the mixture begins to thicken but do not let it get hard. Serve on neat pieces of hot buttered toast. Sprinkle with chopped parsley.

This is delicious for breakfast or high tea.

HERRING ROES ON TOAST

Soft roes
Butter
Salt/Pepper
Lemon juice
Hot buttered toast

Method. Wash the roes and dry them, then cut in convenient sized pieces. Heat the butter until very hot, then fry the roe lightly. Season rather highly with pepper, salt and a few drops of lemon juice, and lay on hot buttered toast. Pop them into the oven for a few minutes to heat right through and serve garnished with parsley.

NOTE. A few fried mushrooms, chopped and cooked in butter, can be added to the top of the roes when they are spread on the toast and make a tasty addition. If you do not like mushrooms, you can fry some skinned tomatoes in butter, season well and serve on top of the roes on toast.

NAVARRO EGGS

1 large or 2 small onions
2 large tomatoes
Pepper/Salt
1 teaspoon chopped
   parsley
4 eggs
2 oz butter

Method. Chop up very finely the onions and the tomatoes and mix thoroughly with the seasonings. Melt the butter in a saucepan and add the well-beaten eggs. Stir well and add the onion and tomatoes and cook over a gentle heat, stirring all the time. When cooked, pile on rounds of buttered toast and serve very hot.

MOCK CRAB TART

6 oz short crust pastry
2 tomatoes
¼ lb grated cheese
1 egg
Little milk
Salt/Pepper

Method. Line a pastry tin with the pastry, and then make filling. Beat egg well in a bowl, add milk, cheese, salt, etc., and mix well together. Skin tomatoes, cut up in thin slices and place in bottom of the pastry. Cover with the egg-milk-cheese mixture and bake in a moderate oven for 20 minutes or until firm. Can be eaten hot or cold.

JAMAICA BACON FOR BREAKFAST

4 rashers of bacon
2 bananas
Seasoning
A little flour

This makes a nice change for breakfast when the eggs are scarce or expensive, or if you just want something different in the morning.

Method. Peel the bananas and cut them in two lengthwise. Season with white pepper and salt and roll them lightly in flour. Now fry the bacon rashers and when ready, keep them warm on a hot dish. Put the pieces of banana into the bacon fat and fry them until nicely browned. Place a piece of banana on each piece of bacon and serve all very hot.

KIDNEY TOAST

2 sheep's kidneys
A small piece of butter
½ teaspoon flour
1 teaspoon chopped
    shallot or onion
2 tablespoons stock or
    water
Seasoning
Hot buttered toast
Chopped parsley

Method. Remove skin and fat from the kidneys and chop them fairly finely. Melt a piece of butter the size of a walnut in a small saucepan, put in the chopped shallot or onion and cook for 2 or 3 minutes without browning. Add the kidney and stir it over the heat until cooked (4 or 5 minutes). Sprinkle in the flour, season to taste, and moisten with about 2 tablespoons good stock or gravy, or in the absence of both, water. Cook a minute or two longer, then arrange the mixture neatly on hot buttered toast cut in pieces, and sprinkle lightly with finely-chopped parsley. Serve very hot.

NOTE. The flour can be left out and the yolk of an egg stirred in just before serving. The shallot or onion can be left out if you do not like the flavour, particularly if you are thinking of this dish for breakfast.

HOT CHEESE SANDWICHES

Bread and butter
Grated cheese
Seasoning
1 egg
½ teacup milk
Fat or butter

Method. Spread about six slices of bread with butter, mixing a little mustard or cayenne with the butter before spreading. Trim the crusts off, then sprinkle the slices with as much grated cheese as the butter will take. Press the cheese well on, place two slices together, and then cut in convenient sized pieces. Beat up the egg on a plate and mix it with the milk and a pinch of salt. Dip the sandwiches into this and let them soak for a minute or two, then fry in a little hot fat or butter, browning nicely on both sides. Serve hot, sprinkled with a little grated cheese.

LIVER AND MUSHROOM TOAST

¼ lb calf's liver
½ dozen mushrooms
1 egg
Seasoning
1 oz butter
2 tablespoons gravy or
  top of milk
½ dozen rounds of bread
Chopped parsley

Method. Wash the mushrooms and chop them roughly. Wash and dry the liver and cut it into tiny dice, then fry both liver and mushrooms in the butter until cooked and tender. Season fairly highly with cayenne, salt and a little lemon juice if available. Beat up the egg with the gravy or top of milk, pour into the saucepan and mix all together quickly until the egg begins to thicken. Arrange this mixture neatly on rounds of fried bread or hot buttered toast if preferred, sprinkle with chopped parsley, and reheat in the oven for a few minutes. Serve on a hot dish on a paper doily.

MINCE RISOTTO

½ lb cooked rice
½ lb chopped cooked meat
2 or 3 spring onions
Margarine or dripping
2 tomatoes, sliced
A little hot water
Salt/Pepper to taste
2 rounded tablespoons
  grated cheese

Method. Chop the onion and fry lightly in the melted fat, then add all the other ingredients except the cheese. Cook till moisture is absorbed, then stir in the cheese. When well-mixed and thoroughly hot, pile on a hot dish and serve in a border of green vegetables or mashed potatoes.

POACHED EGGS WITH POTATOES

4 eggs
4 or 5 cooked potatoes
Seasoning
2 tablespoons grated
  cheese
1 tablespoon melted
  butter

Method. Poach the eggs, place them on a hot dish and sprinkle with pepper and salt. Have ready 4 or 5 well-cooked and mealy potatoes, and rub them through a wire sieve or put them through a vegetable presser on top of the eggs. Sprinkle the grated cheese and melted butter over the top and brown quickly in a hot oven or under the grill.

POACHED EGGS WITH CHEESE

4 eggs
1 teacup white sauce
3 tablespoons grated
  cheese
3 tablespoons bread-
  crumbs
Pepper/Salt
A little butter

Method. Butter a fireproof dish and sprinkle it with half the breadcrumbs and the cheese. Poach the eggs and place them on top. Then pour over the sauce, and put the rest of the cheese and breadcrumbs on top. Dot with butter and put in a hot oven to melt the cheese and lightly brown the top.

POTATO CROQUETTES

1 lb cold boiled potatoes
1 dessertspoon chopped
    parsley
Seasonings
Yolk of egg
1 oz butter
Breadcrumbs

Method. Mash the potatoes and rub through a sieve. Melt butter in pan, mix in potatoes and parsley and cook for about 2 minutes. Turn out on to a plate to cool. Form into shapes, coat with egg and breadcrumbs, then fry in deep fat. Drain well on kitchen paper, place a parsley sprig on each and serve.

POTTED CHEESE

6 oz cheese
1 oz butter
Cayenne pepper
A pinch of mace
¼ teaspoon made mustard
1 teaspoon Worcester
    sauce
Clarified butter

Method. Any scraps of good cheese can be used for potting, and it makes a delicious filling for sandwiches and savouries of different kinds. Remove the rind and either chop or grate the pieces, then pound it with the above proportion of butter, or maybe a wee bit more if the cheese is very dry. Sometimes salad oil is used instead of butter. Season rather highly to taste and beat until a smooth paste is formed. Pack into small pots and run some liquid clarified butter over the top to preserve it.

Potted cheese will keep for weeks.

POACHED EGGS WITH SHRIMPS

6 eggs
6 rounds of toast
1 teacup white sauce
Fresh or potted shrimps
Pepper/Salt

Method. Heat the sauce in a small saucepan and add enough potted or shelled fresh shrimps to thicken the sauce well. Poach the eggs and lay them on the hot buttered toast. Season the sauce with pepper and salt to taste and pour it over the eggs. Serve very hot.

RICE SAVOURY

5 oz rice
1 oz cooking fat
1 tablespoon chopped
    onion
1 pint stock
2 oz grated cheese

Method. Melt the fat in a thick saucepan and lightly fry the onion. Add the rice, and fry over a strong heat until it becomes transparent. At this point, pour in the hot stock (preferably white stock, from chicken, veal, etc.), and reduce the heat. Let everything simmer for just over 20 minutes without stirring. At the end of this time, the rice should have absorbed the stock. Remove pan from the heat and stir in the grated cheese, gently, without breaking the rice.

A green salad makes a nice accompaniment to this dish.

PORRIDGE

¼ lb oatmeal (medium)
1½ pints water
Salt to taste

Method. Put the water on to boil. When boiling, sprinkle in the oatmeal, stirring all the time with a wooden spoon. Keep stirring till the porridge is perfectly smooth and beginning to thicken. Add salt to taste (English palates may prefer it to be sweetened with sugar or syrup). Lower the heat and let the porridge simmer gently till the oatmeal is soft and swollen (½–¾ hour). Give it a stir occasionally as it simmers, to prevent sticking, and if it gets too thick, add a little more boiling water. Serve with milk, or if you can spare it, cream.

NOTE. If you want to shorten the cooking time, you can leave the oatmeal soaking in the water overnight.

MOULDED EGGS

5 eggs
2 oz cooked ham
1 tablespoon chopped parsley
Seasoning
Butter
1 or 2 tablespoons top of milk
5 pieces hot buttered toast

Method. Take five moulds or small cake tins and grease them carefully with butter. Chop the ham finely, mix with the chopped parsley, and coat the moulds carefully with this mixture. Break a fresh egg into each, season with pepper and salt, pour about a teaspoon top of milk over each, and dot with a small piece of butter. Put the moulds in a tin with hot water to reach halfway up the sides and poach in the oven till set. Turn the eggs on to the hot toast, put a sprig of parsley on top, and serve.

NOTE. Lightly browned breadcrumbs can be used instead of the ham and parsley, and, if you prefer it, you can spread the toast with a little savoury paste.

POACHED EGGS WITH MINCED LEFT-OVERS

4 eggs
4 rounds hot toast
¼ lb cooked chicken or veal
2 oz cooked ham or tongue
2 tablespoons gravy
Seasoning
Chopped parsley

Method. Mince the meat and ham or tongue very finely and heat it in a small saucepan with the gravy to moisten it. Season to taste and spread neatly on the rounds of hot buttered toast. Poach the eggs and lay one on top of each round and sprinkle with a little finely-chopped parsley. Serve at once and very hot.

TO MAKE scrambled eggs go a bit further, you can always add cooked green peas, and diced carrots and beans, not to mention a little chopped chive or grated raw onion.

RICE-MEAT LEFT-OVERS

1 oz margarine
Rice
Onion
Tomato
Curry powder, if liked
Diced meat, sausage,
    shrimps, or chicken

Method. Melt margarine, or a little olive oil if preferred, in a saucepan. Put in sliced onion and cook till soft, then add whatever quantity of Patna rice you wish and cook until it is clear, then a little curry powder if you wish. Add your sliced tomato, and your left-over meat, shrimps, chicken, etc., and 2 cups of cold water for every cup of rice. Cook until it is all tender and well-blended.

This makes a very economical dish for as many as you have to cater for, depending on the amount of rice used.

SARDINE SAVOURIES (1)

7 or 8 sardines
½ oz butter
1 shallot or small onion
¼ teacup white sauce
1 oz grated Parmesan
1 tablespoon bread-
    crumbs
Seasoning
7 or 8 pieces fried bread

Method. Chop the shallot or onion and cook for a few minutes in the melted butter, but do not let it brown. Then add the white sauce, cheese and seasonings, and mix thoroughly. Turn on to a plate to cool. Choose small sardines, drain them from their oil and trim off the tails. Prepare some fingers of fried bread and spread them with some of the above mixture. Lay a sardine on top of each and cover with more of the mixture. Sprinkle with breadcrumbs and place in a hot oven long enough to warm through. Serve at once, sprinkled with parsley.

SARDINE SAVOURIES (2)

3 or 4 sardines
1 egg
1 dessertspoon butter
1 or 2 tablespoons milk
¼ teaspoon anchovy
    essence
Seasoning
Buttered toast
Chopped parsley

Method. Dip the sardines in hot water, which will loosen the skins, then scrape off skins, take out bone, and chop fairly finely. (You can use any small broken pieces of sardine for this dish.) Put butter and milk into a saucepan and heat gently, then add the egg without beating it, the minced sardine and seasoning, and stir over the fire until the mixture begins to thicken. Draw the pan to the side, put the lid on, and let the last few moments of cooking take place without any heat underneath. Give a final stir and pile on fingers of buttered toast, sprinkle with chopped parsley and serve at once.

HORSERADISH sauce, added to scrambled egg or spread on the toast on which poached eggs are placed, will give an excellent flavour. Warm the sauce a little before using.

SARDINE CHEESECAKE

6 oz plain flour
2 oz margarine
2 oz cooking fat
4 oz grated Cheddar
   cheese
Salt/Pepper

FILLING

2 tins small sardines
2 oz grated Cheddar
   cheese

Method. Sieve flour with salt and pepper and rub in fats. Mix in the grated cheese, and bind with a little cold water to a nice pliable consistency. Place a flan ring on a baking sheet. Roll out the cheese pastry and fit it into the ring, pressing it well down on to the baking sheet and against the sides of the ring. Trim off the edges neatly. If you have no flan ring, use an ordinary straight-sided tart tin, but be careful when removing pastry case.

Bake in a hot oven for 10 minutes, then lower the heat to moderate for another 10 minutes. Slip off the flan ring and continue baking for another 5 minutes. Leave pastry case on baking tin until cold and then transfer it to a serving plate.

For the filling, drain oil from the sardines and arrange them in a circle in the pastry case, tails to centre. Sprinkle grated cheese in the centre and round outer edges of flan. Place a little chopped tomato, cucumber or olives on top, to decorate, if you wish.

SAUSAGE ROLLS

Sausages
Rough puff pastry

Method. Skin the sausages. Divide each into two and roll in hands which have been dipped in seasoned flour. Place a piece in the centre of an oblong of rough puff pastry cut to size. Fold over. Seal the edges with cold water and pinch together. Score the top twice with the knife, and paint top with milk or egg. Bake for 10 minutes in a hot oven, then 35 minutes in a cooler oven. Serve at once if possible. NOTE. These are also excellent eaten cold.

SAVOURY LAYER CASSEROLE

(1) Sliced apple
   Tomatoes
   Bacon
   Sausages
   Mashed potatoes

(2) Sliced apple
   Tomatoes
   Bacon
   Baked beans
   Breadcrumbs

Method. Grease a casserole and place in it, either the ingredients which are listed in group (1) or those listed in group (2). For the best results, it is advisable to place them in the dish in the order in which they are written. This means that if you are using group (1) the top layer will be mashed potatoes, and if you are using group (2) the top layer will be breadcrumbs. Put into a quick oven and bake for ½ hour.

SEA FOOD PANCAKES

BATTER
4 oz flour
½ teaspoon salt
1½ breakfastcups milk
2 eggs
1 teaspoon melted butter

FILLING
1 oz butter
1 oz flour
½ cup fish stock
½ cup hot milk
½ lb cooked white fish
2 oz mushrooms
Seasoning

Method. Make batter as follows : Sift flour and salt in basin. Make a hollow in centre and drop in eggs. Gradually add milk and then melted butter, drawing in flour from sides and beating. Spread batter thinly over the whole surface of a smooth, greased hot pan or girdle, and when just firm toss or turn with a fish slice. The pan must be hot enough to cook the pancakes quickly, otherwise they will be tough. Do not fold, but keep them hot on a plate or tin over a pan of boiling water.

Now make the filling as follows : Make a rich white sauce in the usual way, with butter and flour, mixed to a roux. Add slowly, stirring all the time, fish stock and hot milk and cook till thick and smooth. Now add up to ½ lb of any cooked white fish (also a poached scallop if you like), and 2 oz of washed and lightly fried mushrooms. Mix all together, season well, and heat through until all is piping hot.

To serve, place pancake on each warmed plate. Put a good spoonful of the creamed fish in the centre of each pancake and fold in three. Put extra creamed fish at the side. Sprinkle with paprika and garnish with chunks of fresh lemon, if available.

SCOTS POTATO FRITTERS

½ dozen large potatoes
2 eggs
1 tablespoon bread-
  crumbs
1 tablespoon ham (lean)
Dripping

Method. Parboil the potatoes, and cut them in thick slices (about ¼″). Beat up the eggs with the finely-grated breadcrumbs and grated ham, dip each slice of potato in this mixture and fry in plenty of good hot dripping.

NOTE. These are excellent by themselves, or for serving with any kind of fried meat.

SCOTCH EGGS (1)

3 hard-boiled eggs
4 oz sausage meat
1 gill stock
1 oz butter
1 oz flour
Seasoning
Little extra flour
Breadcrumbs
Beaten egg

Method. Prepare panada consisting of melted butter into which flour, stock and seasoning has been stirred. Place this panada on plate and allow to cool. Mix with sausage meat.

Roll egg in flour, having shelled it first of course, then cover it with the sausage meat mixture. When covered, roll in flour, then beaten egg and bread-crumbs, and fry in deep fat. Serve in halves.

SCOTCH EGGS (2)

4 hard-boiled eggs
⅓ lb pork sausage meat
A little flour
Egg
Breadcrumbs

Method. Shell the eggs and roll them in a little flour, keeping them whole. Season the sausage meat with a little more pepper and salt and divide it into four equal portions. Wrap one portion round each egg, keeping the shape of the egg as much as possible, and using a little flour to prevent it sticking to the hands. Then coat the eggs with beaten egg and fine white breadcrumbs, pressing the crumbs well on. Lower them into boiling fat, and cook fairly slowly until a golden brown colour.

NOTE. Unless the sausage coating is fairly thin and the eggs cooked slowly once they are in the boiling fat, the pork will not cook sufficiently, and as you know, to be wholesome, pork must be thoroughly cooked through and through.

SKIRLY

2 oz butter
1 large sliced onion
1 rasher of bacon
1 piece of liver
1 peeled tomato
2 tablespoons oatmeal
2 dessertspoons stock

Method. Fry the onions slowly in the butter. When three parts cooked, add bacon cut into small pieces and liver, thinly sliced. When browned, add diced tomato and oatmeal. Mix together with the stock and cook for a few minutes longer. *For 2 persons.*

SPANISH OMELETTE

Eggs as required
1 small teaspoon cold
    water to each egg
Cooked diced potatoes, or
    French beans or globe
    artichokes, diced
Seasoning

Method. Fry the diced vegetables in butter, beat up the eggs with the water and seasoning as required and cook it on top of the vegetables. Turn it like a pancake and cook on the other side.

Can be eaten hot as usual, or cold for a picnic dish.

SPAGHETTI A L'ITALIENNE

3 oz spaghetti
1 teacup tomato sauce or
    purée
Warm water
1 oz butter
2 or 3 oz grated cheese
Seasoning

Method. Break the spaghetti in pieces and put into a saucepan with enough warm water to cover. Add the butter and simmer slowly till quite tender, adding more water if necessary. When cooked and the water nearly all absorbed, add the tomato sauce or purée and season to taste. Cook a few minutes longer, adding grated cheese at the last. Serve with toast.

SAVOURY OMELETTE

1 oz bacon fat
2 eggs
1 teaspoon chopped
    parsley
Little cooked shallot
Pepper/Salt
Grated ham

Method. Beat egg yolks well, then mix into them the ham, parsley, shallot and season well. Whip the whites stiffly and fold carefully into the mixture. Have the fat with a faint blue smoke rising, then turn the gas down to *low*, pour in the mixture and stir gently with a spoon two or three times. As soon as the omelette shows signs of setting, fold with a palette knife towards the handle of the pan. When firm underneath, tilt the pan slightly to spread any soft mixture against the heat. Serve *at once*.

SIMPLE PALIATTI

Small tin spaghetti in
    tomato sauce
2 oz rice
1 oz margarine
1 onion, chopped
1 tomato, sliced

Method. Melt margarine in a saucepan and lightly fry the onion and tomato. Add the washed rice and go on stirring until all the fat is absorbed. Add a small cupful of water and simmer until the rice is cooked. More water may be added if necessary. When rice is cooked, stir in the spaghetti, and heat all through thoroughly. Pile on hot buttered toast and serve.

STEAMED EGG SAVOURIES

Eggs as required
Chopped ham
Grated cheese

Method. Grease some cups or moulds well with butter and into each break one egg. Strew chopped ham on top and cover with grated cheese. Place in a pan of boiling water and allow to steam for 15–20 minutes, or until the eggs are set and the cheese cooked.

TONGUE RAMEKINS

4 or 5 oz cooked tongue
2 eggs
2 tablespoons milk
½ teaspoon made mustard
½ teaspoon chopped
    shallot or onion

Method. Put 2 egg yolks and 1 egg white into a basin with the mustard and milk and beat until light and frothy, then add the finely-chopped tongue and shallot or onion, and mix all together. Grease some little fireproof or paper ramekin cases, three parts fill them with the mixture, stand them on a tin and bake in a moderate oven until set. Have ready the remaining egg white beaten to a stiff froth, pile a little on the top of each ramekin and return to a cool oven until the white is set and lightly browned. Serve hot, garnished with a little chopped parsley.

WELSH RAREBIT

¼ lb Cheddar cheese
2 tablespoons milk
Pinch of cayenne
¼ teaspoon made mustard
A little butter
Hot buttered toast

Method. Grate or shred the cheese and put it in a saucepan with the milk and seasonings. Stir over a gentle heat till the mixture is perfectly smooth and beginning to thicken. Butter the toast, cut into neat pieces, place on a hot dish and pour the cheese mixture over. Everything must be very hot, and it should be served at once because the cheese quickly hardens.

NOTE. If you can spare them, one or two egg yolks can be added just before serving. This makes a richer mixture and prevents the cheese hardening so quickly. A mild-flavoured cheese is best for rarebit. Or you can poach an egg for each person and serve on top of the rarebit. This makes it more of a meal, and is a great favourite in canteens frequented by actors when we want something quick and nourishing.

SWISS SUPPER BREAD

Bread
2 eggs
Cheese

Method. Cut several thick slices of bread into rounds or strips. Beat the eggs in a basin and add enough grated cheese to make a thick spreading consistency. The amount of cheese will depend on the size of the eggs. Spread the mixture generously on to one side of the bread, then fry the pieces rapidly, browning first the plain side and then the cheese-egg side. Should be eaten immediately while crisp and hot. Parsley can be added to the mixture, if desired.

Preserves and Wines

I have been making jams and jellies since I was a little girl, and hardly ever buy jam of any kind. Once you start to make your own preserves, you will find it hard to be satisfied with anything else. Home-made jams and jellies can turn the plainest tea into a feast. The chutneys enhance the dullest cold meat. I hope you will be bold and try some of the home-made wines.

JAMS, JELLIES AND MARMALADE

DRIED APRICOT JAM

2 lbs dried apricots
5 pints cold water
7 lbs preserving sugar
4 lemons
A few shredded almonds

Method. Wash the apricots and put them into a large basin, covering them with the water, and let them soak for 3 days. Then put water and fruit into a preserving pan with the sugar, and add the grated lemon rind and the strained juice. Bring carefully and slowly to the boil and then boil for 20–30 minutes or until the jam will set.

NOTE. I always add a few shredded almonds to this mixture as it gives a delicious "extra." Three days may seem a very long time to soak the fruit, but I have found this method the best of all the recipes I have tried and it really makes the fruit soft and tender when cooked. In very hot weather examine for mould.

APPLE JELLY

4–6 lbs cooking apples
1–2 oz root ginger
Sugar to equal juice
Water to cover

Method. Cut up the apples, just cover with water, and over the side of the pan hang a little bag containing the root ginger. Bring to the boil, and simmer gently for 1 hour until fruit is quite soft and pulpy. Strain through a jelly bag and leave until cold. To every pint of juice allow a pound of sugar. Bring to the boil and cook rapidly until the jelly sets when tested. If you wish, you can also add the juice of a lemon in the final boiling for extra setting qualities, and you can put the rind in with the first boiling. NOTE. Keep skins on apples, and use cores too.

APRICOT AND PINEAPPLE JAM

1 lb dried apricots
2 8 oz tins or 1 15 oz
  tin pineapple
3 lbs sugar
3 pints water

Method. Cut apricots and pineapple finely. Cover with water and juice and soak for 24 hours. Put in buttered pan and bring gently to the boil. Boil for 20 minutes. Add warmed sugar and boil for 8–10 minutes. Test for setting, pot and cover.

BLACKBERRY AND APPLE JELLY

2 lbs apples
2 lbs blackberries
Water to cover
Sugar

Method. Wash the apples, cut them up, keeping skin on and cores and everything, and put them in a jelly pan. Add the cleaned, washed blackberries, and barely cover all with cold water. Bring to the boil and simmer for 1 hour, crushing fruit with back of wooden spoon or potato masher to extract all the juice. Strain through a jelly bag overnight. Next day, allow ¾ lb sugar to each pint of juice. Bring the juice to the boil, then add the warmed sugar, stirring all the time after sugar is added. Boil briskly and start testing after 15 minutes. When a few drops jell in a saucer, it is ready. Pot and cover as usual.

BLACKCURRANT JAM (1)

3½ lbs blackcurrants
  (washed and picked)
4 pints water
7 lbs sugar
Small piece unsalted
  butter

Method. Put fruit, water (and butter if used), in large jelly pan, bring slowly to boil, and simmer until fruit is really soft (about ½ hour). The butter is excellent for keeping the fruit soft and juicy. Add sugar, bring slowly to boil again and boil rapidly for about 15 minutes, or until it sets when tested. Pot and cover.

BLACKCURRANT JAM (2)

To 3 lbs blackcurrants allow 1 pint rhubarb juice and 4 lbs sugar

Method. Rhubarb juice is made by cutting rhubarb into small pieces (do not peel it, as the skin helps to give a nice pink colour), and putting into a large jar with just enough water to moisten the bottom. Cover the jar and steam in a saucepan of water or cook in the oven till you have drawn out all the juice. Then strain through a sieve or jelly bag. This has a very delicate flavour and was often used in the old days instead of water.

The blackcurrants should be as ripe as possible. Strip them from the stalks, wash them, put into a preserving pan with the correct proportion of rhubarb juice, bring slowly to the boil and let the currants simmer slowly for 15 minutes. Warm the sugar and add it to the currants, stirring constantly now, and boil for 20–30 minutes or until the jam will set when tested.

NOTE. Red currant juice can be used instead of rhubarb, but this will give more of its own flavour than the rhubarb which, as I have said, is very delicate.

ECONOMICAL BLACKCURRANT JAM (3) (from Wales)

2 lbs blackcurrants
5 lbs rhubarb
7 lbs granulated sugar

Method. Cover the chopped, cleaned rhubarb with 5 lbs of sugar, stir and leave for 3 days, stirring each day for a minute or two.

Add the blackcurrants and the other 2 lbs of sugar and stir well, then bring all slowly to the boil in preserving pan and start testing after 20 minutes. When set, pot and cover as usual.

NOTE. There is no taste of rhubarb in this mixture, and it is very economical when the blackcurrants are highly priced.

DAMSON JAM (1)

3 lbs damsons
3 lbs sugar
1 pint water

Method. Wash the fruit, add the water and bring slowly to the boil in a preserving pan. Simmer until the damsons are cooked and soft. Add the sugar, stir till dissolved and bring slowly to the boil. Boil very quickly and remove the stones as they rise to the top. Test for setting. Pot and cover while hot.

DAMSON JAM (2)

Damsons
¾ lb preserving sugar to
    each lb of fruit

Method. Remove the stalks from the damsons, then wash them, and put a slit in the side of many of them so that the stones will slide out easily when cooked. Put them into a preserving pan and let them stand by the fire or over a very gentle heat till the juice begins to flow. Now bring the fruit to the boil and add the proper proportion of warmed sugar. Boil until the liquid will set readily when tested, and remove as many of the stones as possible during the cooking. Pot and cover as usual.

DAMSON AND APPLE JAM

8 lbs damsons
2 pints apple juice
10 lbs sugar
Water to cover

Method. Make the apple juice by boiling quartered, unpeeled apples in enough water to cover them, cooking for 1 hour, and dripping through a jelly bag overnight. Wash the damsons, and stone as many as possible. A few of the stones can be cracked and the kernels blanched, tied in muslin and used for flavouring, but be sure you do not let any escape into the jam for they are too bitter to eat.

Put the prepared damsons into the preserving pan with the proper proportion of sugar and apple juice and stir carefully until boiling. If any more stones bob to the surface, remove as many as you can. Boil the jam for 20 minutes or until it sets when tested. Pot and cover as usual.

BLACKBERRY AND APPLE PRESERVE

Equal quantities of apples
    and blackberries
1 lb sugar to 1 lb pulp
A little water

Method. Wash the apples, cut them in slices without removing the skins and cores. Pick the blackberries carefully, throwing away any that are unsound. Put both fruits into the preserving pan with just enough water to keep them from burning and cook until reduced to a pulp, stirring frequently. Rub through a hair sieve, leaving only skins and seeds. Return the sieved pulp to a clean preserving pan with sugar in the proportion given and stir constantly for 20 minutes or so until it is firm. If this is put in small pots it can be turned out in the shape when you want it, and it is excellent served with blancmange or with cream.

WHEN making scrambled eggs, a pinch of baking powder helps to make them lighter and go further.

BLACKBERRY or BRAMBLE JELLY

Blackberries
Preserving sugar
Water to cover

Method. Pick and look over the berries carefully, then put them into a preserving pan and nearly cover them with cold water. Bring slowly to the boil and bruise them well with a wooden spoon to get out all the juice. Then let them boil slowly for $\frac{3}{4}$–1 hour, bruising them down again occasionally, until you are sure all the juice has run out. Strain through a jelly bag and let it drip all night. Measure the juice, return it to a clean preserving pan and bring to the boil. Boil for 15 minutes, then add sugar, allowing $\frac{3}{4}$ lb to each pint of juice, and boil both together until the jelly sets. Pot in the usual way.

CRAB APPLE JELLY

8 lbs crab apples
4 quarts water
Preserving sugar

Method. Wash the apples, cut them in two and put them in a preserving pan with the water. Bring to the boil and cook slowly until the apples are soft and broken. Strain all night through a jelly bag, and next day measure the juice and return it to the preserving pan with 1 lb of warmed sugar to each pint. Boil together till the jelly will set when tested, then pot and cover in the usual way.

GOOSEBERRY AND RED CURRANT JAM

3 lbs red gooseberries
1 gill red currant juice
3$\frac{1}{4}$ lbs sugar

Method. To obtain the red currant juice, stalk the currants and put them in a double saucepan or into a jar placed in a saucepan of boiling water and let them cook till all the juice is drawn out. Then strain either through a jelly bag or a hair sieve, letting the juice drip all night.

Top and tail the gooseberries, wash them thoroughly, and put them into a preserving pan with the red currant juice. Heat slowly and when boiling, cook for 15 minutes. Add the warmed sugar gradually, and boil again till the jam will set when tested, stirring constantly. Pot and cover as usual.

GOOSEBERRY JAM (1)

4 lbs green gooseberries
6 teacups water
7 lbs sugar

Method. Cut gooseberries up, having topped and tailed them. Boil fruit and water for 1 hour. Add sugar and boil for 1 minute. Test, pot and cover.

GOOSEBERRY JAM (2)

4 lbs green gooseberries
4 lbs preserving sugar
¼ pint cold water

Method. Choose fresh young gooseberries before the skins are too hard. Top and tail them and wash them. Put the sugar into a preserving pan with the water, let it dissolve, then bring to the boil. Add the gooseberries and boil all together gently until the jam will set readily when tested. Pot and cover as usual.

GREEN GOOSEBERRY JELLY

Green gooseberries
1 lb preserving sugar to
  each pint juice
Water to cover

Method. Choose gooseberries before they are ripe. Top and tail them and wash them thoroughly. Put into a preserving pan and just cover them with cold water. Bring to the boil and simmer until they are well broken, stirring occasionally. Strain through a jelly bag overnight.

Next day measure the juice and return it to a clean preserving pan. Add 1 lb of sugar to each pint of juice, stir until the sugar is melted, then boil 15–20 minutes, stirring occasionally, until it sets when tested. Skim well and pot and cover as usual.

LEMON CURD

6 oz loaf sugar
2 oz unsalted butter or
  margarine
2 lemons
2 eggs

Method. Grate the lemon rinds and pour lemon juice and rinds over the sugar. Leave to soak for a few minutes. Then melt the butter or margarine in a jar or pan standing inside a larger pan of boiling water, on the stove. Add the sugar-lemon mixture to the melted fat, then add the eggs which have been thoroughly beaten until light and frothy. Stir all together over a slow heat with a wooden spoon until it thickens. Leave to get cold. Do not make larger quantities, as this does not store well.

MEDLAR JELLY

Medlars as required
Water to cover
¾ lb preserving sugar to
  every pint of liquor

Method. Wash ripe medlars, put them in a pan and cover them with water. Simmer very slowly until they become a pulp. Strain overnight through a jelly bag and next day put into a clean preserving pan, allowing ¾ lb preserving sugar to every pint of juice. Bring to the boil and boil rapidly until it sets when tested on a cold saucer. Pot and cover in the usual way.

LOGANBERRY JELLY

Loganberries
Water
Preserving sugar

Method. Take the stalks off the loganberries and put them into a preserving pan with just enough water to keep them from burning. Cook them over a very gentle heat until reduced to a pulp, stirring frequently. Strain through a jelly bag and, when every drop of juice has run out, measure it and return to a clean preserving pan. Add 1 lb of sugar to every pint of juice and stand the pan in a warm place till the sugar is melted. Then bring to the boil, skim if necessary and boil for 20 minutes or till the jelly sets when tested. Pot and cover in the usual way.

PLUM JAM (1)

6 lbs plums
½ pint water
4½ lbs sugar

Method. Wash the plums and stone them, if liked (or skim stones from the surface when jam is boiling). Put the fruit in preserving pan with the water and cook slowly until the skins are tender (about 45 minutes). Add the warmed sugar, stir till dissolved, bring slowly to the boil, then boil briskly for 10 minutes or till jam sets when tested. Let it cool for 10 minutes to prevent plums from rising in the jam jars, stir up again, then pot and cover in the usual way.

PLUM JAM (2)

Plums
Preserving sugar

Method. Wipe the plums or wash them, then weigh them and allow ¾–1 lb sugar according to the acidity of the fruit. Score the plums across or, if time permits, cut them in halves and take out the stones. Spread the plums and sugar on a large dish in layers and let them stand overnight. Turn all into a preserving pan, bring slowly to the boil and boil steadily, stirring occasionally until the jam will set when tested. All the stones which rise to the surface should be removed if this has not already been done. If you like, you can crack a few of the stones, blanch the kernels and add them to the jam to improve the flavour. Pot and cover in the usual way.

SALT and vinegar make cucumber tough and indigestible. When making cucumber sandwiches, put the salt on the bread and butter, not on the cucumber. But, paradoxically, if you cover the sliced cucumber with salt and leave for an hour or so before making the sandwiches, then pour off all the liquid which has been drawn out and rinse off the cucumber, you will make it easier to digest.

QUINCE JELLY

Quinces
1 lb sugar to 1 pint
    quince juice
Water

Method. Peel, quarter and core the quinces. Weigh the pieces and put them into a preserving pan with 2 teacups water to each pound of fruit. Simmer slowly till the fruit is quite soft, but do not let it get too pulpy or the jelly will not be clear. Strain through a hair sieve or a jelly bag without pressing the pulp. Measure the juice and put it into a clean preserving pan with the given proportion of sugar. Bring slowly to the boil and boil quickly for 15–20 minutes. Pot and cover as usual, after testing for setting.

RASPBERRY AND RED CURRANT JAM

Raspberries
To 1 lb raspberries allow
  1 gill red currant
  juice and 1¼ lbs sugar

Method. Make the red currant juice as instructed for the gooseberry and red currant jam.

Pick the raspberries, removing the stalks, then weigh them and put into a preserving pan with red currant juice. Bring to the boil and boil for 10 minutes, then add the sugar by degrees and boil till the jam will set, stirring almost constantly. Pot and cover as usual.

RED CURRANT JELLY

6 lbs red currants
2 pints water
Sugar

Method. Wash the currants, removing the stalks, and put in preserving pan with the water. Simmer until tender (40–45 minutes). Strain through a jelly-bag and leave to drip overnight. Allow 1 lb sugar to each pint of juice. Bring the juice to the boil, add the warmed sugar and stir till this is slowly dissolved, then boil briskly for 10 minutes, or till jelly sets when tested. Usually 10 minutes is sufficient, as this jelly sets readily.

RHUBARB AND GOOSEBERRY JAM

4 lbs dark red rhubarb
4 lbs green gooseberries
6 lbs preserving sugar
Grated rind of 1 lemon
¼ pint water

Method. Cut washed rhubarb into small chunks, wash gooseberries, top and tail them, and put the prepared fruit into preserving pan with the water. Simmer very gently until both rhubarb and berries are tender, then stir in the warmed sugar and lemon peel. Bring slowly to the boil, then boil quickly until a little of the jam tested on a saucer will set.

RHUBARB AND GINGER JAM

7 lbs rhubarb
4 oz crystallised ginger
7 lbs preserving sugar

Method. Wash and cut up the rhubarb into inch length pieces. Soak in a basin in layers with cut-up ginger and the sugar for 24 hours. Turn into preserving pan, bring slowly to the boil (stirring all the time) and boil briskly for 30–35 minutes. Test, skim, pot and cover.

STRAWBERRY JAM

4 lbs strawberries
4 lbs sugar
4 small lemons

Method. Add the strained juice of the lemons to the strawberries and bring very gently to boiling point, with as little heat as possible under the pan. Boil for 20 minutes. Add sugar, 1 lb at a time, stirring all the time, letting it dissolve slowly and boil for 10 minutes or until set. Pot and cover.

VEGETABLE MARROW JAM

6 lbs marrow
6 lbs preserving sugar
2 oz whole ginger
3 lemons
¼ teaspoon cayenne

Not many people make this jam, but we used to have an Irish neighbour who made it, and we begged "pieces" spread with it when we were children, we found it so unusual, so if you would like to try it here it is.

Method. Cut the peeled, seeded marrow into pieces the size of a walnut. Cover with sugar and leave overnight in a china or earthenware dish. Put into a preserving pan next day with the juice of the lemons, and the rind, ginger and pepper tied loosely in a muslin bag. Add no water. Boil steadily for about 1 hour. When ready, it should look like preserved ginger. Pour into pots and cover in the usual way.

ORANGE JELLY MARMALADE

3½ lbs bitter oranges
4 lemons
8 lbs preserving sugar
7 pints water

Method. Grate the orange and lemon rinds and keep them aside. Cut up the remainder of the fruit and add to the water, with the pips. Bring slowly to the boil and boil for ½ hour or until skins are very soft. Put into a jelly bag and strain over a bowl containing the rinds. Leave dripping overnight.

Next day put the jelly and rinds on to boil and, when almost at boiling point add the sugar and bring slowly to the boil again. Boil fast for 7 minutes (or up to 10 minutes). Test for setting, pot and cover.

MIXED FRUIT MARMALADE

1 grapefruit
1 sweet orange
1 lemon
4 pints water
5 lbs sugar

Method. Wash fruit and put all through the mincer, keeping any stones separate in a little of the measured water. Boil pulp and water for 20–30 minutes, adding the water in which stones steeped, then stand for 24 hours. Boil again, with sugar added, until set (about ¾–1 hour). Pot and cover as usual.

TANGERINE MARMALADE

3 lbs tangerines
1 lemon
1 grapefruit
4 quarts water
4–5 lbs preserving sugar

Method. Wash the fruit, remove tangerine rinds and shred, then tie those shreds in muslin. Roughly cut up the tangerines and the other fruit complete with their rinds. Put into a large basin covered with the measured water and soak overnight. Turn into preserving pan and simmer for about 2 hours till the quantity is reduced by a third. Remove bag with tangerine rinds after 45 minutes, but keep them aside. Strain the fruit through a jelly-bag, measure and add 1 lb sugar to each pint of juice. Bring to the boil, stirring well and boil briskly for 20–30 minutes. Rinse tangerine shreds and add them to the pan 5 minutes before dishing. Cool marmalade for 10 minutes, stir up again, pot and cover.

THICK MARMALADE

4 lbs bitter oranges
4 sweet oranges
2 lemons
10 pints water
Sugar

Method. Quarter the oranges and lemons and remove the pips. Soak the pips in water overnight, then strain. Put all the fruit through the mincer, with the exception of the sweet orange skins, which are not used, and soak in a basin with the water overnight.

Next day put the mixture into a preserving pan, add the strained pip water and boil for 1½–2 hours, keeping the quantity of liquid to two-thirds or more. Turn into a basin and again leave overnight.

Now measure, and to every pint of pulp and juice, allow 1½ lbs sugar. (The quantity should be about 8 pints of pulp and juice and 12 lbs sugar.) Boil for about 30 minutes. Test, and when ready, cool slightly. Pot and cover when cold.

This makes about 15 lb pots of marmalade.

TO PREVENT jam from mildew, dip rounds of greaseproof paper in the white of an egg. Place these circles on top of the jam and seal in the usual way.

CHUTNEY AND PICKLES

APPLE CHUTNEY

4 large cooking apples
½ lb large muscatels
½ lb ordinary raisins
1 large onion, grated
1 lb demerara sugar
½ pint brown malt vinegar
1 teaspoon salt
2 teaspoons mixed spices

Method. Chop the apples finely into a large bowl and over them pour the sugar. Add the grated onion, raisins, chopped muscatels, salt and spices, and cover this mixture with the vinegar. Put a plate on top and leave until next day. Bring to the boil and cook gently for 20 minutes. Bottle and cover.

This will keep for months.

PICKLED RED CABBAGE

2 firm red cabbages
Salt
1 quart brown vinegar
½ oz peppercorns
½ oz allspice
¼ oz whole ginger
¼ oz cloves
2 or 3 drops cochineal

Method. Remove any decayed and outside leaves from the cabbages. Cut in quarters and remove all the hard stalk from the centre. Then take each quarter and with a sharp knife cut across in very fine shreds. Spread this on a large dish, sprinkling a good handful of fine salt over each layer. Place another dish on top and let this stand for two days. Strain off the liquid, shake the cabbage dry in a salad basket or a strong cloth and put it into stone or earthenware jars. Put the vinegar into a saucepan, add to it the spices tied in muslin, and boil together for a few minutes to let the flavours become really absorbed in the vinegar. Add the colouring, cool and strain. Pour this spiced vinegar over the cabbage, using enough to cover it, and cover the jars tightly.

This pickle will be ready for use in 2 or 3 days. It will keep for several months but it loses some of its crispness after a time.

GREEN TOMATO CHUTNEY

3 lbs green tomatoes
3 large onions
1 pint vinegar
½ lb raisins
1 lb demerara sugar
1 teaspoon ground ginger
1 tablespoon salt
½ teaspoon pepper
1 oz crushed mustard
   seed

Method. Cut tomatoes in small pieces. Slice onions. Put on a dish and sprinkle salt on them, leave overnight. Next day put all ingredients into enamel or aluminium pan. Bring to boil and simmer until mixture is thick and soft. Stir often especially after tomatoes thicken.

Pour into jars and cover. Can be used at once.

GOOSEBERRY CHUTNEY (1)

1 lb green gooseberries
1 lb rhubarb
1 lb sultanas
1 lb onions
1½ lbs moist brown sugar
½ teaspoon cayenne
2 tablespoons salt
1 tablespoon ground
    ginger
1 quart malt vinegar

Method. Wash and chop the gooseberries, rhubarb, raisins and onions (or put them through the mincer if preferred). Then put them in a lined pan with the other ingredients and cook slowly for about 3 hours, adding more vinegar if the chutney reduces too much.

Put into small jars and cover when cold.

GOOSEBERRY CHUTNEY (2)

2 lbs green gooseberries
¼ lb shallots
¼ lb sultanas
1 lb demerara sugar
1 teaspoon cayenne
    pepper
2 teaspoons ground
    ginger
2 teaspoons salt
1 pint malt vinegar

Method. Top and tail gooseberries, put in preserving pan with the other ingredients, and simmer gently for 1½ hours. When the gooseberry skins are tender, chutney is ready for potting.

The flavour improves with age, so try to keep for a little while before using.

MIXED FRUIT RELISH

6 oranges
3 lbs seeded raisins
2 lbs blackcurrants
2 lbs granulated sugar
3 pints cold water

Method. Peel the oranges and put skins through the mincer. Slice oranges very thinly and put into a basin with the water. Add the minced skins to this mixture and leave to soak overnight.

Next day turn into a preserving pan, and add the raisins, the picked blackcurrants, and the sugar. Boil for about 2 hours, stirring frequently. Pot in glass jars and cover when hot.

This is delicious with cold meats, and the mixture keeps well even after the jars are opened.

PICKLING BRINE

¼ lb coarse salt
1 quart water

Method. Dissolve salt in the hot water, strain and use cold.

This is excellent for use with vegetables which are improved by soaking in brine before pickling, as it helps to soften and flavour them.

TO PICKLE ONIONS

1 quart small silver onions
1 quart white wine vinegar
1 oz white peppercorns
½ oz allspice
3 or 4 cloves
1 dessertspoon salt

Method. Choose very small onions for pickling. Peel them under water. Put all the other ingredients into a saucepan and bring to the boil, removing the scum as it rises. Simmer for a few minutes to let the vinegar become well flavoured with the spices. Dry the onions, throw them into the boiling vinegar and let them cook for 5 minutes or until they turn clear. Pour them into a strong jar or bottle, cork or tie down securely, and keep for a month before using.

RHUBARB CHUTNEY (1)

2 lbs rhubarb
3 large onions
¼ lb sultanas
¼ lb preserved ginger
1 tablespoon curry powder
1 teaspoon white or
    cayenne pepper
1½ tablespoons salt
¼ lb brown sugar
1 breakfastcup malt
    vinegar

Method. Cut the rhubarb and the onions as finely as possible and stew in as little water as possible. When tender, add the other ingredients, making sure the ginger also is finely chopped. Turn the mixture into a basin, cover with a plate and allow to stand for 12 hours. Pot and cover.

RHUBARB CHUTNEY (2)

½ lb chopped raisins,
1 lb rhubarb, chopped
1 onion, chopped
1 apple, chopped
1 tomato, chopped
¼ lb sugar
1 pint malt vinegar
1 teaspoon salt
1 teaspoon ground ginger
Pinch mixed spice
Pinch cayenne pepper

Method. Put all the ingredients into a lined pan and bring to the boil. Boil for 1 hour, stirring frequently, and pot and cover as usual.

This chutney can be used within a week, but all chutneys are really improved with keeping, to mature a little.

PICKLING VINEGAR

1 quart vinegar
2 teaspoons peppercorns
1 teaspoon allspice berries
Piece of root ginger
Blade of mace
Good pinches of cayenne
    pepper and salt

Method. Boil all ingredients together in the vinegar for 5 minutes. Strain through a jelly bag or piece of muslin and use—*hot* for soft pickle; *cold* for hard pickle.

BEET JELLIES

Beetroot
Vinegar
Water
Raspberry jelly

If you do not like the way beetroot discolours the other ingredients in a salad, you might like to try serving small individual beet jellies, each on a lettuce leaf.

Method. Prepare cooked beetroot, cut it up into small pieces and cover with a mixture of half water and half vinegar. Take a pint packet of raspberry-flavoured jelly cubes and dissolve in a little hot water, then add the pieces of beetroot and make up to a pint with the liquid in which they were soaking. Pour into little moulds to set.

HOME-MADE WINES

BEETROOT WINE

4 lbs beetroot
4 lbs sugar
1 large orange
1 lemon
1 lb raisins
1 oz yeast, spread on toast
8 pints water

Method. Clean and slice beetroot and put in pan with 5 pints of water. Boil for fully 1 hour. Strain and add 3 pints of water and bring to blood heat.

Transfer to a crock, together with sugar, juice of lemon, juice of orange, and raisins. Float the toast, yeast side down. Cover crock and leave for 2 weeks.

Strain and return to crock for another 2 weeks, then bottle. Put corks in loosely for first 3 days, then gradually tighten when it is ready to drink.

Do not disturb during fermentation.

RASPBERRY VINEGAR (from Yorkshire)

1 lb raspberries
1 lb sugar
1 pint pure malt vinegar

Method. Put raspberries and sugar into large basin and leave overnight to draw the juice. Next day boil together with the vinegar for 20 minutes, adding a few cloves if desired. Strain and bottle.

This is excellent for sore throats and chests and can also be served with pancakes or Yorkshire pudding.

LEMONADE PUNCH

1 lemon
2 tablespoons water
1 tablespoon raspberry syrup
1 tablespoon caster sugar
Soda water
Ice

Method. Put the strained juice of a lemon into a large glass with the water, sugar and raspberry syrup. Add some crushed ice and fill up with soda water. A thin slice of lemon can be placed on the top.

NOTE. Other fruit syrups can be used, and a little brandy can be added if desired.

HOME-MADE LEMONADE

2 lemons
Sugar to taste
2 sprigs of washed mint
Boiling water

Method. Grate the lemon rinds or peel thinly with potato peeler, leaving all the pith behind. Put rinds in a heat-proof jug and squeeze over them the juice of the lemons. Cover with caster sugar to your own taste, then boiling water (1 pint), and the mint sprigs. Stir up with a wooden spoon to blend thoroughly, then leave until cold. Chill in refrigerator if possible.

Alternative recipe. If you want to keep the lemonade for any length of time, use this method. 1 tablespoonful in a tumbler of cold water or soda water makes a refreshing drink at any time.

Wipe 3 lemons, peel the rind off very thinly, then halve them and strain out the juice. Now put the lemon rind and juice in a large jug with 1½ lbs loaf sugar and 1 oz tartaric acid and pour in 1 pint boiling water. Stir frequently until nearly cold, and when quite cold, bottle and cork tightly.

BOSTON CREAM

1 oz tartaric acid
1½ pints boiling water
¾–1 lb loaf sugar
2 teaspoons lemon essence
1 egg white
Baking soda

We used to love this when we were on holiday in the North of Scotland. It makes a delicious summer drink. *Method.* Pour the boiling water over the sugar and tartaric acid and let them stand until cold and dissolved. Then add the lemon essence and the white of egg beaten to a stiff froth, and bottle for use. Pour about a wineglassful of this mixture into a tumbler, nearly fill with cold water, stir in a pinch of baking soda, and drink while bubbling up.

SHERRY

1½ lbs sugar
1 lb raisins
2 small potatoes
4 pints cold water
½ oz fresh yeast
Toast

Method. Boil sugar, raisins and potatoes in the water for 5 minutes. Turn out into a stone jar and on top lay a ½ slice of toast spread with the yeast. Cover jar lightly with lid but do not have it tight. Leave in the dark for 4 weeks, stirring each day. Strain through muslin and put in bottles, adding ½ teaspoon sugar to each bottle. Leave corks loose for a day or two then cork tightly. Leave as long as possible to mature, say 2 months.

IF THE jam goes mouldy on the surface with too long keeping, scrape off the mouldy part, turn the rest into a pan and boil up again. Store in perfectly clean jars and it should be fresh again.

Wines

RUM PUNCH

3 pints cold water
1 lb loaf sugar
4 oranges
1 lemon
½ pint strong tea
½ pint rum

Method. Put the sugar and water into a saucepan add the thinly peeled rind of ½ lemon and 1 orange, stir till dissolved, then bring to the boil and boil for 5 minutes. Remove from the heat and add the juice of the lemon and all the oranges, the tea (which must be well made and strong and strained carefully), and ½ pint of good rum. Strain carefully and serve either hot or cold.

SAKI WINE (Chinese)

4 medium-sized potatoes
1 lb rice
3 lbs sugar
1 lb blue raisins
8 pints water
1 oz yeast
Toast

Method. Put rice into crock and pour boiling water on top. Let it stand for a day to enable rice to soften. Add the rest of the ingredients, and half a slice of toast spread with yeast, yeast side downwards. Leave to ferment.

Stir daily, after fermentation starts. Strain and bottle any time after 3 weeks. Put corks in loosely for first 3 days, then gradually tighten, when it is ready to drink.

TEA PUNCH

2 pints tea
2 lemons
1 orange
3 oz sugar
Crushed ice

This makes a most refreshing drink in hot weather. *Method*. The tea must be strong and well made, and it should be poured boiling hot over the sugar and the grated rind of the orange. Add the juice of the lemons and let the liquid stand till completely cold. Strain, add the orange cut in thin slices and free from pith, and serve the punch in tall glasses with a little crushed ice if available.

NOTE. Other fruits can be added, such as shredded pineapple, strawberries, bananas, etc., and a little soda water can be mixed with the punch before serving. And of course, if you want to make it a little stronger, you can add a little good brandy or rum to the punch.

UNCLE TOBY'S PUNCH

1 lemon
3 lumps sugar
1 wineglass boiling water
1 wineglass rum
2 wineglasses hot stout

Method. Rub the rind of a lemon on 3 lumps of sugar. Put them in a large jug with the juice of the lemon and the wineglass of boiling water. Add the rum and the hot stout. Mix, strain and add more sugar if necessary.

FRUIT CUP

Assorted fruits
Red or white wine
1 tablespoon sugar
Rum
Soda water

This is a good way of providing for a crowd, as inexpensive red or white wine can be used.

Method. Cut up 1 apple, 1 orange, ½ lemon, a small piece of cucumber if available, some cherries and some grapes and let the wine stand on them for an hour or two. Add about 1 tablespoon sugar, and before serving, a little rum and as much soda water as desired.

Confections and Toffees

It is always fun to make your own candies and sweeties, and I think your sweet tooth will fasten happily on to many of the recipes in this section.

BARCELONA TOFFEE

1 lb granulated sugar
1 teacup water
1 dessertspoon vinegar
1 oz butter
6 oz Barcelona nuts
Pinch of salt
1 teaspoon vanilla essence

Method. Put all the ingredients, except the nuts, into a saucepan and stir until dissolved. Then boil till the toffee breaks crisply when tested in cold water. Add the nuts (shelled, toasted and chopped roughly), then pour out on an oiled tin and when cold break in pieces.

COCONUT DATES

1 lb stoned dates
¼ lb desiccated coconut

Method. Put the dates in the oven for a few minutes to soften. Then with a fork beat in the coconut. Roll into small balls and leave to harden.

COCONUT BALLS

6 oz ground almonds
6 oz caster sugar
1 teaspoon almond essence
Egg white
Cochineal
Desiccated coconut

Method. Put the ground almonds and sugar in a basin. Add the almond essence and form into a paste with white of egg, but do not get it too soft. Divide this paste and colour one half pink with a few drops of cochineal. Form all into small balls, roll in desiccated coconut, pressing the coconut well on, and place on a papered tray to dry.

Confectionery

ALMOND or WALNUT TOFFEE

1 lb granulated sugar
3 oz butter
¼ teacup water
Pinch of cream of tartar
3 oz almonds or walnuts

Method. If you use almonds, blanch and split them, dry in the oven, then arrange them with the flat side downwards on a greased tin. If walnuts are preferred, toast the shelled nuts for a few minutes in the oven, then spread them out on a greased tin. To make the toffee, melt the butter in a saucepan, add the sugar, water and cream of tartar, bring to the boil and then boil without stirring until the toffee is brittle when tested in cold water. Pour over the nuts and leave to set. Then break in pieces as required.

BUTTERSCOTCH

1 lb light brown sugar
4–6 oz butter
⅛ lb syrup
1 tablespoon water
Pinch of cream of tartar
½ teaspoon vanilla
¼ teaspoon lemon essence

Method. Melt the butter in a saucepan, then add the syrup, sugar and water, and dissolve slowly over a gentle heat. Bring to the boil, stirring all the time, add the cream of tartar and boil till the toffee breaks crisp when tested in cold water. Flavour to taste and pour on to an oiled or buttered tin. When set, mark in squares and break in pieces when cold. If you are keeping the toffee for any length of time, wrap it in wax paper when cold and store in a tin box.

NOUGAT

1 lb icing sugar
4 oz clear honey
3 oz sweet almonds
1 tablespoon pistachio nuts
1 or 2 oz glacé cherries
4 egg whites

Method. Sieve the sugar and put it into a bowl in a saucepan of boiling water to come well up the sides. Add the egg whites and honey and mix well with a whisk. Keep mixing until the mixture is white and thick. This will take about 30 minutes, and be sure the water does not boil down too much so that the bowl will be kept evenly hot. When ready, remove from the fire and stir in the shredded and well-dried almonds and pistachios, and the cherries cut in small pieces. Have ready a small square or oblong biscuit box, greased at the sides, and with the bottom lined with wafer paper. Pour the nougat mixture into this, pressing well down. Cover with more wafer paper and put a weight on the top. When cold, cut in convenient-sized pieces with a very sharp knife, and if not to be eaten at once, wrap the pieces in wax paper.

TO PREVENT fried bread going soggy, do not put any fat in the pan. Spread the slice of bread lightly on both sides with margarine before frying in a dry pan. It will toast to a dry golden brown.

222

FUDGE

¼ lb margarine
8 tablespoons sugar
8 tablespoons golden
   syrup
1 tin condensed milk
Vanilla essence

Method. Melt the margarine in saucepan. Add sugar and ½ teaspoon vanilla essence and bring very slowly to the boil. Add syrup and condensed milk (the inexpensive quality will do). Keep stirring until it thickens and turns a deep golden brown. Remove saucepan from the heat, and beat till the mixture gets really thick and fudgy. When it is turning sugary at the sides of the pan it is ready. Turn it out into tins and, if possible, keep for a week until it really dries out. Any kind of nuts may be added—chopped almonds, walnuts, etc., and these should be stirred in just before pouring.

CHOCOLATE FUDGE (1)

1 lb granulated sugar
½ pint milk
2 oz unsweetened
   chocolate
1 oz butter
1 cup chopped nuts
Vanilla essence

Method. Grate or shred the chocolate and put in a saucepan with the sugar, butter and milk. Heat slowly over a gentle heat, stirring all the time till melted. Then simmer, stirring occasionally till the mixture forms a soft ball when tested in water. Remove saucepan from the heat, stir in the nuts and flavouring, and beat till the mixture gets really thick and fudgy. Pour into oiled tin, mark in squares with the back of the knife and cut in pieces when cold. NOTE. If you want a richer mixture, you can use cream or condensed milk instead of ordinary milk.

CHOCOLATE FUDGE (2)

2 oz unsweetened
   chocolate
2½ teacups evaporated
   milk
1 tablespoon syrup
1 teaspoon vanilla essence
1 teacup chopped walnuts
2 teacups sugar

Method. Put in a saucepan the shredded chocolate, milk, sugar, syrup, and cook over a gentle heat, stirring till the sugar dissolves and the chocolate is melted. Bring to the boil, cover and cook for 2 or 3 minutes to stop crystals forming.
Take the lid off and cook to soft-ball stage, stirring constantly. When it gets to the soft-ball stage, take off the heat and add the butter. Let it cool to lukewarm heat without stirring. Add the vanilla when the mixture is cool. Beat vigorously until it is thick and loses its gloss. Stir in the chopped nuts and quickly spread it on a greased tin and mark into squares. Break when cold.

IF LETTUCE or watercress go limp, leave them to soak in a basin of cold water to which you have added a spoonful of sugar, and they will freshen and crisp up in less than ½ hour.

AMERICAN COCONUT CUBES

2 breakfastcups brown
    sugar
1 breakfastcup fine
    coconut
Barely ¼ cup milk
1 tablespoon butter
Pinch of salt

Method. Put all the ingredients in a saucepan and stir over a gentle heat till the sugar has dissolved. Bring to the boil, and continue boiling and stirring till a little of the mixture forms a soft ball when tried in cold water. Take off the fire, beat till fairly cool, turn into a lightly buttered tin, smooth with the blade of the knife, and cut into little cubes when sufficiently set, using a sharp knife.

RUSSIAN TOFFEE (1)

¼ lb brown sugar
¼ lb white sugar
¼ lb butter
1 teacup cream
1 teacup golden syrup
Vanilla essence

Method. Dissolve the butter in a lined saucepan, then add the other ingredients and flavour nicely with vanilla. Boil till the toffee feels crisp when tested in a little cold water. You must keep stirring all the time, and when it is ready, it will draw away cleanly from the sides of the pan. Pour into a well-greased shallow tin, mark across in squares and when nearly cold, cut in pieces with a very sharp knife. Wrap the pieces in wax paper.

RUSSIAN TOFFEE (2)

1 lb granulated sugar
¼ lb butter
1 teacup cream
2 tablespoons water
Vanilla essence

Method. Use either brown or white sugar for this recipe. Melt the butter, then add the sugar and water and stir over a gentle heat till boiling. Add the cream and boil again, stirring all the time, until the mixture thickens and hardens when a little is tested in cold water. Remove from the fire, add about a teaspoonful of vanilla essence, and when the mixture has stopped bubbling, pour into a greased shallow tin. When nearly set, mark in squares with a knife and when cold, break in pieces and store in a tin box.
NOTE. Take the pan off the heat before adding the cream. This is a very rich toffee and is excellent for storing in an airtight tin with a close-fitting lid.

CRISP TREACLE TOFFEE (1)

1 lb brown sugar
¼ lb fresh butter
¼ lb tin black treacle
A little vinegar

Method. Melt butter, stir in sugar, then treacle, and stir all the time until it comes to the boil. Then boil without stirring for 10 minutes. Test for brittleness, flavour with vinegar and pour into a tray large enough to form a thin toffee.

TREACLE TOFFEE (2)

1 lb brown sugar
1 lb black treacle
1 oz butter
1 dessertspoon vinegar

Method. Put the black treacle in a saucepan with the sugar and the butter and let it melt over a gentle heat, stirring all the time. Stir till boiling, and stir till it breaks crisp when tested in cold water. Flavour with the vinegar, pour in an oiled tin and break in pieces when cold.

PEPPERMINT CREAMS

1 lb icing sugar
1 white of egg
Few drops peppermint oil
1 tablespoon water

Method. Sieve the icing sugar into a basin and moisten with the egg white and water. Work with the hands into a smooth soft paste, and flavour with a few drops of oil of peppermint. When it is pliable and free from cracks, roll the paste out to $\frac{1}{8}''$ thick on a board that has been sprinkled with sieved icing sugar. Cut into rounds with a tiny cutter, and leave aside on a sheet of greaseproof paper sprinkled with caster sugar to prevent sticking. Press the scraps together and roll out again until everything is used up. Leave till dry, and they are ready for eating.

Invalid Cookery

Invalid cookery can be very monotonous, both for the cook and for the patient, and I have tried to give an appetising and interesting selection of recipes which I hope will gladden the appetite of the really ill and of the convalescent.

APPLE CREAM

2 baked apples
1 small carton double cream
Squeeze of lemon juice
Sugar to taste

Method. Remove the pulp from the baked apples and rub it through a fine wire or hair sieve, scraping the sieve well underneath to get all the pulp free. Add to it the cream (or custard if preferred), a squeeze of lemon juice, and sweeten to taste with caster sugar. Beat well for a few minutes and serve in a small glass dish. A few biscuit crumbs can be sprinkled on top, if liked.

BANANA CUSTARD PUDDING

1 or 2 bananas
Sugar
Grated lemon rind
1 teacup milk
1 egg
A little butter

Method. Peel and slice the bananas with a silver knife, or a fruit knife (to prevent discolouring), and lay them at the foot of a greased pie-dish. Sprinkle with sugar and grated lemon rind. Beat the egg with the milk and strain over the bananas. Dot with butter and bake in a moderate oven (about 20 minutes).

BEEF TEA

¼ lb lean beef
½ pint cold water
Salt (if allowed)

Method. Shred the beef with a sharp knife and put in a stone jar with the cold water. Stand the jar in a pot of water at the side of the fire or stove, and bring slowly to the boil. Add salt, if allowed, and let it infuse till it is a rich dark colour. Strain and serve with toast.

BLACKCURRANT DRINK

1 dessertspoon black-
    currant jam
½ pint boiling water
Squeeze of lemon juice
A little sugar

This is a grand cold cure, and very easy to prepare. *Method*. Put all the ingredients into a jug and stir well. Cover and stand by the side of the stove, or in a pan of boiling water for 15–20 minutes. Strain through a fine strainer or piece of muslin, and drink it hot.

BUTTERED APPLES

2 apples
1 oz butter
½ oz sugar
Pinch of cinnamon

Method. Peel the apples, cut in halves, and remove the cores. Lay in a fireproof dish, well greased with some of the butter, and sprinkle with sugar and a little cinnamon or grated lemon rind if preferred. Dot the rest of the butter on top, cover with a lid or greaseproof paper and bake in a moderate oven till the apples are soft and lightly coloured (½–¾ hour).

CORNFLOUR CHARLOTTE

4 or 5 finger biscuits
¼ pint milk
1 level tablespoon corn-
    flour
1 teaspoon sugar
1 dessertspoon butter
Few drops of vanilla
Red currant or other
    bright-coloured jelly

Method. Take a good-sized mug or jampot with straight sides, grease the bottom with salad oil or melted butter, then line the sides with finger biscuits split and neatly trimmed, fitting them closely together. Put most of the milk on to boil with a piece of butter the size of a walnut. Mix the cornflour smoothly with the rest of the milk, and stir it into the rest. Stir over a gentle heat till boiling, then cook for a minute or two. Add sugar and vanilla or any other preferred flavouring. Cool slightly, then pour it into the lined mould. Leave it aside till cold, then turn out and decorate the top with a little red currant or other bright jelly.

NOTE. Arrowroot or rice flour can be used instead of cornflour, if preferred. A tablespoon of cream or an egg yolk can be added instead of the butter.

STEAMED CHOP

1 mutton chop
Pinch of salt
A little butter

Method. Wipe the chop with a damp cloth, trim off most of the fat, and lay it in a greased plate over a pan half full of boiling water. Sprinkle with a little salt, cover with a piece of greased paper, then with the saucepan lid. Keep the water fast boiling to give enough steam, and if it boils away too much, add more boiling water. Cook for 15–20 minutes, then turn the chop and cook the same length of time on the other side. Serve at once with the juice that has run from it.

This is one of the most digestible ways of cooking a chop for an invalid, and it has a most delicate flavour.

EGG AND RUM

1 teacup milk
1 tablespoon rum
1 dessertspoon sugar
Pinch of salt
Pinch of nutmeg
1 egg yolk

This is a good old-fashioned recipe for cases of exhaustion.
Method. Put the egg yolk, rum, sugar, salt and nutmeg into a cup or small basin and beat together with a fork. Add the milk, either warm or cold, just as you prefer, and mix all together. Pour into a tumbler and serve.

EGG FLIP

1 egg white
1 teacup hot milk
A little sugar

Method. Beat up the egg white to a froth, but do not let it get too stiff. Put it into a tumbler and gradually pour on the hot milk, stirring all the time. Add a pinch of sugar if you like it sweet, or if preferred, a pinch of salt.

EGG NOG

1 egg
1 tablespoon sherry
1 dessertspoon sugar

Method. Mix the egg yolk and sugar in a small basin till creamy. Add the sherry, then the egg white beaten to a stiff froth. Mix lightly but thoroughly, and serve in a glass. Brandy or rum can be used instead of the sherry.

EGG WITH CREAM AND BRANDY

1 egg white
1 tablespoon cream
1 tablespoon brandy
Sugar

Method. Beat up an egg white to a stiffish froth, add cream and brandy, mix well, sweeten to taste and serve in a glass.

FISH CUSTARD

1 egg
2 tablespoons milk
1 tablespoon cooked fish
Pepper/Salt

Method. Any nicely cooked fish will do for this. Chop it finely and season with pepper and salt. Beat up the egg with the milk and add the fish to it. Pour into a well-greased cup or small basin and cover with greased paper. Steam slowly until set (10–15 minutes). Turn out when ready and decorate with a little sprig of parsley.

FISH SOUP

½ lb white fish
½ pint cold water
¼ teacup milk
½ oz butter
½ oz flour
A little chopped parsley
Salt to taste

Almost any white fish can be used for this, but haddock, whiting or plaice are among the most suitable. *Method.* Wash the fish carefully, cut in pieces without removing the skin and put into a lined saucepan with the water and salt and bring slowly to the boil, removing the scum as it rises. Cook for a few minutes until the fish loses its transparent appearance, then lift out a few neat pieces, take off the skin and any bone, and put aside for serving in the soup. Let the remainder cook slowly until all the goodness is drawn from the fish (about 1 hour), then strain through a fine sieve or strainer. Clean the saucepan to get rid of any scum, and put in the butter. Let it heat, then blend in the flour till smooth, and add the fish liquor and the milk and stir till boiling. Add the fish pieces you kept aside, the chopped parsley, and cook for a minute or two longer. Serve very hot.
NOTE. A more savoury soup can be made by adding a few pieces of chopped vegetables to the fish, but this is not so plain for an invalid. If you want a richer soup, you can add an egg yolk. Put the yolk into a basin and pour the hot soup slowly on to it, stirring all the time. Again, for a richer soup, you can use 1 or 2 tablespoons cream instead of milk.

FISH STEWED IN MILK (1)

1 small filleted sole or
    plaice
1 tablespoon bread-
    crumbs
A pinch of nutmeg
¼ teacup milk
A small piece of butter
Salt

Method. Wipe the fish with a damp cloth, season lightly with salt and make up in little rolls. Put these into a basin with the milk, breadcrumbs, butter and seasoning. Cover with a saucer or greaseproof paper and steam until tender (about ½ hour). Serve on a hot dish, garnished with a sprig of parsley.

STEWED FISH (2)

1 filleted fish—whiting,
   haddock, sole or
   plaice
1 tablespoon bread-
   crumbs
¼ teacup cold water
1 teacup milk
¼ oz butter
1 teaspoon chopped
   parsley
White pepper/Salt

Method. Wipe the fish with a damp cloth and cut into small neat pieces. Rinse out a lined saucepan with cold water to prevent the fish sticking to it, and lay the fish at the bottom. Sprinkle over them a little salt and white pepper, pour on the milk and water, and cook gently with the lid on until ready (10–15 minutes). Lift out the fish on to the serving plate and keep hot. Add the breadcrumbs and the butter to the water and milk in the pan, and stir over the heat till the breadcrumbs swell and thicken the sauce. Sprinkle in the finely-chopped parsley, then pour this sauce over the fish.

NOTE. You can cook this dish in a small fireproof casserole.

FRUIT TART

1 small sponge finger, or
   2 finger biscuits
1 egg
1 teaspoon caster sugar
¼ teacup milk
1 large apple
2 tablespoons water
1 dessertspoon sugar

Method. Stew the apple with the dessertspoon sugar until soft, and put it at the bottom of a small greased pie-dish. Cut the sponge finger or the finger biscuits in slices and lay them on the top. Separate the yolk from the white of the egg, beat up the yolk with the milk and pour over the sponge cake. Let it stand for a few minutes, then bake in a moderate oven for 10–15 minutes. Meantime, beat the egg white to a stiff froth, fold in the teaspoon of caster sugar, and pile it on top of the pudding when it is ready. Return to the oven to set and lightly brown the meringue. Lift out and sprinkle with sugar.

NOTE. Any other stewed fruit can be used instead of apples.

HADDOCK or WHITING, STUFFED AND BAKED

1 whiting or small haddock
2 tablespoons bread-
   crumbs
A little chopped parsley
2 tablespoons milk
1 egg yolk
Grated lemon rind
Small piece of butter
Pepper/Salt

Method. Clean and skin the fish, and cut off the head. Make a stuffing with the breadcrumbs, parsley, a little grated lemon rind, pepper and salt, and bind together with egg yolk. Fill the opening in the fish with this mixture, then place it in a fireproof dish. Pour the milk round, cover and bake quickly for about 15 minutes. Remove the cover, sprinkle the fish with a few dry breadcrumbs, dot with butter, and brown lightly for another 5 minutes.

MILK GRUEL

1 tablespoon oatmeal
½ pint milk
Good pinch of salt or
   1 teaspoon sugar

This is a favourite dish in Scotland, and we had it very often as children when we were convalescing.
Method. Put the oatmeal and milk into a basin and mix together, then cover with a plate and let it stand for at least ½ hour, stirring now and then.

Strain off the milk into a small lined saucepan, pressing the oatmeal as dry as possible, so that all the goodness will go into the milk. Stir this milk over a gentle heat till boiling, then simmer slowly for 10 minutes. If it is too thick, you can add a little more milk. Season with salt or sugar according to taste. (We had salt in Scotland.) A small piece of butter can be added at the last, and a spot of brandy, if desired. Gruel must be served very hot.

RABBIT STEWED IN MILK

¼ a young rabbit
1 teacup milk
Small bunch of herbs
1 teaspoon flour
Small piece of butter
Seasoning

Method. Blanch the cut-up rabbit by putting in a saucepan with enough cold water to cover, bring to the boil, and pour this water away. Rinse in fresh cold water, put into a jar or basin with the milk and seasonings (herbs are optional) and place in a saucepan with enough hot water to reach half-way up the sides. Cover the jar with a lid or strong greaseproof paper, and the saucepan with a lid, and simmer gently until tender (1–2 hours). If the water boils down too much, you must add more. When sufficiently cooked, lift out the pieces of rabbit and keep them hot. Pour the milk into a saucepan, and remove the herbs, if used. Blend the flour with a little cold milk in a basin and add to the milk. Stir over a gentle heat until it boils and thickens, and add more seasoning if necessary. Stir in the butter, and pour this sauce over the pieces of rabbit to coat them nicely.

NOTE. Small rolls of bacon can be served round the dish, if liked.

STEAMED PUDDING

2 tablespoons suet, grated
2 tablespoons bread-
   crumbs
2 tablespoons flour
2 tablespoons sugar
2 egg yolks, or 1 whole egg

Method. Mix all the ingredients well together, adding a little milk if necessary. Put into a greased basin, cover with a cloth or greaseproof paper, and steam for 1 hour.

STEAMED MUTTON AND RICE

1 mutton chop
1 teaspoon whole rice
Pinch of salt
1 teacup cold water
1 small stick of celery

Method. Wipe the chop with a damp cloth, trim off nearly all the fat, and put it into a jar or basin with the salt, water and the well-washed rice. Wash and brush the celery, removing any brown parts. Cut into fine shreds and add to the ingredients already in the jar. Cover with a lid or strong piece of grease-proof paper, and place the jar or basin in a saucepan with enough boiling water to come half-way up the sides. Put the lid on the pan and steam slowly until tender (1½–2 hours). If the water boils down, you must add more. When ready, lift the chop on to a hot plate, and pour the rice, etc., round it.

NOTE. If you do not like the flavour, you can leave out the celery. The jar containing the chop can be placed in a moderate oven instead of in the saucepan of boiling water if more convenient.

Miscellaneous

This is a small collection of recipes difficult to place in any of the other categories, and deals among other things with haggis, stovies, and a few recipes for accompaniments to various dishes.

SALTED ALMONDS

¼ lb almonds
½ tablespoon salad oil or
   clarified fresh butter
Fine salt

Method. Blanch and dry the almonds. The quickest way is to let them sit in the boiling water for a few minutes till the skins loosen a bit and then they will peel off quite easily. Place them in a moderately hot oven, in a clean baking tin with ½ tablespoon of the best salad oil or clarified fresh butter, and let them turn a light brown on all sides. Keep turning them until they are nicely browned all over. Turn them now on to a sheet of kitchen paper and sprinkle them generously with fine salt. When cold, shake off the loose salt and the almonds are ready to serve. Alternatively, they can be kept in a glass jar till wanted.
NOTE. Walnuts and peanuts can be treated in the same way, or a mixture of nuts if preferred.

FRIED BREADCRUMBS FOR GAME

Take some stale white bread and rub it through a sieve to make fine breadcrumbs. About a cupful is generally enough. Melt about 1 oz butter in a frying pan or in a tin in the oven, put the crumbs in and stir them about gently until lightly browned, dry and crisp. They should absorb all the fat. Serve on a small dish with a paper doily under them.

APPLE AND CELERY SALAD

2 or 3 apples
1 head celery
1 or 2 gherkins
Oil and vinegar dressing
A little lettuce

Method. Using the white inside portion of the celery only, wash it, cut it in fine shreds and let it lie in cold water for at least ½ hour. Then drain and dry it well in a cloth. Choose sharp juicy apples, and peel, core and slice them very thinly. Put the celery and apple in a basin, and pour over enough oil and vinegar dressing to moisten them (made with oil, vinegar, pepper, salt, made mustard, and sugar). Mix together very lightly. Line a salad dish with nice crisp lettuce leaves, arrange the salad on top, sprinkle with chopped or shredded gherkins and, if you like, sprinkle also a few chopped nuts on top.
NOTE. This is an excellent accompaniment to roast pork or goose.

STOVIES

Potatoes
Butter or dripping
A little water
Salt/Pepper
Onions

Method. Melt the dripping and toss chopped onions in it. Add quartered potatoes, and *just enough* water to prevent them sticking or burning. Sprinkle with salt and pepper. Cover closely and simmer very gently until soft and cooked. At the very end, you can add a tablespoon of medium oatmeal to give extra nourishment and dry the outsides of the potatoes.
NOTE. The essence of stovies is that they must be kept as dry as possible and if the potatoes are not in danger of burning (keep shaking them about), do not add any water at all. It is only added to keep the food safe.

CUCUMBER SALAD

Cucumber
White pepper/Salt
2 or 3 spring onions
Oil and vinegar dressing

Method. Choose a fresh green firm cucumber, and peel and slice it as thinly as notepaper. Always start at the thick end and work towards the stalk for better flavour. Lay the slices on a plate with the onions which have been washed and thinly sliced, and cover liberally with salt. Lay another plate on top and let the mixture stand for ½ hour, then pour off all the liquid which has accumulated, and you will find this makes the salad more digestible. Arrange the slices neatly in a salad dish and pour the oil and vinegar dressing over (made with oil, vinegar, pepper, salt, made mustard and sugar).

BAKED BANANAS (for serving with chicken)

Bananas
Brown sugar
Lemon juice
Bacon

Method. Cut one (not-too-ripe) banana per person, in half lengthwise. Place banana halves in a shallow buttered oven dish—preferably one that can come straight to the table. Shake a teaspoonful of brown sugar over them and a squeeze of lemon juice, and cover with strips of thin streaky bacon. Put on top shelf of oven for 15–20 minutes, and serve with fried or roast chicken.

BREAD CROUTONS FOR SOUP OR GARNISHING

Use bread not less than a day old, and cut off the crust. Cut in slices about $\frac{1}{2}$" thick, then in strips, and then into even squares. Or cut in small rounds or fancy shapes with a vegetable cutter, or triangles, just as you please. If the bread is a bit soft, let it dry on the rack above the fire or in a cool oven for a little while. These croûtons can then either be fried in boiling fat or in butter in a frying pan, or on a greased tin in the oven. Drain well on kitchen paper before serving. They should be crisp, dry, pale golden and very hot.

EASY GLAZE FOR COLD MEAT

$\frac{1}{4}$ pint stock or water
$\frac{1}{2}$ oz gelatine
1 teaspoon meat extract

Method. Dissolve the gelatine in the stock or water, then add the meat extract, and boil until reduced to about half the quantity, stirring frequently. Season if necessary, strain, and let it become almost cold before using. Paint this over any of your cold galantines, using a brush, and painting all over in even, straight strokes. If one coat is not enough, let the first one cool and brush the meat over again until it has a rich brown shiny surface. In the meantime, keep the glaze in a melted condition by putting the pan or jar containing it in a saucepan half full of hot water.

TO MAKE BROWNED BREADCRUMBS

Break some stale bread or crusts into small rough pieces, put them on a baking tin and bake them in a cool oven till brown and crisp. The more slowly they are done the better. Crush the dried bread with the rolling-pin and when reduced to crumbs, pass them through a wire sieve. These crumbs are so useful for various cookery purposes. If they are only slightly coloured, they will do very well for egging and breadcrumbing and are more economical than fresh white crumbs. Store in a jar with a lid.

CANDIED PEEL

Although you can buy candied peel easily, some people still prefer to make their own, and if you feel like doing so, here is the way to do it. Peel should be sound and fresh. Cut it in convenient-sized pieces and soak in salted water for a few days. Then drain off the water and put the peel in a lined saucepan with fresh cold water to cover. Bring to the boil, and simmer slowly till the peel is quite tender. Drain again and put the peel into a basin. Now measure 1 lb of granulated sugar and ½ pint of water to six skins, and boil sugar and water together for 10 minutes. Pour this syrup over the peel, cover the basin, and stand in a cool place for a week. At the end of this time, pour off the syrup into a clean saucepan and bring it to the boil. Then add the peel and let it boil until clear and very little syrup shows in the saucepan. Turn out on to a greased tin or dish, sprinkle with sugar, and set in a warm place to dry and candy. When it is quite dried and candied, store in a jar with a lid.

DUMPLINGS TO SERVE WITH MEAT

6 oz flour
2 oz suet
1 teaspoon salt
½ teaspoon baking powder
A little milk or water

Method. Chop the suet very finely and mix it lightly with the flour, salt and baking powder. Bind all together with water or milk and knead lightly. The dough should be soft without being sticky. Make it up into small balls, using floured hands, and cook them for 15 to 20 minutes along with the meat with which they are going to be served. The water *must* be kept simmering all the time they are in it, or the dumplings will be heavy.

MAYONNAISE OF TUNNY FISH

Lettuce
Tunny fish
Mayonnaise sauce
Chopped parsley
Pepper

This is a very attractive way to serve tinned tunny fish. *Method.* Take the heart of a nice firm lettuce and separate the leaves carefully, being careful not to break them. They should be as near to the shape of a scallop shell as possible. Wipe very gently with a damp cloth, or wash if necessary, but they must not get limp. Mix the tunny fish with well-seasoned mayonnaise, and put some of this in the centre of each leaf, decorated with chopped parsley, and a sprinkling of black pepper. Arrange neatly on a round dish with all the stalk ends of the lettuce leaves towards the centre. Any extras can be added for decorative effect, such as halved tomatoes snipped with scissors to form little baskets, or thinly-sliced cucumber, or radishes cut to form little flowers.

SWEET CORN SOUFFLE (American)

1 tin sweet corn
1 oz margarine
1 oz flour
½ pint milk
Salt/Pepper to taste
2 eggs
3 oz grated cheese

Method. Empty the tin of sweet corn into fireproof glass dish. Melt the margarine and into it stir the flour, then add the milk, and season to taste. Add the yolks of the eggs, and 3 oz cheese, grated, and bring it gently to boiling point. Do not cook fast or the yolks may curdle. Whip the egg whites to a stiff froth, fold into the sauce, and pour all over the sweet corn. Leave room for the soufflé to rise in the cooking. Bake for ½ hour in a moderate oven until nicely browned and cooked through.

XMAS FRUIT SYRUP (for the children)

Strained juice of
 12 mandarins
Rinds of 6 mandarins
4 quarts of boiling water
4 lbs preserving sugar

Method. Strain the juice into a basin. Add grated rind, cover and stand for 12 hours. Dissolve the sugar in the water and bring to the boil. Chill. Then stir strained juice and rinds into it, and serve when required. Can be bottled and sealed if not all required at once. If desired, soda or tonic water can be added to this syrup when serving, to make a sparkling drink. NOTE. To give an exotic flavour, add 12 tablespoons shredded pineapple just before serving.

MINCEMEAT

2 oz raisins
2 oz currants
2 oz sultanas
2 oz shredded suet
1 oz mixed peel
1 oz brown sugar
1 chopped apple
Rind of ½ lemon
1 tablespoon lemon juice
¼ teaspoon ground ginger
¼ teaspoon cinnamon
½ teaspoon mixed spice
Pinch salt

Method. Clean the raisins, currants and sultanas and chop them. If not already done, chop the peel. Mix all these ingredients together with the apple in a large basin and stir in the sugar, spices and salt. Grate in the rind of ½ lemon and stir in the lemon juice. If liked, brandy or rum may be used instead of lemon juice. Mix thoroughly with a wooden spoon. Pack in a jar or jars, pressing down tightly and cover. Keep for several weeks to allow flavour to develop before it is required for mince pies.

TO CLARIFY BUTTER

Put some good salt butter into a small lined saucepan and bring slowly to the boil, then simmer gently for a few minutes. Draw the pan to the side and let it stand until the butter has stopped bubbling. Now take off all the froth from the top with an iron spoon, and pour the clear oil into a dish ready for use, leaving any sediment in the saucepan.

Miscellaneous

MEALY PUDDINGS

1 lb medium or coarse
   oatmeal
¼ lb beef suet
2 onions
Salt/Pepper
Long pudding skins

This is a delicious and most savoury pudding which my mother-in-law used to make, and if you can obtain the pudding skins from your butcher, you might like to try this very Scottish recipe. It is just sausage skins you ask your butcher for, and he may be able to spare you some.

Method. Put the oatmeal in the oven, spread out on tins, and toast it to a light golden brown, turning it over now and then so that it can colour evenly. Chop the suet finely, using a little flour if necessary, and skin, scald and chop the onions finely. Now mix oatmeal, onions and suet together and season fairly highly with pepper and salt. Tie one end of the pudding skin and spoon in enough of the mixture to make a fair-sized sausage, then tie again, leaving enough room for the mixture to swell in the cooking. Proceed to make more sausages in the same way, tying them at both ends so that they can be cut separately afterwards. When all are ready, prick them well with a fine needle to prevent the skins bursting, put them into a saucepan of slowly boiling water, and let them simmer for ½ hour. When the puddings are required, you can either toast them a few minutes in front of the fire or in the oven, lay them in gently boiling water, or sit them on top of a simmering stew.

TO CLARIFY FRYING FAT AND DRIPPING

When fat becomes brown and discoloured after a lot of use, it can be clarified by melting it, and pouring into a large basin half full of warm water. Stir well to wash the fat and put it aside to cool. When it is cool, the fat will have risen and formed a cake on top of the water. Lift this off, scrape away any sediment which may lie underneath, wipe the fat dry and put it aside for future use. Throw away the water of course.

CUCUMBER CANDLESTICKS

1 cucumber, cut flat at
   both ends
2 tomatoes, chopped
Cold flaked fish, or peeled
   shrimps or prawns
A little mayonnaise
Seasoning if required
2 tomatoes, sliced

Method. Cut the cucumber into 2″ chunks, scoop out the seeds and mix them with the chopped tomatoes, the fish, and seasoning if required. Bind all together with a little mayonnaise. Pile into the hollow left in the centre where seeds have been scooped out, and sit each "candlestick" on a flat slice of tomato.

SCOTCH HAGGIS

I have been asked so often how to make haggis, that although I feel few people will be brave enough to tackle this, or even be able to find all the ingredients, for interest's sake I give you the recipe below, taken from a very old cookery book which is at least 100 years old. You will see there is nothing very mysterious about the ingredients, but the quantities are vast, and if you do feel like trying this mysterious dish, you could cut down these quantities to suit your own requirements. I give the details exactly as I obtained them from this old book.

The liver, heart and
    tongue of a sheep
A sheep's paunch
1 to 2 lbs onions
½ lb oatmeal
¼ lb suet
Salt/Pepper
Some stock or gravy
A pinch of nutmeg
A pinch of mace

Method. Thoroughly cleanse the paunch, washing it first in cold water, then plunge it into hot water and scrape it on both sides. Cut it so as to form two or three small bags in which to cook the haggis, sewing up any holes and openings with a needle and strong cotton. Allow the bags to remain in cold water until wanted.

To make the mixture, take the heart, liver and tongue, and wash them well in salt and water, and then boil them slowly for 1½ hours. Meanwhile, chop the suet, scald and chop the onions, and toast or bake the oatmeal until a golden brown. When the meat is ready, drain and dry it, and mince it finely, removing any parts that are uneatable. Mix the minced meat with the other ingredients, and season rather highly with pepper, salt and a little spice as shown in the list of ingredients. Moisten with stock or some of the liquor in which the meat was cooked, but do not get it too wet. Drain and dry the bags, fill them three-parts full with the mixture and sew them up. Prick the skins here and there with a needle, plunge the haggis into a saucepan of boiling water with a plate at the foot, and allow them to boil slowly at least 2 hours, pricking them occasionally to prevent them bursting. After cooking, a haggis will keep for several days, and only require re-boiling for a short time when wanted. It must be served very hot on a folded serviette. A small hole is cut in the skin and the filling taken out with a spoon. No sauce or gravy is required. NOTE. The liver, heart and tongue of a lamb will make a more delicate haggis than those of the sheep.

TO MAKE the most of spring cabbage, squeeze every last drop of water out between two plates after it is cooked, then chop a lump of butter through it and add a good dash of black pepper.

ADD a few stoned grapes to the white sauce you are serving with the fish, and see how you add a touch of novelty and of luxury to the dish.

TOMATO APPETISERS

Skinned, sliced tomatoes
Fresh chopped parsley
Salt/Pepper
Lemon juice

Method. Over the skinned sliced tomatoes, put fresh chopped parsley, salt and pepper, and a good squeeze of lemon juice.

TOMATO RING

1 pint of tomato juice
1 envelope of powdered
    gelatine
Filling for centre

This is a very decorative way of serving a summer-time salad.

Method. Melt the gelatine according to the directions on the packet, mix with the tomato juice, and pour into a ring. When set and cold, turn out carefully and fill the centre with anything you choose. This can be a mixed vegetable salad, a green salad, hard-boiled eggs and potato, a fish mixture, etc.

INDEX

INDEX

Sheep's heart, 39
Sherry, 217
Short crust pastry, 167
Shortbread, 173
Shortbread, coconut, 171
Shortbread, thin, 175
Shortbread biscuits, 174
Shortbread biscuits, almond, 170
Shortbread biscuits, Ayrshire, 169
Silver and gold pudding, 122
Skirly, 200
Smoked haddock omelette, 70
Smoked haddock pasties, 71
Smoked haddock savoury, 70
Smoked haddock with egg sauce, 69
Snaps, brandy, 172
Soda loaf, 178
Sole with mushrooms, baked, 77
Sole with shrimp stuffing, 76
Soufflé, baked apple, 106
Soufflé, baked fish, 80
Soufflé, cauliflower, 90
Soufflé, fish, 83
Soufflé, ground rice, 120
Soufflé, sweet corn, 239
Soufflé with pineapple, rice, 119
Soufflés, little ginger, 117
Soup, Angus potato, 19
Soup, cabbage, 15
Soup, celery and rice, 15
Soup, fish, 230
Soup, Italian minestrone, 15
Soup, lentil, 16
Soup, onion, 16
Soup, Paddy's potato, 19
Soup, pig's feet, 17
Soup, simple, 13
Soup, tomato, 17, 18
Soup, tomato and green pea, 17
Soup, velvet, 18
Soup, watercress cream, 19
Soups, 13-19
Soused mackerel, 73
Southern stew, 29
Spaghetti à l'Italienne, 200
Spanish cod, 68
Spanish omelette, 200
Spanish pudding, 122
Spanish stew, 51
Sponge, plum, 118
Sponge, strawberry, 155
Sponge, treacle, 121
Sponge pudding, 121

Sprats, baked, 79
Sprats, fried, 79
Spring stew, 39
Sprouts, braised, 101
Sprouts with cheese sauce, Brussels, 101
Steak, bachelor, 22
Steak and kidney pie, 31
Steak and kidney pudding, 24
Steak and rice kedgeree, 34
Steaks, minced veal, 43
Steamed pudding, 114, 232
Stew, Australian, 21
Stew, Belgian, 23
Stew, Irish, 36
Stew, mutton, 38
Stew, Southern, 29
Stew, Spanish, 51
Stew, spring, 39
Stew in casserole, 38
Stovies, 236
Strawberry flan, 168
Strawberry jam, 211
Strawberry rice cream, 129
Strawberry sponge, 155
Strawberry tart, open, 165
Stuffing, chestnut, 140
Stuffing, forcemeat, 32
Stuffing, mushroom, 141
Stuffing, potato and celery, 141
Stuffing, sage and onion, 141
Stuffing, sausage, 142
Stuffing, special potato, 141
Stuffing for turkey, 142
Stuffings, 140-142
Suet dumplings, 30
Suet pastry, 161
Sultana bread, 180
Summer pudding, 128
Supper bread, Swiss, 202
Swedish lemon ring Madeira, 156
Swedish meat balls, 35
Swedish rice, 118
Sweet corn cobs, 91
Sweet corn soufflé, 239
Sweetbreads, lamb's, 38
Sweets, cold, 123-130
Swiss apple tart, 168
Swiss hazelnut biscuits, 173
Swiss roll, 157
Swiss supper bread, 202
Syrup, Xmas fruit, 239
Syrup gingerbread, 159
Syrup sauce, 136